TALKING THE WALK:
Should CEOs Think
More about **Sex?**

TALKING THE WALK:
Should CEOs Think More about **Sex?**

How gender impacts management and leadership communication

DR JULIA HELENE IBBOTSON PhD, FHEA

iUniverse, Inc.
Bloomington

TALKING THE WALK: SHOULD CEOs THINK MORE ABOUT SEX? HOW GENDER IMPACTS MANAGEMENT AND LEADERSHIP COMMUNICATION

iUniverse books may be ordered through booksellers or by contacting:

iUniverse
1663 Liberty Drive
Bloomington, IN 47403
www.iuniverse.com
1-800-Authors (1-800-288-4677)

ISBN: 978-1-4697-8838-8 (sc)
ISBN: 978-1-4697-8839-5 (ebk)

Printed in the United States of America

iUniverse rev. date: 02/23/2012

CONTENTS

TABLES USED IN THE TEXT

DEDICATIONS

To my dear daughter Tam, who is a true professional and also a wonderful mother to two of my delightful grandchildren, Charlie and Zoe. Keep talking the walk!

ACKNOWLEDGEMENTS

I would like to thank Professor David Young who had nothing but positive encouragement throughout the long process of my extensive research and writing, and Professor Gwen Wallace who so thoroughly critiqued my work, gave me so much support . . . . and who made me delete all my semi-colons! Many thanks also to Professor Elaine Millard and Professor Marie Parker-Jenkins who have given me so much encouragement over the years. All four have been, and will continue to be, dear friends. I thank them for their faith in my ability.

Thanks are also due to my editor for her patience; I hope that it was rewarded by the end result.

Finally, and perhaps most importantly, I would like to thank my family who let me fly.

ENDORSEMENTS FOR TALKING THE WALK: SHOULD CEOS THINK MORE ABOUT SEX. HOW GENDER IMPACTS MANAGEMENT AND LEADERSHIP COMMUNICATION.

"This is an excellent piece of work, meticulously researched and presented." *Professor David Young, University of Derby, England, author of Work-based Learning Futures (2009)*

"Dr Julia Ibbotson is a very talented teacher, writer and leading academic . . . . positive and inspiring . . . Julia has produced high quality work . . . she is an excellent researcher." *Dr Deirdre Hughes OBE, founding director iCeGS, director DMH Associates, England*

"Dr Julia Ibbotson has maintained her commitment to gender and leadership over several decades manifested in her personal, professional and academic life. Her proposed book builds on a lifetime of experience and insight coupled with a style of writing which would make this an accessible book worthy of publication. Added to this, the under-recruitment and promotion of women into senior positions in the workplace continues to be a timely and on-going challenge for most societies and this would make a valid contribution to the debate". *Professor Marie Parker-Jenkins, professor of educational research, University of Limerick, Ireland, and author of Aiming High (2007)*

"Dr Julia Ibbotson's work will prove invaluable to those wishing to challenge and transform a current culture of testosterone-fuelled competition into one that pays more attention to change through collaboration and concern for the development of all members of a working team. Drawing from her own and others' experience, Julia suggests that male dominated institutions have much to learn from the management styles of the women they employ. She presents her scholarly research, based on deep probing into the working of educational management, in a style that is accessible and engaging to the general reader. Her work has an important message at a time when serious questions are being raised about how the lower standing of women in all branches of management might be addressed." *Professor Elaine Millard, author of Differently Literate (1997), Gender in the Secondary Curriculum: Balancing the Books (1998), Popular Literacies, Childhood and Schooling (2005), and professor of education at Birmingham City University, England*

"a great writer" *Peggy Fellouris, author of Dancing in the Rain (2011) , Massachusetts, USA*

"a most talented writer" *Nancy Mills, California, USA, travel writer and founder of <u>www.thepiritedwoman.com</u>*

GLOSSARY

DfE	UK Department for Education (at different dates referred to as DfES and DCSF)
EO	Equal Opportunities
ERA	Education Reform Act
INSET	In-service Training
LEA	Local Education Authority (now Local Authorities)
LMS	Local Management of Schools
NC	National Curriculum

PREFACE

"Women are a powerful and growing force in the global economy," says Alison Maitland in "Women Mean Business" (Raconteur Media 2010), and yet "women are scarce in senior management. They represent 15% of executive committee members of the 101 biggest companies in America, just 7% of this top management layer in Europe's largest companies and 3% in Asia, according to the Womenomics 101 survey published by Wittenberg-Cox." She adds "The business world is learning that the persistent gender gap—in terms of leadership, as well as occupational segregation and pay—needs to be addressed in the interests of not only fairness but also of economic competitiveness and the governance of society's institutions." And so, she concludes, "It is time for CEOs to get serious about sex."

It is here that I need to confess my bias: I am a woman(as well as an academic, seasoned researcher, teacher and writer) and one who has on numerous occasions wasted a great deal of time writing applications for promotions to higher leadership roles, only to end up frustrated and bruised. So I do have a personal subjective take on this. But I also happen to think that women make good leaders of teams (I wouldn't have applied for so many senior positions if I hadn't thought so). I do understand the disappointments. And I do feel strongly that women can contribute in a special way to the management and leadership of institutions. I did have a successful career in leadership when I was eventually given the opportunity to prove what I was worth—when finally a male assessor decided to take a chance on me. We professional and business women have a lot to offer and we should not feel disheartened by the (often male) assessors on the promotion panel.

So many women give up on the battle up the ladder in the corporate or professional world, and start their own businesses or professional consultancies. I applaud their determination and their success. But what a pity. Because Maitland goes on to claim that "there is a strong body of research showing that gender-balanced teams are more innovative and that companies with more women in leadership enjoy better financial results than all-male ones." She refers to two separate reports by Catalyst and Mckinsey.

In this recession and post-recession period, I would argue that women in middle/senior leadership and management positions are more likely to create teams which collaborate and are receptive to other ideas, and that, more than ever, we need creative solutions and consensus. This is not to take an overly simplistic view of masculine and feminine differences in leadership communication, but to advocate that both approaches are needed in senior leadership teams. And that there are occasions when the "stereotypical women's" approach of collaboration and consensus is the more effective way forward. Feminine communication is more strategic and risk-aware, and therefore can be more successful especially in times of recession.

"Men could benefit from learning from women how to be more risk-aware and how to consider why someone says or does something before responding," claims Professor Cary Cooper, from Lancaster University Management School, UK (Raconteur Media 2010). However, it is also possible that women's more consensus-based, team-building style of leadership communication may make us less likely to step forward for individual promotion.

We women tend to compare ourselves, often unfavourably, with others: *should I go for that promotion? Am I really ready for it? Or do I need more experience/training/qualifications to compete with other candidates?* Whilst men tend to say: *"I've put in a lot of work for the business/I'm the senior colleague here/I'm ready. I deserve this promotion"* and they just go for it. We women talk about our teams, our colleagues, the youngsters we've nurtured through the company, and hang back for ourselves. Men talk about themselves and know what they're worth. They are confident about interview and selection panels (research shows that men perform better in such situations than women). They are confident about their ability to do the job—even if eventually it transpires that they can't "cut it".

And so this book presents a study which explores issues of management communication from a gender perspective. The study was based on management teams in secondary schools (pupils aged 11-18 years) in the UK. However, its findings, I believe, are somewhat more universal and apply to many other types of institutions. But that is another research study and another book!

My study outlined in this book arose from a concern regarding the imbalance of men and women progressing to middle and higher management posts in secondary schools in England. This is shown in the statistics published by the UK's Department for Education (DfE) in a series of documents historically over twenty years. Current research indicates that this picture has not essentially changed by 2011. Indeed, the National College for Leadership of Schools and Children's Services (2009) reports that women are significantly under-represented in senior leadership in schools, especially in secondary schools (p34).

It also arose from my own personal struggle to advance my teaching and educational leadership career: on three occasions, as a school teacher seeking senior management positions, I was selected for a shortlist of six/seven equally experienced and well qualified candidates where only one was male. Who got the promotion? The man in each case. No, that wasn't a scientific study, only personal anecdotal reflection, but it got me thinking. I embarked on a long quest to analyse the twenty previous years of gendered promotional data. The picture became very clear: women were, and are still, sidelined for promotion. I talked to many CEOs and senior managers. And the gist was the same: *it's all about image, it's all about looking and sounding like a strong leader.*

So I investigated the possibility that there are gender differences in management communicative repertoires which have the effect of undermining women's chances of promotion to higher leadership positions.

In other words, do women "talk the walk", as men seem to? I argue that the organisational culture and the linguistic repertoire of "communities of *educational* practice" (Eckert & McConnell-Ginet 1992, Lave & Wenger 1991, Bergvall 1999, Holmes & Meyerhoff 1999, Wenger 2002, Hammersley 2004) reflect the values and ethos of the school-team of teacher practitioners, and that this influences women's career prospects.

Using case studies of four middle managers of both sexes in each of four secondary schools in one Midlands county of the UK, I observed team meetings, audio-recorded, and analysed them as a non-participant research observer. I transcribed key sequences and, using the framework of discourse analysis. I investigated whether there were linguistic differences between the male and female middle managers. I wanted to (a) analyse the way that language reflects management style (Hymes 1977, Arreman 2002, Baxter 2003), and (b) explore the possibility that communication differences might influence the under-representation of women in management posts.

My research used qualitative methods, based on the post-modern constructivist approach to gender as a social construct, and on a dialectical approach to linguistic theory, focusing on the role of context, pragmatic speech activity and the function of utterances within interactions. The originality of the enquiry is that it uses discourse analysis of real managerial transactions by male and female middle managers taking place in regularly scheduled meetings in the workplace. I also investigated the organisational culture of the four schools, in which the meetings were set. I used a content analysis of documents and semi-structured interviews with the head-teachers in each case.

Much of the research into gender linguistics over the last two or three decades has been of a feminist orientation and focused on one interpretation: that there are distinct gender differences in language use which reflect very different management styles and that women are, by default, negatively valued as potential managers. The argument has been that women's style is interpreted as falling short of a valued masculine model of language and management which is regarded as the norm.

However, in this book I argue that communication processes are *different* for men and women, because they bring different *frame and schema* to their interactions. Although this may mismatch the style valued by their assessors for promotion, the language of male and female middle managers is also influenced by frames other than that of gender, such as that of the middle manager role and that of the organisational culture of the school. I explore the usefulness of the Community of Practice model (Wenger 2002, 2004), which has developed over the last few years, as a tool for describing language variation between genders, across organisational cultures and within shared enterprises, since it can be used to explain the overlapping sets of shared linguistic traits between different linguistic groups.

My findings indicate a correlation between feminine-oriented linguistic practices in a community of educational practice and head-teachers' linguistic repertoire and, significantly, access of women to middle and senior managerial and leadership roles. In other words, if the senior manager is a woman (or a man who uses feminine styles of communication), then the acceptable language of leadership is that of team-building, consensus, collaboration, creativity, risk-awareness and receptivity to ideas. Women are more likely to be valued and to gain leadership and higher management roles in such a context. Conversely, women are less likely to gain promotion within an institution where the masculine style of communication is favoured and where the acceptable language of leadership is that of status, self-orientation, power and command.

I argue in this book that any community of practice which is developed from a feminine management style, and is reflected in linguistic strategies typifying the feminine end of the continuum (Cameron 1997, Wodak 1997), is more likely to be represented by team building, others-orientation and supportive practices (Statham 1987, Ozga 1993). I conclude that linguistic practices reflect the values of the community of educational practice and affect women's promotional prospects. Care needs to be taken by CEOs, including headteachers, that essentially feminine strategies of leadership reflected in communication styles are enabled and empowered in order to grow successful institutions for the future.

Following on from this, I suggest in the final chapter, implications for professional development, for men **and** women, in the realms of leadership communication. How can we women project the expected image for leadership? Can we women be taught to "talk the walk"? And, perhaps more importantly, should we?

Dr Julia Ibbotson, University of Derby, England, January 2012
juliaibbotson@btinternet.com

INTRODUCTION

SO WHAT ARE THE ISSUES?

The study underpinning this book explores issues of management and communication from a gender perspective within secondary schools. It arose from a concern regarding the clear male/female imbalance in progress to middle and senior management posts in secondary schools. Its starting point was the statistically significant shortfall of women managers in secondary schools at middle management/team leadership level and above in England and Wales, as published by the UK's Department for Education (DfE) over a period of twenty years, which reinforces the notion of the "glass ceiling" (Davidson and Cooper 1992). The main concern of the argument is regarding possible sociolinguistic barriers for women in reflecting the *valued* management style in secondary schools and therefore resulting in this imbalance in women's promotional opportunities.

The UK's DfE publications, "Statistics of Education: Teachers, England and Wales" include, amongst other statistics, tables showing teacher distributions by sector, sex, age, and salary level. Over the past twenty, or even thirty years, the statistics demonstrating distribution by sex in junior, middle and senior management posts in secondary schools in England and Wales have changed very little.

Across these years, these statistics showed that over twice as many women as men enter the profession in the UK secondary school sector at age 25 and below, although this discrepancy has evened out by age 35-39. Totals across all age groups showed that there were more men than women in teaching (101 to 97 thousand) in 1992, but a slightly decreased ratio of men to women (8:9) in 1997. Yet in 1992 the percentage of men at age 35-39 still on main scale salary dropped below 20% and this marked the point at which men forge ahead of women in terms of management positions. Men were then clustered at 4 management points (old scale D) from this age onwards. There were twice as many men as women on this level (middle management) and above (senior management) from this age upwards. For women, however, those on main scale never dropped below 25%, and those gaining management posts were clustered at 2 management points (old scale B), that is junior management level, across all age groups.

In 1997, the picture was much the same. The equivalent middle management salary level was then called the 14-17 pay spine level (roughly equivalent to the old 4 management points, previously scale D), and men again forged ahead at age 35-39 to this level and above. By age 40-44, men outnumbered women by 2:1 at this salary level and above, and by age 45-49 by 3:1.

In the 2001 edition, "Teachers in England", which includes pay distribution for England and Wales, statistics showed that again, men forged ahead of women at age 35-39 at the 14-17 pay spine level and above. The percentage of women at that level had slightly increased through age bands 40-44, 45-49 and 50-54, therefore slightly more women were gaining middle management posts. However, men still outnumbered women in middle and senior management posts by a little less than 2:1 up to age 49, then more than 2:1 after age 50.

The report by Powney, J et al (2003) found that "female head-teachers are substantially more likely to believe that gender has played some negative role in their careers: 26% of female head-teachers reported that gender had had some negative impact on their career, compared to only 3% of male head-teachers" (5.2.6, p49). The report indicates that a staggering 71% of female teachers consider that gender is an important factor in career progression (6.5, p59).

In the past ten years, the UK has developed an amended professional structure in which incentives have been introduced for teachers who want to remain in the classroom rather than take on management posts. This has, to a limited extent, advantaged women teachers, but the status of "advanced teacher" and "excellent teacher" have done little overall to raise more women into higher management posts.

Indeed, the National College for Leadership of Schools and Children's Services (2009) reports that women are significantly under-represented in senior leadership in schools, especially in secondary schools for the 11-18 year olds (p34). The issue appears to be a continuing challenge and one which needs further significant investigation.

The focus

There are clearly many reasons, including sociological and psychological, for this discrepancy, but my focus on this was to investigate one area in depth: whether there are any linguistic reasons which might influence the situation. A literature review of gender management theory, outlined in chapter one, suggested that there are differences in male and female management style and a review of gender linguistic theory, outlined in chapter two, suggested that there are differences in male and female linguistic style. Identified features of gender differences in management style and in language use correspond closely.

The literature suggested the concept of an identifiable "feminine" style of management most associated with women. This was also associated with linguistic usage employed by women in interactions which was identified as interpersonal, interactive, participative, and unifying, as opposed to the "masculine" style which was identified as assertive, status-engrossed, and dominating and was most associated with men.

Therefore, I wanted to focus on (a) investigating whether such linguistic differences between men and women are demonstrated within real managerial contexts, (b) analysing the way that language use reflects management style, and (c) exploring the possibility that linguistic differences influence the under-representation of women in middle and senior management posts.

The use of terms

In this work, I have defined **gender** as not referring to a biologically-defined sex category but to the social distinctions drawn between men and women, in other words, socially constructed attributes, learned behaviours. I have therefore used the terms "**feminine**" and "**masculine**" when referring to gender differences in language usage and repertoires, and in management style, in order to indicate tendencies on a continuum, in other words, gender as a continuous variable, for example "more or less feminine". However, I have used the terms "**women**" and "**men**" when referring to biological sex categories, for example in discussing statistics on salary differentials as used by the DfS and management structures in schools. I have used the terms "**female**" and "**male**" (a) when referring to the interconnection of the two, that is, the clusters of traits at each end of the continuum, or (b) when applying an adjectival modifier to refer to the nouns "women" and "men".

I have defined **discourse analysis** in the linguistic use of the term in this research context, as the analysis of the following:

(1) speech events (or utterances) within interactive spoken texts (or connecting sequences),
(2) the organisation of these texts and the ways in which parts of the texts are connected, and
(3) the devices used for achieving textual structure as part of the interactional process.

This is a matter of sociolinguistics, the subdivision of linguistics which deals with the social aspect of language, or language specifically seen within social contexts (see O'Grady 1997).

The research base

Previously, much of the work in theory and research into gendered language and management has been shaped by the dominance/difference debate and often by attempts to support or deny negative stereotypes of women's repertoires. I wished to explore what *actually* happens in management communications.

In my study, I wished to investigate the existence of any possible gender differences in language use between middle managers/ team leaders in case studies of four secondary schools and to explore the way that language use reflects management style. I also wished to investigate whether this suggested one reason for the under-representation of women in middle and senior management posts.

The basis of the work was therefore:
- to explore gender differences in communication styles within real managerial transactions.
- to consider how language works as part of the management process
- to consider whether any feminine speech repertoires disadvantage women as managers beyond junior management level

The aims of my work were:

- to elucidate within real managerial transactions of middle managers, gender differences in the strategic use of language in interactions with their teams
- to explore senior managers' perceptions of middle management skills and characteristics which might be seen to affect promotion prospects
- to evaluate the extent to which, as a result, women might be negatively valued as managers at different levels.

Little research has been published on investigations into supposed gender differences in communication styles within real managerial transactions. The originality of my argument lies in the fact that it does this, using discourse analysis, and that it will contribute to an understanding of gender issues in relation to specific management communications.

As I wanted to study real contexts in which middle managers communicate with their teams within normal school situations, I audio-recorded scheduled team meetings inside secondary schools. I then transcribed them for discourse analysis. I analysed quantitative data to an extent, in that the regularity of occurrences of specific speech traits was an important factor, but I took an interpretative approach to the discourse analysis of the meeting as a whole, in order to investigate the way in which the manager used his/her speech repertoires within the transaction. I explored what actually happened linguistically between the manager and the team, and compared the differences between men and women in different schools, focusing on three key areas which I had identified from the literature as reflecting the greatest differences in management style:

- dealing with status;
- handling conflict/conflict resolution;
- and decision-making.

I also explored the influence which the different organisational cultures had on the context of the meetings, and whether there was any significant difference between schools headed up (led) by men or women. In other words whether a school with a female headteacher (principal) demonstrated a different type of organisational culture from a school headed by a man, and whether this affected the linguistic repertoires presented by both male and female middle managers. I also explored, within semi-structured interviews, the opinions of headteachers (principals) on the desired characteristics of middle managers, in order to consider the evaluation of skills/characteristics in making decisions about promotion. I used data from the schools to indicate the actual management structure by sex in each case.

My study, therefore, investigated the relationship between these evaluations and gender-based communicative performance and considers whether feminine linguistic strategies, and therefore female managers, are negatively valued. My argument arose from my investigations into the communication process itself within a specific context (middle management team meetings in secondary schools), and into gendered language repertoires, specifically gender differences in language use.

My research questions were as follows:

- how does language work as part of the management process in real managerial transactions, and how does it reflect the skills and characteristics of middle managers?
- are there differences in men's and women's linguistic repertoires which may reinforce senior managers' perceptions of management performance?
- do senior managers' perceptions of valued middle management skills and characteristics favour men over women?

The argument

My argument, or thesis, is that, exemplified by my case studies, communication processes are different for men and women; that these differences arise from the different agenda (frame/schema) which they bring to the situation; that there is an identifiable "middle management agenda" which is gender-free; and that the feminine linguistic repertoire mismatches, in some areas, the style valued by, especially, male headteachers, who constitute the majority of promotion assessors.

I argue that the linguistic framework of the Community of Practice (Wenger 1998, Bergvall 1999, Holmes and Meyerhoff 1999) is a useful tool for describing language variation between the genders, across organisational cultures, and within shared enterprises, as it can be used to explain the overlapping sets of shared linguistic traits between different linguistic communities. This is especially so given the importance of current change experienced in schools and school management practices, as explored by Hargreaves (1998), and his notions of collaboration being developed into "contrived collegiality". I would argue that while the practice of collegiality or collaboration involved an advantage for women because the feminine frame focuses on empowerment and support, the practice of contrived collegiality can also involve an advantage for women because the feminine frame also focuses on consensus.

Finally, I argue that it is more necessary than ever, in the current climate of change, to recognise and value the contribution of the "feminine" linguistic and management style to a balanced management team within a school, and that there are advantages in this for the future development of school management. I outline implications and strategies in chapter eight.

An outline of the argument through the chapters

In chapter one, therefore, I review the existing literature in order to establish the major debates over the last three decades regarding the role of communication in management and the gendered styles of management and communication. Broadly, these focus on the differences between the genders in style and effectiveness, and the clusters of traits associated with each gender. The identified clusters which demonstrate a consistent pattern throughout the literature show that men tend to be associated with a more detached, rational, tough, depersonalised style in management behaviour and communication strategies, whereas women tend to be associated with a more supportive, empowering, collaborative style. I develop the argument (which is pursued further in chapter two) that men and women bring different "frames" (world views) to the managerial situation, and to management in their chosen communication strategies. However, perceived masculine styles have been given normative status, leaving feminine styles deficient by default. In many cases, the literature ignores feminine styles altogether and focuses on a gender-blind argument on management styles which nonetheless in fact concentrates on styles associated with masculine clusters. Shakeshaft (1989) argued that this "world view" focused through a "male lens" assumes that it is representative of both genders, and assumes that effective women managers will use masculine managerial techniques.

Dr Julia Helene Ibbotson PhD, FHEA

This view would therefore reinforce the entrenchment of the "glass ceiling effect" (Davidson and Cooper 1992) upon which my study is based, using DfS statistics showing the shortfall in women's access to middle and higher management levels in secondary schools compared to men's.

However, while Davidson and Cooper, Shakeshaft and Evetts (1994) argued that traditional management values and indeed embedded structures for management behaviours and strategies often advantage men, nevertheless they all argued, along with Loden (1987) and Strachan (1993), that feminine styles can be more effective especially in an educational context.

A consideration of the literature on organisational culture prompted me to develop the argument that in schools the perceptions of teachers within an organisational culture which seeks to value a "fellow professional" frame in discourse style, may well effect the managerial linguistic repertoire adopted within that school, moving it towards more feminine linguistic strategies of enabling, empowering, and collegiality.

I conclude this part of my argument by reasserting that if men and women approach management and communication situations with different agendas, different frames, which give rise to different linguistic strategies, yet also use the linguistic strategies perceived as required by their role as middle managers, the research base needs to take this into account and consider the context (of the organisational culture and of the interaction itself) in order to gain insights into gendered linguistic strategies.

Since I establish in chapter one the importance of language and communication in the manager's role, I develop this argument **in chapter two,** where I explore the ideas generated by the debates on language differences, in a critical analysis of applied studies of the differences between male and female linguistic repertoires. I review the literature in order to establish the major debates in gender linguistics over the last three decades, and track the development of ideas. I argue that the deficiency model of gendered language use, especially propagated by Lakoff (1975) was based only on a scientific enumeration of **forms** of language used by men and women, whereas an analysis of the **function** of utterances within the interactional context is required. In my fieldwork analysis I concentrate on function as opposed to form, in other words the recognition of the importance of the context of any interaction, and therefore of the pragmatics operating within that interaction. In chapter two, I provide the rationale for this, citing the published literature in support.

In chapter two, I outline the differences identified in published research between men's and women's linguistic usage. These were grouped around the female profile of cooperation, unity, building relationships, and rapport, and around the male profile of competition, striving for status, and task achievement (Schick Case 1988, Tannen 1992.) Men were found to use speech features which suggested authority, dominance and status differentiation, while women were found to use speech features which suggested support, facilitation and empowerment of others.

I go on to discuss an explanation given by some linguists for the existence and significance of these differences, the concept of the different "frames" brought to any interaction by women and by men (Coates 1993, Shakeshaft 1989, Tannen 1992,1994). These are at times referred to in the literature as "world views" or "intentions", but all refer to the effect on linguistic variation of those identities men and women assume by gender. I argue that, again, there is a danger in interpreting the masculine style as the norm because it is regarded as more authoritative and dominant, and the feminine style as deficient by default. I suggest that the communicative competence expounded by Hymes (1971) may be interpreted differently by men and women if they belong, or see themselves as belonging, to different speech communities or linguistic subcultures. Additionally, the use of the frame and schema theory goes some way to explaining the way we use past experiences and understandings to shape linguistic usages, for example in gendered linguistic repertoires among others.

Finally, in chapter two, I suggest that model of the Community of Practice (Eckert 1990, Eckert and McConnell-Ginet 1992, Bergvall 1999, Holmes and Meyerhoff 1999) provides a useful tool for exploring the similarities and dissimilarities in gendered talk in my study of middle managers' communication strategies in team meetings in schools. This model provides a tool for investigating a number of linguistic diversities, not only that of gender but also the interlinking frames arising from the shared practices, shared enterprises, and shared pragmatic repertoires of other group memberships, such as (in my study) that of middle managers in the context of their team meetings, or that of the organisational culture of the school in which the team meetings take place.

In chapter three, I outline the methods I pursued and the rationale for my choices. I discuss the epistemological and methodological issues involved in this particular study and explain my position as researcher. I outline my decision to use a qualitative approach, to use case studies and to take the role of non-participant observer in my fieldwork, audio-recording team meetings, so that I could examine first hand the language of pre-existing social groups undertaking real tasks in the way that they do regularly as part of their work commitment. I outline my research design and discuss issues of validity and reliabilty.

I argue that my approach owed much to (1) Dell Hymes' 1977 ideas on the "ethnography of speaking", or the necessity of investigating the functions of real speech events, (2) the concept of gender as a social construct (Cameron 1992,1997, Coates 1993, Tannen 1992,1994, Wodak 1997), and (3) the post-modern constructivist approach, whose advocates reject the view that there is a true knowledge "out there" and argue that "the social world is constructed and shaped by members of society" (see Abbott and Wallace 1997). I argue against the positivist approach linked to quantitive research methodology in which, it is argued, the researcher is not involved subjectively or personally in the research process. I argue for a position which reflects the post-modern constructivist approach, rejecting the view that the sociologist can be a dispassionate and uncritical "scientific" observer and arguing that, in social research, insights can be gained through a subjective interpretation of the events we describe.

I explain that, as with previous researchers in sociolinguistics, I have used the dialectical approach to linguistic theory, emphasising the role of context, the pragmatic speech activity within an interaction, the "function" (Dell Hymes 1977 as above, Graddol and Swann 1992, Coates 1993). I argue that if men and women tend towards different world views, and bring to speech events different agenda and frame/schema (Minsky 1975, Goffman 1974,1981, Gumperz 1982, Tannen 1994) this will shape the creation of different linguistic repertoires to reflect them. Discourse analysis in this research is closely interlinked with semantics and pragmatics. I outline the problems inherent in analysing and interpreting these but I argue the necessity of this in order to achieve insights into the workings of language in the chosen context.

However, I also argue that I have used what is termed by O'Grady et al (1997) as "social network analysis", as a non-participant observer in the case studies. I argue that I needed to establish a rapport with the managers whose interactions I was studying, so that there was a basis of trust, yet maintain a level of objectivity and detachment to the **proceedings** of the meetings I audio-recorded and analysed. In this way, the managers were not participants with me in a co-operative enquiry. In this chapter, I also discuss a similar interlinking of objectivity in investigation and subjectivity in interpretative analysis in the semi-structured interviews with the headteachers. I explore the issues involved in the dynamics of the conflicting elements of the study and the way in which these determined my choice of research methods so that I could find the most appropriate way of addressing the research questions.

I also outline in chapter three the ethical issues involved in my methodology, chronologies of the processes involved in the fieldwork and the discourse analysis.

In chapter four, I show the first stage of my exploration of the organisational cultures of the four schools I was using in my case studies. This chapter outlines the information I acquired from a review of each school's documents: the school prospectus, any available Equal Opportunities policies or investigations, and documents on the staffing structure which indicated the distribution of management posts by sex. I discuss my subjective interpretation of the findings. My main findings were that women were seen to be under-represented at middle and senior management levels in all four schools in my study, that they were clustered in junior management / assistant roles, that women in higher management posts were more likely to be in pastoral roles. More importantly, my argument is that there was no difference in the existence of these features whether the headteacher was male or female (although in schools with a female headteacher women had a slightly greater access to academic management roles than in schools with a male headteacher), and that there was little difference in schools where documentary evidence suggested an awareness of gender issues in professional development.

In chapter five, I explore another aspect of the organisational culture of the schools, outlining the process and my interpretation of the semi-structured interviews with the four headteachers, in which I aimed to gain insights into their evaluations of the skills and characteristics they required from their middle managers. I discuss the issues involved in the research methods used, the subjectivity of the linguistic pragmatics involved and of my interpretations of the outcome. I also discuss the implications of the results in terms of their possible influence on the organisational cultures of the schools in my study. I found that the most highly valued skills/characteristics for effective middle management were those associated with the feminine style in the literature. This appeared the case in both schools with female heads and in one of the schools with a male head. However, the other male headteacher tended to demonstrate a greater valuing of the masculine management style. Although the valuing of many features of the feminine style suggests a female-friendly organisational culture generally within all four schools, I argue that the differences could also provide an influence on the organisational culture in which the middle managers are operating and on their chosen linguistic repertoires.

Chapters six and seven comprise (a) the transcriptions of the key areas of the team meetings recorded (the areas which I selected to indicate the manager's use of language in order to establish status, deal with critical incidents, handle conflict and make decisions), (b) the analytical commentaries on each interaction and (c) an indication of the patterns emerging from the data. I discuss my findings which indicate differences of language use between men and women in three key areas of establishing status, handling conflict and decision-making. In these two chapters, I analyse more than six hours of meetings, involving two male and two female middle managers from one school, and one male and one female manager from another school (both schools having male headteachers) and find that there were clear themes inhabiting the data. Patterns of gender linguistic differences in interactional strategies used by the managers were becoming clear. The cluster of linguistic strategies used by both men and women included the use of topic control, statives and declaratives, first person statives and professional jargon. I argue that these constitute a common "middle management speak" which reflects the experience of and pragmatic understanding of a community of practice (common group "frame" for language) within middle management. The differences in linguistic strategies between men and women in three of the key areas (establishing status, handling conflict, and decision-making) notably included men's use of imperatives, floor dominance, dismissal of empowerment and distancing strategies. Women's linguistic strategies, in contrast, included empowerment of others, support/co-operation/consensus strategies, deflection of conflict, apology and self-correction. I argue that these constituted a common "gender speak" which reflects the experience of and pragmatic understanding of a community of practice within each gender, in other words the "frame" which each gender brings to the interactional event. I argue additionally that individuals' value weightings of these separate but linked frames or communities of practice provide the key to individual idiolects. This was seen clearly in the language of the male manager of the school whose male headteacher demonstrated the greatest valuing of masculine management style. This manager's linguistic strategies tended to move nearer to the masculine end of the continuum than any of the others. I argue that the community of practice in this school's organisational culture influenced this particular male manager to foreground his masculine frame more emphatically.

Having identified clear patterns in chapters six and seven, in two of the schools, I decided that the most appropriate way forward was to interrogate the rest of my data in the light of these emerging patterns, and to investigate whether these patterns were confirmed in the other two schools studied.

In chapter eight, I identify the detail of the comparative linguistic analyses emerging so far, and test this against the data found in critical sequences within the three key areas of gender difference from the remaining two schools. I found that the linguistic strategies used by both male and female managers in these two schools with female headteachers tended towards the feminine end of the continuum, with strategies mainly focused on co-operation and consensus. I argue that the gendered community of practice, as far as the men were concerned, had become subsumed under the greater influence and importance of the school community of practice.

I argue that each individual's idiolect (analysed in the commentaries on each manager's linguistic usage in the meetings recorded) is composed of strategies from a number of repertoires from sociolects arising from the communities of practice to which they belong, for example gender, managerial, professional, and the specific school community. I argue that these are informed and shaped by the shared experiences, shared pragmatic understandings and shared discourse structures and strategies within each group. I argue that although linguistic strategies differentiated by gender are significant, there are also other influences on language choices in any repertoire, and that these are influenced by membership of communities of practice other than that of gender, which may be foregrounded during interactions.

In conclusion, I reassert my argument, exemplified in the case studies, that there are differences in the way that male and female middle managers use linguistic strategies in managerial interactions with their teams these differences arise from the different frames they bring to the situation; these frames can be identified as communities of practice in which shared experiences and pragmatic understandings shape discourse gender variation in linguistic usage is part of a continuum of both sexes' gendered linguistic practices there is an identifiable middle management frame which is common to both genders gendered linguistic practices may be subsumed under other linguistic practices, for example that of the field of educational management or of the particular school itself and its organisational culture the feminine style of management is valued in theory by both male and female headteachers, although in practice there is a significant under-representation of women at middle and senior management levels the feminine linguistic repertoire may mismatch the management style **incipiently valued** by male headteachers who form the majority of assessors for promotion to senior levels of management

Finally, I argue that especially in the current climate of change it is important to maintain a balanced management team and to value the feminine linguistic and management style in the practice of promotion within schools and other institutions. I outline the implications and strategies for the future development of school management, and address the issue: do women "talk the walk", and should they be expected to?

CHAPTER ONE

WHAT IS THE CONTEXT OF THE RESEARCH STUDY?

Introduction

In this chapter, I outline the relevant ideas which I have identified in the literature as having a bearing on my research study. In my study, I have concentrated on issues of gendered language repertoires and I explore the relevant literature on this area in chapter two. Perceptions regarding the sociological reasons for gendered differences in management and communication style have been discussed extensively elsewhere (for example, Loden 1985, Shakeshaft 1989, Davidson and Cooper 1992, Tannen 1994) and it is not my intention in this study to retread the same ground. It is, however, relevant to look at what these differences are and at the linguistic reasons for such gendered differences. I am particularly interested in exploring the communication process itself, in a specific context, that of middle managers' team meetings in secondary schools. I am investigating what happens in these situations and what is significant about these events and processes, with specific reference to gender language.

However, in this chapter, I also investigate previous research into gender differences in management style, and literature on organisational theory and management theory, especially perceptions of comparative effectiveness. This provides an interesting background to my data, so that I can gain insights into gender differences in the specific communication process under study.

Throughout the book, I argue that communication processes are different for men and women because of their different "agendas" (frames) **as** men and women, which they bring to the situation. I also argue that

1

there are other repertoires which middle managers use, regardless of gender, but which arise from the "agenda" of the middle manager role itself.

The concept of gender

Giddens (1989) defines sex as "biological or anatomical differences between men and women" and gender as "concerning the psychological, social and cultural differences between males and females" (p158). In this thesis I define the term "gender" as a socially constructed category based on sex but referring to the social distinctions drawn between men and women, as opposed to the biologically defined category referred to as "sex". "Gender" in this study refers to the socially constructed attributes or traits which tend to be attributed to each sex, as argued in Cameron (1992, 1997), Coates (1993, 1998), Wodak (1997). My argument is based on the idea that discourse is a social practice and so gendered identities are constructed through and embedded within interactional discourse, as opposed to being simply reflected in language. Therefore, this study looks at not only the differences between men and women's language but also their similarities in specific contexts. It is a concept of gender as a variable, not as an absolute, in the way that a biological sex category is. In a linguistic context I argue that differences between men and women in language use are not, and cannot be, absolute, but are identifiable as clusters of traits, or tendencies, at a point on a continuum. In other words, a woman's linguistic usage may be more or less "feminine" in character, or nearer or further from the feminine end of the continuum. She may also display some linguistic tendencies which are nearer to the masculine end of the continuum. For this reason, I have used the terms "feminine" and "masculine" when referring to gender differences in language use and repertoires, and to tendencies in management styles. On the other hand, I have used the terms "women" and "men" when referring to the biological category admitted on birth certificates/ the census/ application and registration forms, and thus used by schools and the DfS to identify distribution of posts by sex. I have used the terms "female" and "male" as either simply an adjectival modifier from the nouns "woman" and "man", or when referring to the clusters at each end of the continuum. I am, of course, like Coates (1993) aware of the technical use of the term "gender" in linguistics as a grammatical category, used in many romance and Germanic languages. However, as this thesis concerns only English speakers and as there are no longer any such grammatical categories in modern English, unlike Coates, I do not anticipate there to be a confusion in the use of the term.

Communication in management

The literature on organisational theory and management theory makes it clear that communication can be regarded as a major activity of the manager in all fields, not only in educational management. Oral communication face-to-face with team members is the most significant part of this. Martin and Willower (1981) outlined a Mintzberg-type study of American school principals, albeit "elementary school" who were found to spend more than 70% of their time in communication of some sort, including more than 50% spent in oral interactions with colleagues. Studies by Kmetz and Willower in 1982 and Berman in 1982 supported these findings.

Management studies such as those undertaken by Pitner (1981), Kmetz and Willower (1982), and Gross and Trask (1964,1976), although small case studies, began to suggest that men and women use this communication time differently, and use different communication approaches in their interactions. Research into gender management styles, for example Loden (1985), Statham (1987), Shakeshaft (1989) and Ozga (1993), indicated that linguistic distinctions may arise from men and women's differing aims and intentions as managers. In chapter two, I outline research which indicates that gendered linguistic differences may arise from men and women's different intentions, not only as managers, but also as men and women (Tannen 1992).

Therefore, an evaluation of these communications must take into account these differing intentions as well as the differing linguistic-stylistic features themselves. An interpretation of female style and effectiveness may be based on a male stereotype as a norm (a deficiency model), not taking into account other frames which a female might bring into the situation and which might influence her choice of linguistic repertoire (a difference model).

The idea of interpreting language within a sociocultural context, reflecting Saussure's "language is a social fact", underpinned the philosophy behind Dell Hymes' use of the term "ethnography of communication" in the early 1970s. The perspective of this present study is not linguistics as a system of input/output data-handling analysis, but an exploration of social interaction: framing language meanings as a way of handling people in situations, controlling interactions and interpersonal relationships. The difference between men's and women's use of linguistic strategies in these interactional situations can be seen as inextricably linked to their sociocultural positions and their culturally conditioned meaning systems, assumptions and inferences. The relationship between language and thought in this context is an important facet of this perspective and brings into play the question of how far men and women can be said to belong to different speech communities.

As Stevenson (1993) wrote,

> "For language to be used in communication, however, linguistic knowledge must be linked to knowledge in other domains. Such a link can be found in the way that words activate both syntactic knowledge and concepts in other domains." (p306)

If gender can shape people's position in society, values and thought processes, and we need to look to feminist thought here, then it could also be said to be linked closely to language use, communication strategies, and the functions and intentions underlying them. Fasold (1990) identified this problem:

> "The question should be 'what differences in interactional strategy between men and women are there, and how do they reveal the structure of society with regard to the sexes?'
> "(p106)

The present study explores how language is used as the main tool for executing these strategies in the specific context of management within the secondary school.

The sociocultural context of a specific secondary school is therefore an important area to explore in terms of the background to a study of gendered managerial language use within it. There may, for example, be implications of specifically "teacher" preconceptions and expectations of management role and style which are different from those of other organisations, or indeed from those of other schools. Is there a colleague-based approach recognised between fellow professionals, for example the expectation of autonomy in the classroom, which affect the managerial communication style between managers and their teams which is both expected and delivered? Is there an organisational culture within a particular school which emphasises a special approach between teachers and pupils / teachers and teachers, which differs from that of another school? These are issues which I return to in later chapters in the light of my research study.

Gender issues of management

I looked at published studies of gendered management style in a variety of managerial contexts as well as the specific context of the secondary school because I wanted a broad basis for comparison. I then explored the findings from studies of gendered linguistic traits in order to investigate whether there was a correlation between women's management style and women's linguistic traits, which I explore in chapter two. A number of studies have investigated women's management style in different management contexts, not only that of educational management. A review of this literature shows that a pattern emerges from the research. This pattern relates closely to that identified by linguists investigating women's language traits across a variety of social and management situations, and the pragmatic or semiotic context for them. Value-laden attitudes towards particular management and communication styles are also explored in this literature, questioning whether the perceived or actual feminine style may be regarded as in some way deficient to the masculine norm.

Lindsay Darking (1991) used a number of case studies to illustrate women's experiences of attitudes towards them as managers. She argued that the "Headmaster" tradition has merely been replaced by a more managerial model in schools, which still takes its characteristics from an essentially masculine model, such as that of analytical detachment, rational problem-solving, and toughness, all traditionally attached to the male stereotype. She wrote:

> "a Local Government Management Board study found that the tough, competitive approach to management in local authorities meant that women who tried to do things differently—for example, by working in a more democratic and open way—were seen as ineffective by almost everyone in the organisation, including other women."

However, she also describes female college Heads who are trying more collaborative, democratic and open styles of leadership in what appears to be a successful and effective way, although they too had encountered prejudicial attitudes towards their own particular style of management. Darking's point is that if this style is perceived as essentially female and is negatively value-laden because of its "deviation" from the conventional masculine model, then this could produce an inherent barrier to status for women in general and have grave implications for recruitment.

Other literature also explores the idea of an essentially feminine style of management and communication. Jenny Ozga (1993) identified the feminine style as "enabling". In her collection of profiles and anecdotes, she drew out a pattern of skills associated with the women managers in her study. These were interpersonal and interactional skills: those associated with communication, with a sensitivity to people's feelings and responses, and those motivated by a desire for consensus and unification, a desire for working towards common goals. Marilyn Loden (1985) also identified a similar set of skills characterised by female managers. She identified interpersonal skills of listening, a concentration on empowering others not self, and an expertise in teamwork and participative management. These identified patterns in the literature are interesting in the light of my own findings outlined in chapters 6, 7 and 8.

Ozga's and Loden's identification of characteristically feminine skills of management and communication need not necessarily preclude males: men might also positively value interpersonal skills and a desire for consensus. It is important not to assume a male "opposite" to these characteristics, however temptingly this might fit with a masculine stereotype of management behaviour. However, other studies indicated that men do tend to take a different slant from women on the choices they make in managerial and communicative repertoires. Anne Statham (1987), for example, in her study of gender-based management, claimed that women tended to use a more task-engrossed, person-invested style, while men may use a more image-engrossed, autonomy-invested style. The phrase "may use a more . . ." appeals to me as it implies a choice of style repertoire, rather than a rigid gender identity. Statham was concerned to stress that the feminine style should not be regarded as deficient in terms of some masculine norm, but merely different in terms of a spectrum of behaviour, and that both styles may produce misunderstandings, misinterpretations, and hence resentments and negative perceptions from the other gender.

It is also important to note that Statham was not making the (female) people-oriented, (male) task-orientated distinction used in the past, but one which is rather based on an extroverted/introverted orientation. Davidson and Cooper (1993) also pointed out a study by Ferrario in which women managers scored more highly than men in "consideration" and "initiating structure": in other words, they showed an emphasis on team management with a high regard for people **and** for task.

The view that women choose to use different styles from men because of their different "world view" or perspective was explored by Charol Shakeshaft (1989). This diverges from the view that women use different styles because they inherently lack the kind of leadership qualities traditionally perceived as owned by men. Her work criticised the "androcentric bias" in theory and research, where the world is viewed through a "male lens" and then the assumption made that this is representative of both genders. She criticised the bias which embodied the "conception of leadership as that which men who are designated leaders do" (p154). The "no difference" (or gender blind) view which implies that successful women managers are those who use the same managerial techniques as men, neglects to account for any other repertoires used by males and females in addition to those in common between the genders. Shakeshaft argued:

> "All of the "no difference" literature looks at the ways men manage and then asks, "Do women do these things too?" Not surprisingly, for the most part, women do, indeed, do them . . . What is not investigated in these studies, what isn't even conceptualised, are the activities that women undertake and their motivation for doing so that are in addition to and different from those that men perform" (pp166-167).

In order to support her view, she quoted studies by Kmetz and Willower (1982) and Pitner (1981) where women school managers were found to spend more time in support and advisory roles, and in contacts with students and teachers than men. She also outlined work by Gross and Trask (1964,1976) who found that women showed a higher task attention than men; they exerted more control of teachers' professional activities by discussing classroom problems; they kept informed about children, by monitoring more closely and receiving reports more frequently. In other words, they used a more involved and "hands-on" approach. Again, these patterns are interesting to note as I explore the issues arising from my own findings in later chapters.

Shakeshaft's ideas were concerned with management behaviour, but within the linguistic field the same idea is also supported by reference to the frame and schema theory (for example, Goffman & Minsky 1974, Gumpertz 1982) which is used to explain differences in the ways in which interlocutors shape discourse. The basis is that we use our past experiences, social and linguistic, to shape our present usage. Thus, men and women, amongst other social groups, bring to their discourse different frames. The idea was developed by Tannen (1992) in her concept of gendered "frames" and in the Community of Practice model outlined by Bergvall (1999) and Holmes and Meyerhoff (1999). Both of these are pursued further in chapter two.

Yet characteristics of the traditional masculine model still seem to be valued generally in our society, the toughness, detachment, dominance outlined earlier in this chapter, despite a certain lipservice paid to "political correctness" (begun in the 1980s) and being "in touch with the feminine side". Apart from the implication in this idea that some kind of inherent "female-ness" exists as opposed to the social construct of gender characteristics, there is also the implication that women lack the valued masculine qualities above. Indeed, there is even a tendency to deride women who do display them, as "unfeminine". Davidson and Cooper (1992) pointed out the significance of linguistic labelling: a man is a "leader" whereas a woman is "bossy"; a man is "constructive and showing initiative and persistence" whereas a woman is "nagging".

If there is a perceived legitimacy of leadership associated with conforming to the dominant style, that is, in most secondary schools and colleges, masculine, then the feminine style is seen in terms of the deficiency model. It follows that there are then pressures on women to adopt a more masculine style for themselves. The most popular response in recent years has been to invest in assertiveness training for women managers. Davidson and Cooper (1992) claimed that a woman's assumed role in society (support/unity/peacemaking) extends to her style in management roles, and that this may cause stress and a pressure to adopt masculine managerial attributes in order to become more "assertive, confident, decisive, delegatory"(p47). They added that current criteria (in the 1990s) for judging good management focused on these skills rather than on team-building and supportive behaviour. One factor contributing to the "glass ceiling effect" could be this perception of female style: how women come across may be valued in terms of the life of the community (the school community included), but not rated highly as leadership quality. This creates a constraint in itself, but also has an effect on women's self-image and self-value, which also might undermine promotional possibilities.

Respondents in Julia Evetts' (1994) study of headteachers' career histories claimed that "the whole business of competitive interview actually suits men a great deal better than women", and that "a lot of business is decided at meetings and that meetings, on the whole, suit men, large formal meetings particularly." Criteria for management, appraisal for management, and the structures for management, look here to be advantaging male managers, yet Evetts and Shakeshaft (1989) both argued that in education the feminine style logically seems more appropriate. In other words, managerial behaviours for an "effective school" correspond with feminine managerial behaviours, for example by emphasising achievement, frequently evaluating student progress, supporting teachers and using compromising and conciliatory strategies for conflict resolution.

On a wider international and organisational level, Loden (1987) also ascribed failure in American companies to a failure to recognise female potential and talent as an essential asset in management. She argued that those companies utilising women's management skills showed increased productivity, employee commitment and greater cooperation. Likewise, Strachan (1993) in her research report of a development programme in New Zealand for female educational managers, acknowledged that there is a female preferred style of management. This, she referred to as "affiliative" and centres it on the importance of relationships, shared decision-making processes, empowerment of others. She concluded that "good educational leadership practice is seen to more closely "fit" with the preferred practice of many women."

The literature, therefore, suggested a pattern of skills characteristic of the female manager in a number of different managerial contexts, not only that of the secondary school. These skills were within the area of interpersonal relationships and interaction, and involve support and empowerment of others being managed. I have also looked at the masculine model of leadership and at the way in which this might be valued more highly than the feminine model in our society. However, I have outlined four items of literature where it is suggested that feminine skills are more effective than masculine skills, especially within the school context. I now move on to consider ideas of managerial style and effectiveness.

Managerial style and effectiveness

During the last three decades, ideas on managerial style have shifted focus. Twenty years ago, they tended to focus on Mintzberg's (1980) model of managerial roles. These included the interpersonal role (figurehead, leader, liaison operator), the informational role (monitor, disseminator, spokesperson), and the decisional role (entrepreneur, resource allocator, negotiator). None of these roles seem to preclude the feminine model outlined above, and almost all require high-level communication skills, some, indeed, the negotiation, consensus-seeking and team-building skills identified as within the feminine style. Leading and controlling, when seen in this light, is also within the concept of the feminine style. Moreover, Hersey and Blanchard's (1982) concept of management, was based on the flexibility of a manager to use four leadership styles deriving from a combination of two basic leadership behaviours, directive and supportive. Thus they recognised the importance of supportive leadership behaviour, which is identified in the literature as a feature of feminine style.

Models of management style have tended to be functional, in the sense that they refer to the activities/operations which managers are assumed to undertake. They also tended to be non-specific to a particular type of organisation, and therefore by nature were generalised. Adair (1988) looked at effective management in terms of three basic functions: task, team maintenance, and individual needs; management style being determined by the way you choose to perform those functions. He found the "Three Circles" model the most useful model of effective management, where the three functions ("needs") were overlapping and interlinked. In this model, the style of a particular manager foregrounded whichever function was appropriate at a given time to him/her.

However, Ball's (1987) use of Weber's "ideal types" applied management theory more directly to the school context. The model allowed for the flexibility of style within the micro-political system of the school, in other words for style switching. Management style, according to Ball, described the way in which managers resolve conflicting functions, those concerned with achieving and maintaining control (domination) and those concerned with ensuring social order and commitment (integration). Control, in the organisational sense, ensuring continuance and survival, and in the educational sense making and implementing policy, might often involve conflict and opposition. Integration, then, was all the more important as a means to deal with the potential or actual conflicts. In organisational terms, the task function (initiating and directing) and the human function (consideration) provided these contradictory pressures.

He claimed:

> "In abstract terms in the school context, leadership styles are both an act of domination (the assertion of ultimate responsibility) and an expression of integration (the focus of identity and common purpose in the institution)." (p83)

Ball's four main styles ("ideal types"), interpersonal, managerial, and political (subdivided into adversorial and authoritarian) were not gender related and took no account of gender differences. This "gender-blindness" reflected the issues raised by Mills (1988) and Shakeshaft (1989) on the way the world tended to be viewed through a "male lens". It was also noted by Evetts (1994). However, Ball's interpersonal style took more account of the feminine characteristics of management identified in the previous section of this chapter, even though his exploration of managerial and political styles owed more to features identified as masculine. The interpersonal style was marked by an emphasis on personal contact and communication, individual negotiations and compromises, and procedures deformalised. In other words, the stress was on the human (consideration) function of the organisation.

Other literature on management style and effectiveness seemed to be characterised by challenges to the traditional masculine model. Clampitt (1991), for example, argued the case for a new model appropriate to modern management. His "Dance technique" of management communication relied on flexibility and a much greater understanding of people, contexts and interpretations, skills accessible to the feminine style suggested in the literature. Benfari (1991) also used a wider basis for the assessment of management style beyond the Myers-Briggs Type Indicators to include needs, motivations, the handling of conflict, and power. An ability to be flexible, to respond to context and people, again seemed to be more relevant to modern management, and to women. However, Darking's (1991) exploration of the traditional and continuing tendency to value the masculine model of management technique rather than the feminine, outlined in the previous section of this chapter, suggested that practice lags behind theory. Little has moved on in this area over the last ten years, mainly, I think, because the focus has been on management of organisational change and on gendered management differences, their nature and sociological causes and effects. Marshall (1995) in her critical review of gender and management research, claimed:

> "I do not think that this question—of whether men and women are really different—will dissolve until fundamental conceptions of management fully move beyond their foundations in male experience and sex role stereotypes." (p58)

On the evidence of the review so far, I would argue that both men and women aim to fulfil the same functions (the activities/operations seen as part of their role) as managers. Their choice of management style simply foregrounds one function over another, yet often is used as a means of achieving another function as well. Both male and female managers may use Ball's interpersonal style in their repertoire, but females may foreground this style as the preferred style in which to achieve a range of functions, while males may use it as only one of many styles, others perhaps being foregrounded instead.

I have looked at gender issues of management style and at theories of effective management. Now I look at how these may be affected by the particular organisational culture, in this study that of the secondary school.

Organisational culture

Mills (1988) and Shakeshaft (1989) both claimed that analyses of organisational culture and of management behaviour (including style and language) within it have often been "gender-blind". However, they argued (and I share this view, which in fact forms the basis of my research) that gender is a sociocultural construct and that as organisations are a key aspect of a given culture, then organisational analysis needs to take account of the relationship between gender and organisational life. This may reveal far-reaching effects within the particular organisation of the school. Mills (in Hearn, Sheppard 1989) discussed the embedding of masculine norms and management style within an organisation. He argued that organisational discourse favours men. He was using "organisational discourse" in its linguistic sense, that is, not only in the sense of speaking itself, but also of interaction that takes place within a whole linguistic context of semantic and pragmatic understandings attached to that organisation. We have already seen, in the section on gender issues of management, that Evetts (1994) explored the idea that in secondary schools interview procedures and formal business meetings tended to advantage men. Sheppard (1989), also, explored the devaluing of women in organisations where there are important differences between men and women in terms of perceptions of such issues as power, leadership and dominance.

On the other hand, Ball (1987) concerned himself with the way in which the micro-politics of the school affect the manager's choice of management style and therefore his/her need to style-switch in order to accommodate different situations and people. Although Bell's work was essentially "gender-blind", he recognised that there is not necessarily one embedded (masculine) norm for management style valued within the organisational culture of the secondary school, and that "managers" per se use whichever style may be expedient on a particular occasion according to those micro-political influences. This, of course, does not necessarily imply that a traditional masculine norm may not be the valued dominant style in a school.

Taking this further, Ozga (1988) looked at the measure of independence which manag**ees** (those in a manager's team) in the secondary school enjoy. She argued that despite the hierarchy within the structure of the school's management, the appointment of workers (teachers) to positions supposedly according to merit, a sequence of those positions constituting a career structure, nevertheless the teachers "work site", that is, the classroom, remains "significantly" independent of that management hierarchy, despite being under the direction of and monitored by the line manager.

Although the progress of centralisation and national initiatives set in place since Ozga's work (see the following paragraph on Hargreaves 1998) undermine her argument, nevertheless, we can still see that, to an extent, this concept of a teacher's independence remains an interesting idea upon which, on the basis of my experience, I would speculate further. A teacher's actual classroom activities do tend to be allowed a certain amount of individual independence (for example, in terms of teaching and classroom management style). It is also clear, in my experience, that a teacher may for various reasons have acquired a greater expertise than his/her line manager in a particular area (for example, in examining a specific paper) and he/she may then be used in the role of consultant to the line manager. Additionally, mana**gees** (those who are managed, or are within a particular manager's team) may represent multi-role positions within the school: a classroom teacher within the Geography department (under the direction of the Humanities Faculty manager) may also be the Deputy Headteacher of the school. This is an issue explored later in chapters 6 and 7 as I analyse my fieldwork. It is possible that such multi-roles, which I would speculate may be reflected in other types of organisation also, will affect the communication style adopted by the manager to his/her managees within a secondary school. These possibilities raise questions which I address in chapters 6 and 7. Does the recognition of a managee's particular expertise, for example, lead to a consultancy frame for the management discourse? In other words, does a middle manager seek to empower his/her managee in recognition of that managee's specialist knowledge or expertise? Does the recognition of the independence of the classroom teacher lead to a more colleague-to-colleague "fellow professional" frame to the discourse style? Do the perceptions of teachers within an organisational culture which seeks to value these aspects, affect the managerial-linguistic repertoire adopted within that school, and also the evaluation of style within the school? And, finally, does this advantage the feminine linguistic and managerial style?

Ten years later, one perception of the way that the organisational culture of the school operates in times of change, is that of Hargreaves (1998). He writes of the undermining of the "existing culture of individualism" (p207) and of the rise of collaboration between teachers in the proliferation within schools of working parties, committees, shared staff development, and so on. Hargreaves claims that "collaborative decision-making and problem-solving is a cornerstone of postmodern organisations" (p17). However, shared involvement in decision-making and constructive resource-building may imply a less hierarchical structure in terms of management participation by non-managerial staff, in other words empowerment, which may affect the managerial-linguistic repertoire mentioned in the previous paragraph. Hargreaves goes on to argue that the hidden danger in such "teacher-led collaboration" may result in administrators substituting "the safe simulation of contrived collegiality". By his term "contrived collegiality", Hargreaves refers to the "compulsory cooperation" required of teachers in, for example, working parties for department development plans structured by **given** whole school development plans, or in "collaboration to implement non-negotiable program and curricula whose viability and practicality are not open to discussion" (p80). Again, it is likely that the operational management of such contrived collegiality would affect the linguistic repertoires especially of middle managers, whose task then could involve treading a thin line between managing contrived (ostensible) empowerment and managing task-oriented scenarios driven by structured rubrics. My section on gendered management earlier in this chapter implies that the different genders may handle this differently in terms of the management style and the interactional repertoires they choose, because of the different frames they bring to the managerial situation. This is an important issue in my research and is argued through later in my chapters 6, 7 and 8.

I have raised some of the issues explored in the literature on organisational culture, especially with regard to that of the secondary school, and begun to indicate where these issues may be of relevance to a study of gendered managerial language. Finally in this chapter, I return to the argument on the social implications/underpinnings of language usage within an organisation and culture, especially as it pertains to gendered choices of language repertoires. In this way, I draw together the issues raised earlier in the chapter.

The ethnography of communication

At the opening of the chapter I stressed the importance of setting this present study within the context of language as a "social fact", a recognition of linguistics as a social activity, reflecting and dependent on the participants' positions in society, their understandings within semantic and pragmatic frameworks.

Dell Hymes' (1974) use of the term "ethnography of communication" encapsulated the idea of speech forms being inextricably bound up with social meaning systems, assumptions and inferences. If speech is dependent on socio-cultural conditioning it will reflect both the commonalities within a social, or work / management, group and also the differences between the "world views" of men and women in the same society, or sub-group. In other words the speech community of the school reflects both the shared norms of interaction between participants but also the divergent norms of different groups, such as gender. This issue is important for my methodological discussion and for the discussion of my results in later chapters.

The view that discourse is a social as well as a linguistic phenomenon is an idea developed by a number of linguists in the past four decades, such as Firth (1964), Halliday (1978) and Stubbs (1983). Firth claimed that "every man carries his culture and much of his social reality about with him wherever he goes" (p66). He identified an interlocutor's use of pragmatic understandings in an interaction as a way of controlling interaction and interpersonal relationships. In other words, a speaker may manipulate the lexis or language structures he/she uses, anticipating the pragmatic understandings the recipient may assume from these choices, and thus control the interaction and its outcome. However, it was Stubbs who developed this idea to accommodate differences of pragmatic understandings within the speech community, analysing exchange structures and claiming that there are "multiple layers of meaning between the literal propositional meaning of an utterance and the act which it performs in context." For Halliday the context was also that "in which the culture itself is interpreted in semiotic terms".

If language is part of the social process and dependent on the culturally conditioned thought processes of the participants, then the very concept of leadership may be entirely different for men and women. We would need to consider the idea that men and women might bring different thought processes to the management role and to management interactions. Gender-blind comparisons of language and behaviour in management are not enough. An understanding of gender-related "agendas" (frame/ schema) is required. Some of those differences identified in the literature have been outlined in the earlier section of this chapter.

Fowler, Hodge et al (1979) went so far as to claim that "power differential provides the underlying semantic for the systems of ideas encoded in language structure" (p2). This semantic could be differentiated by gender, as Fasold (1990) argued, in investigating the differential use of status-marking linguistic forms by gender. An example he gave of the differences in language use between men and women in executing different interactional strategies was interesting and illustrated the area under investigation in the present study: a female "expert" during a research investigation uses this expertise as a resource for her "uninformed" partner or managee, whereas a male counterpart uses the expertise as a competitive advantage over his managee (taken from Leet-Pellegrini 1980).

This, then, comes round full circle to the arguments of Shakeshaft, Ozga and Evetts cited earlier in the gendered management section of this chapter, that women managers operate in their interpersonal interactions from a viewpoint, a "world view", which is "fundamentally different" (Shakeshaft 1989) from that of their male colleagues. In other words, women bring a different frame and schema to their managerial interactions from that of men, and this may affect their linguistic repertoires. How fundamentally different these repertoires may be from men's and how far their repertoire is shaped by a common middle manager frame, which is shared by men, is one of my research questions. However, it is essential that any investigation into the use of linguistic strategies in real managerial transactions is underpinned by a consideration of these issues. This is what I aim to do in this research study.

Summary

In this chapter, I reviewed the literature on management and gender in order to establish the major debates over the last three or four decades regarding management and gender, especially with regard to management style and communication. These tend to focus on the differences between men and women in style and effectiveness, and on identified clusters of traits associated with each gender's management behaviour and communication strategies. These clusters tend to follow a consistent pattern throughout the literature as follows:

- Men tend to be associated with a more detached, rational, tough, depersonalised style
- Women tend to be associated with a more supportive, empowering, collaborative style
- However, in many cases the literature either imbued perceived masculine styles with normative status, thus presenting feminine styles as deficient by default, or

- Focused on a gender-blind approach which ignored feminine styles altogether and concentrated on styles associated with masculine clusters.

I have attempted to show that the latter two approaches demonstrate the way in which traditional management values and embedded structures for management behaviours and strategies have often benefited men, and this argument is clearly shown by Davidson and Cooper (1992), Shakeshaft (1989), and, most particularly, Evetts (1994). The gender-blind and feminine-deficient approaches have been challenged by the four writers cited above and also by Loden (1987) and Strachan (1993), who argued that feminine styles can be more effective, especially in an educational context. Using the literature on organisational culture, I raise the question of whether, in the organisational culture of secondary schools, where a "fellow professional" approach may be valued, this might be more appropriately addressed by a more feminine style of management and communication, one which uses strategies of empowerment and collegiality.

I have focused on the argument of Shakeshaft (1989) that the advocates of the traditional approach reflect a "world view" seen through a "male lens" and assume that effective women managers will (or need to) use masculine managerial styles and strategies. I have argued that this reinforces the entrenchment of the "glass ceiling effect", a term used by Davidson and Cooper to describe the sparse promotional prospects for women above junior management level, and upon which my study is based using DfES statistics.

I have outlined literature on communication in management, which establishes its importance in the manager's role and which indicates a difference in the way in which men and women use communication time with their managees. Using the concepts of the frame and schema theory of communication, which suggests that interlocutors bring their own past experiences and understandings to any interaction, I have begun to present my argument that men and women bring different frames to managerial interactions, which shape their use of communication strategies and their managerial behaviour. In the same way, middle managers may apply their own frame to their interactions with their teams. Thus, I assert in this chapter that

- if men and women approach management and communication with different agendas (frames) which give rise to different linguistic strategies and
- if men and women also bring to the management situation a frame which is perceived as required by their role as middle managers and also gives rise to certain linguistic strategies, then the research base needs to be designed to take into account issues of context, in the sense of the context of the organisational culture and of the interaction itself, in order to gain insights into gendered linguistic strategies in real managerial transactions.

In the next chapter, I take up some of these theoretical debates as I explore the literature on gendered linguistic repertoires in greater detail, focusing on the sociolinguistic debates and the issues which have arisen from changing perspectives over the last three decades. I start with the early debates which reflect those presented in the management literature of the same period. I then focus on the issues arising from more recent applied studies and on the importance of them for this study.

CHAPTER TWO

BUT WHAT DOES THE LITERATURE TELL US?

Introduction

In the previous chapter, I outlined a survey of the literature on which this study is based. It focused on managerial behaviour and communication from a gender perspective and indicated that men and women approach management interactions differently although they may fulfil the same functions at their common level of management (for example middle management level). I also outlined the arguments arising in the literature which suggest that although the masculine style of management and communication is advantaged in many ways, nevertheless the feminine style may be more appropriate in an educational context.

There are a number of issues arising from theory and research, especially with regard to specific gendered language choices, which need to be further explored in the context of this investigation:

- the nature of the relevant debates in sociolinguistics over the last three decades, especially with regard to gender linguistics
- specifically, the idea that men and women bring to managerial interactions different frames (as in the frame and schema theory)
- what the nature of those different frames may be according to gender linguistic theory
- the issues arising from recent applied studies in gender linguistics and the implications for my own study.

I have already suggested that oral communication, face-to-face, constitutes a major part of the educational manager's work. The way that a manager conveys his/her intentions, therefore, must affect the outcome of interactions and determine the success of managerial transactions. However, the linguistic strategies employed in interactions are also the products, not only of the user's socio-cultural understandings, but also of the receiver's. An analysis of the language used should therefore take into consideration (a) the context of use (the discourse) and (b) the understandings of the participants (the pragmatics).

The study of gender linguistics has begun to do this, and this chapter seeks to explore the progress of research over the years and also the issues and findings of more recent research.

Early gender linguistics: discrete speech traits

It is interesting that, in contrast to earlier linguists, more recent researchers have been concerned to place language into the context of use rather than analysing language as if it exists in a pure sense apart from the complexities of human social and interpersonal interaction. The concept of language as part of the socio-cultural context in which it is used, reflecting and informing it, is the underlying foundation of more recent linguists such as Holmes (1984), Coates and Cameron (1989), Coates (1993) and Tannen (1992,1993,1994). However, it was not always so. It is interesting to look at earlier theory in order to cast some light on the stereotypes of gendered language use which underpin some common evaluations even today.

Previous linguists, such as Labov (1972), Trudgill (1974), and Lakoff (1975), identified certain features of "women's language", traits collected and counted without reference to the conversational context in which they appeared. Researchers believed that these traits characterised women's speech as opposed to men's. This research was based on purely quantitative methodology and without using qualitative analysis. In other words, the researchers took account of linguistic "form" only (that is, what the word or syntactic item **is** and how many times it is used) and not the linguistic "function" (that is, what the word or syntactic item **is doing in this conversational context**, its contextual meaning).

Linguistic features suggested by Lakoff (1975) included: (the examples are my own)

- Tag questions, such as "that report is due tomorrow, isn't it?"

21

- Lexical hedges, such as "sort of", "you know" (also known as epistemic modality),
- "Super-polite" forms, such as indirect requests ("I'd really appreciate it if you could . . ."), euphemisms, qualifiers, and disclaimers,
- Rising (question) intonation on declaratives, such as in response to a request for scheduling information ("about two o' clock?"),
- Use of direct quotations as appeal to authority or substantiating own requests, such as "so he said, 'we must have that report by two o' clock'",

all of which suggested to Lakoff a sense of hesitancy and desire for reassurance. Despite the "evidence" being based on questionable research methodology, such as intuitions and general observations, or artificial laboratory conditions far removed from natural informal speech in real interactional contexts, nevertheless much of this research was taken as significant in giving credence to the idea that women's speech is deficient in comparison to the powerful, assertive style of men. It gave rise to **the deficiency model** of women's language. The underlying point here is that Lakoff linked a number of different linguistic features in women's style of speech by the common criterion that they were all expressing uncertainty, thereby characterising women's speech as tentative and powerless. She did not consider the contextual implications of the utterances nor recognise that there could be other linguistic functions (contextual meanings) of these linguistic items other than those of expressing uncertainty.

Other research, such as that by Zimmerman and West (1975), reinforced this view. Their investigation into conversations between mixed sex pairs indicated that men interrupt women, whereas women rarely interrupt men. Male interruptions tended to deny the current speaker's right to speak, and in this research the interrupted speaker was likely to be female, thus females tended to fall silent in mixed sex interactions. This suggested to the researchers that men use this strategy in order to control the conversation, or the topic of conversation, and that male speakers are therefore the **dominant** speakers in a mixed sex conversation. This research reinforced **the dominancy model** of gendered language.

Women were, however, found to interrupt other women in all-female groups, but this type of interaction was different. It consisted of minimal responses (for example, mmm, yeah) or supportive comments which did not deny the other's right to continue but encouraged it, and was reinforced by para-linguistic responses such as nodding and smiling. These effects could be seen as evidence of Cooper's (1995) "active listening" characteristic of women's interactions and not as attempts to control the interaction, but as techniques to create unity and connections between speakers.

The idea that male speakers are dominant and controlling speakers has reinforced the deficiency theory. The deficiency model characterises men's speech as dominant, powerful and therefore, by implication, achieving its purpose, because it is seen as "stronger" and therefore more effective. Women's speech, on the other hand, is seen, by default, as weaker, subordinated, and less likely to achieve its purpose.

The key question here, however, is: what are the purposes of a particular conversation and are these purposes different for men and women? In this case, women could be using different conversational strategies in order to achieve quite different purposes from those of men. For more recent researchers, context is crucial to understanding discourse and the function of particular individual linguistic items within that discourse.

Newer lines of enquiry: the importance of context

Discourse analysis is a framework in which the importance of context is recognised. Stubbs (1983) defined it as "linguistic analysis of naturally occurring connected spoken or written discourse", and includes in this the study of conversational exchanges which refer to the context in which those exchanges take place. He argued that communication is impossible without shared knowledge and assumptions between speakers and hearers. Therefore in discourse analysis, semantics (shared meanings) and pragmatics (shared understandings) are recognised as having an important role in the progress of an interaction and they are dependent on the context. Reflecting J L Austin's idea that utterances are actions, he argued that language and situation are inseparable.

Holmes' (1984) work on the importance of context to the use of tag questions pointed out the danger of taking linguistic features out of context and interpreting them without reference to function. As Coates (1993) points out, in reference to Lakoff's out-of-context, quantitative analysis of "form" only,

> "All this work is based on the questionable assumption that there is a one-to-one relationship between linguistic form (tag question) and extra-linguistic factor (tentativeness)."

Holmes investigated the function of tag questions used by both genders, and suggested that tags could be categorised according to their functions in the interactional process of a conversation. She identified two functional types of tag questions based on whether they expressed a **modal** or **affective** meaning. Modals, for example, might express a degree of uncertainty, asking the addressee for confirmation or reassurance, but affectives have the function of facilitating, supporting or softening the speaker's utterance and are therefore oriented towards the addressee or receiver. Affective tags are more likely to be used by people with more control over the interaction, such as teachers, interviewers or lawyers in the course of their work. In this way, these tag questions have significant use in encouraging participants to contribute to the interaction.

For example, the question, "You produced a report along those lines last week, didn't you?" brings a contributor into the conversation, and provides a supportive framework for that contribution. Likewise, the question "You are going to give me that report today, aren't you?" acts as a softener to what might otherwise have been an imperative, and might perhaps have created a negative or hostile reaction.

Holmes found that the role of the participants in the interaction was significant and that those who were facilitators, for example teachers or interviewers, were more likely to use these kinds of affective tag questions. Amongst the facilitators, women were more likely to use affective tags than men. This type of usage would imply, therefore, that these kinds of tag questions are not necessarily indicators of powerless, unassertive language, but on the contrary, the powerful language of those controlling an interaction.

Other researchers (for example, Holmes 1984, Coates and Cameron 1989, Coates 1993, Tannen 1992, 1994, Holmes and Meyerhoff 1999) have also been concerned with analysing speech traits in actual conversational contexts and have interpreted female traits in quite a different way from the early researchers such as Lakoff, by investigating the speaker's intentions and effects in interpersonal interaction. Their findings interpret female speech as powerful because it is supportive and uses strategies which help to ensure that an interaction proceeds towards consensus and team-building.

These findings align with the idea of women as motivated by the desire for consensus and team focus, rather than as necessarily manifesting "powerless" language. O'Barr and Atkins (1980) for example, suggested that a speaker's role in an interaction was more significant than gender in determining the type of powerful language used, and that women were perfectly capable of choosing to use assertive language if their role in the interaction prompts it. The point is that assertiveness may be shown through cooperativeness, support and solidarity in speech rather than through competitiveness and status-seeking.

However, such speech traits, or clusters of linguistic characteristics as Coates delineates (1993 p112-3), may be "powerful" in some situations, but "powerless" in others. She claims,

> ". . . the differences between the competitive, assertive male style and the cooperative, supportive female style mean that men will tend to dominate in mixed sex interaction." (p117)

The question is whether that domination is effective in relation to the purpose/product of that interaction. The question for the present thesis is also how far these speech traits affect the style and effectiveness of the female manager, and how do they affect an assessor's perceptions of the potential female manager?

Gender perceptions of interactional effectiveness

The desire for team focus and consensus has been identified also by the linguist Deborah Tannen (1992) as a particularly female preoccupation motivating women's speech styles. In her investigation of women in both social situations and more formal work/managerial situations (for example, committee meetings), she found that women tended towards what she terms "rapport talk", that is, using language to make connections with others and to reinforce intimacy and unity. On the other hand, she found that men tended to use language to preserve their independence and to negotiate status ("report talk"). Although there may be an interchanging of motivations, that is, men may also be concerned with making interpersonal connections and women may also be concerned to establish their status and authority, nevertheless, the goals they are fundamentally focused on determine, and are pursued through, their different language styles.

While Zimmerman and West (1975) characterised the genders as either more or less powerful and controlling in mixed sex interactions, Tannen identifies the phenomenon of "interruption" as distinguishable, not in terms of purely gender criteria, but by the criterion of "intent": cooperative interruption, which reinforces unity and tends to be a characteristic of women's speech, and non-cooperative interruption, which asserts status and tends to be used more often by men. These distinctions also have the advantage that they do not imply a deficiency model, but rather a **difference model.**

The model which emerges is one that reveals women as choosing different language styles from men, whether consciously or unconsciously (culturally conditioned). Those styles reflect an approach which is grounded in a desire for consensus, intimacy and harmony in interpersonal relationships. Since management has to be concerned to a large extent with communication with other people, it is interesting to see the common features emerging in the research literature on both management and language styles from a gender perspective (see the section in chapter one on gender management styles).

Furthermore, Susan Schick Case (1988), in a study of the effectiveness of language used by women in management, also identified differences in gender communication. She argued that these differences were focused on women's tendency to use a speech repertoire which is facilitative, personalised and supportive, and men's tendency to use that which is depersonalised and authoritative asserting status and dominance. My previous point regarded the necessity to consider the purpose/product of the interaction before it is assumed that the masculine style is more effective. Schick Case found that in some instances the feminine style was more effective in achieving the purpose of the interaction and in arriving at the task product, and was rated more highly than the masculine style in the evaluation of the team. As a result of her findings, she suggested that institutions should capitalise on the strengths of women's managerial style, viewing it as different and yet equally valid, and not as deficient. Sadly, statistics on middle and senior management figures for women indicate that this does not seem to have materialised over the last 15 years (see Introduction).

When Labov (1972) defined the speech community in terms of "participation in a set of shared norms" he was not acknowledging the possibility of men and women having different approaches to conversational interaction and therefore different communicative styles in their managerial interactions, as recent research seems to suggest. The speech community of the school and indeed of the management of the school, therefore may not be unified in its use of, expectations of, or evaluations of male and female managers' language.

Sociocultural influences in gender language use

The importance of the work of recent linguistic researchers outlined above is precisely that it is not gender-blind, that it takes into consideration the possibility of men and women using language for different purposes. It departs from the notion that language has an immutable and set reference quite independent from the users of that language, and it considers the effect gender might have upon the user and receiver of linguistic events. In other words, it reflects Fasold's (1990) exploration of the differences in interactional strategies between men and women and the way they reveal the structure of society with regard to the sexes. If language is the major tool for executing these strategies, then linguistic usage may tell us a great deal about the way in which the sexes view their position in regard to the sociocultural environment in which they find themselves. This is the notion of gender, because of the different experiences the sexes have in society, shaping values and thought processes, and of these different values and thoughts being identified in speech patterns and repertoires (Sydie 1987).

We see this idea reviewed in Shakeshaft's (1989) detailed exploration of the different "world view" of men and women. She argued against the dangers of viewing the world through the "male lens" and for the reality of the different female style arising inevitably from the unique "world view" of the female. Her premise was that women choose to use different managerial and linguistic strategies and styles based on the fact that they experience a "different reality" from men.

This concept suggests that women experience a different set of linguistic "meanings" from men by which their world is framed. Tannen (1994) claims that

> "no language has meaning except by reference to how it is
> "framed" or "contextualised" "(p11)

In her chapter on Power and Solidarity (1993) she argues that the same linguistic strategies may create dominance or powerlessness in different contexts, and that there is a need to analyse meanings in specific contexts and not to generealise on the basis of a particular linguistic variable. She writes that there is a

> "danger of linking linguistic forms with interactional
> intentions such as dominance." (p183)

This reflects Coates' (1993) point on the dangers of linking linguistic form with extra-linguistic features.

Tannen stresses that linguistic strategies are potentially ambiguous and polysemous (having more than one meaning or interpretation). Therefore, in any given interaction there lies the potentiality for misinterpretation and misunderstanding in terms of the receiver and the assessor of the speech event. Again, it is important to look at the strategy or variable within the context of its use and of its user.

Coates (1993) identifies a number of areas in which "miscommunication" might take place due to the different interactional intentions (along the lines of Tannen's (1992) concept of "frames"). For example, she lists tag questions and interruptions which I have previously identified, the need to make links between topics of conversation or between contributions, topic shifts, self-disclosure, verbal aggression, and the value of listening. For the purpose of this thesis, such misunderstanding of a communicational strategy is interesting from the perspective not only of the male receiver in any particular speech event but also of the appraisal of the strategy within a sociocultural context. It implies the need for an identification of and exploration of the linguistic correlates of gender. This exploration might be based on the assumption that the differences found between the sexes reflect subcultural differences or reflect the social dominance of men in our society. In many ways, both of these angles are significant in any investigation into intentions and motivations in communication strategies. If Coates says "speech is an act of identity" (1993 p161), then men and women's identities assumed by gender will have a distinct bearing upon their linguistic variations and upon their interpretations of the appropriacy of particular interactional strategies. What might become a problem is if the dominance theory becomes subsumed by the deficiency model. In other words, there is still a danger of interpreting women's linguistic variables and different strategies in terms of falling short of the male model simply because masculine speech is regarded as having dominancy features and therefore is assumed as a norm and judged as superior to feminine speech styles.

However, the concept of communicative competence is useful here. The term was first used by Hymes (1971) to refer to what a speaker needs to know in order to use linguistic forms appropriately, such as internalised sociocultural norms. He argued that in order to become an effectively functioning member of a speech community a speaker must internalise far more than the grammatical and phonological rules which Chomsky (1965) referred to as linguistic competence. This sociocultural knowledge is therefore revealed in speech events by the participants. The idea that men and women might be regarded as belonging to different subcultures linguistically and constitute different speech communities, in certain respects, informs and is informed by the study of the different communicative competencies of men and women.

Common to people of both sexes is the use of an appropriate exchange structure within an interaction. Sociocultural learning or experience demands that generally in transactional interaction we use a structure of exchanges which follow a pattern, a two part exchange of question-answer or declarative-response, or three part exchange of initiation-response-feedback (Sinclair and Coulthard 1992). These direct the "moves", as Coulthard (1992) refers to them, within transactions. Coulthard argues that context is an important variable in interpreting speech acts, both for the participants concerned and for researchers undertaking discourse analysis. Dysfunction may arise if the pattern is varied because of one speaker's dominance or interruption of others. The different world views of men and women may influence their use of, or response to, or interpretation of, such variation.

It might be that the norms for women's speech patterns arise from experience of small more intimate group interaction, where solidarity and co-operation are important, whereas the norms for men's speech patterns arise from the experience of large public group interaction, where competition and individual status-gaining are important. These differences in experiences between men and women, which may influence gendered behaviour, may be seen in evidence even from early childhood games, where girls tend to play co-operatively in small groups while boys play competitively in larger groups. Of course, it is beyond the scope of the present thesis, and not its primary concern, to analyse the many sociocultural influences themselves which might have a bearing upon the reasons for the differences in gender linguistic usage. But it is important to acknowledge that these sociocultural influences could have an effect on choice of language use.

Researchers using the frame and schema theory as a tool for understanding interactional events, explain differences in structuring discourse by arguing that we use past experiences to shape, and to understand, present usage (Goffman 1974,1981, Minsky 1975, Gumperz 1982). Minsky argued that, as in the processes of artificial intelligence, when a person encounters a new situation, they select from memory a substantial structure ("a frame") to adapt to fit to that new situation, the same process being used in linguistic situations. Goffman also argued that people define their interaction with others in terms of a frame or schema which is identifiable and familiar and provides them with the semantic and pragmatic framework with which to shape their transactions. Gumperz refers to the same idea when he argues that socio-cultural knowledge is needed in "conversational inference", "the situated or context-bound process of interpretation, by means of which participants in an exchange assess others' intentions, and on which they base their responses" (p153). He includes in his definition of frame, the role taken by the physical setting, the participants' personal background knowledge, attitudes towards each other, assumptions concerning role and status relationships as well as social values associated with various message components. In other words, men and women would use their different gendered behaviours to shape their language repertoires and their pragmatic understandings of others' language strategies. Tannen's (1992) gendered "frames" develop this concept.

A recent model, which has gained more widespread acknowledgement during the course of my research, is that of the Community of Practice. This moves on from the idea of speech communities and communicative competence. The Community of Practice is defined by the membership of the group and by those practices in which the membership engages as a joint enterprise, gender being one of the diversities which impinge upon the group (Bergvall 1999, Holmes and Meyerhoff 1999).

Holmes and Meyerhoff define the Community of Practice (the term having been introduced by Eckert and McConnell-Ginet in 1992) as a "tool for the description of language variation that bears a strong resemblance to fundamental principles of social identity theory". It is a speech community which essentially arises from a shared enterprise and involves a "shared repertoire of joint resources for negotiating meaning". It is based on mutual engagement in an enterprise, and membership and practices of the group arise out of this dimension only, therefore there may be diversities within the group, it is not necessarily egalitarian or consensual. Bergvall (1999) argues that those using the Community of Practice approach as a tool for analysing interactions focus on the constructive practices of the group and emphasise the "mutability in gendered linguistic displays across groups". Therefore they do not mark "intra-group variation as deviant, but as part of a continuum of all people's gendered practices." Advocates of this approach move on from both models of gender linguistic variation outlined in this chapter, the deficiency and the difference models, to a model of diversity which challenges the assumption of dualised differences in gendered language variation studies.

It is a useful tool for my present study because it accommodates the notion of masculine and feminine tendencies in linguistic usage, along the lines of a variation continuum, rather than a distinct dichotomy of usage between men and women. It can also be used to explain other influences on language strategies used by managers in their interactions, other than gender. Eckert and McConnell-Ginet(1992) argue that the model enables the researcher to abandon assumptions common to many language and gender studies: for example, that gender can be in some way isolated from other aspects of social identity and that the linguistic manifestations of gender are the same across different communities. It therefore explains variation within gender categories and likewise similarities across gender categories. The model also includes reference to "core" and "peripheral" members of any community of practice, those members who are likely to use the linguistic practices of the community to a greater or lesser degree according to the strength/extent of their involvement with it.

In my work the model may be applied to those linguistic usages which arise from the shared enterprise of team meetings in secondary schools and the perspectives and shared world views through which the community that comes together in such meetings engage. These pragmatic understandings may be shared by people of both genders, yet the membership of other communities of practice (for example, gender) may also provide diverse linguistic strategies, especially those reflecting dominance or leadership within the community. The model provides a useful framework for exploring the similarities and dissimilarities in gendered talk in the common situation of the team meeting in schools.

Summary

In this chapter, I have given a brief survey of the development of gender linguistics as a study area of sociolinguistics. I have indicated that the analysis of gender differences in speech patterns began with the assumption of a deficiency model which took as its norm the speech patterns more often used by men. Speech features identified out of context as traits of "women's language", and as deficient, were associated with hesitancy and powerless language (for example Lakoff 1975). Women's language, therefore, became commensurate with subordinated and deficient language. Such notions of a stereotypical "women's language" still commonly exist in social folklore.

I have reviewed the work of some of the more recent researchers in this field, who have been more concerned to analyse women's language repertoires within their context of interactional use, the function of linguistic usage as opposed to its form (for example Holmes 1984, Schick Case 1988, Coates 1993, Tannen 1992, 1993, 1994). These researchers claim that feminine speech traits need not be characterised as powerless, but often as powerful language assuming a feminine interactional purpose of establishing solidarity, consensus and interpersonal relationships. These researchers have moved away from a deficiency to a difference model of gender language variation. The gendered speech features I have identified in the literature are grouped around the following profiles:

- women use speech features which suggest support, facilitation and empowerment of others; these reflect a profile of co-operation, unity, building relationships and rapport
- men use speech features which suggest authority, dominance and status differentiation; these reflect a profile of competition, striving for status and task achievement.

I have argued that there is a danger in assuming that the masculine style is the norm because it is seen as more authoritative and dominant, and the feminine style as deficient by default.

I have reflected on the issues in the literature of different gender-based understandings and interpretations of communicational events and I have suggested that these might be formed by women's different experiences of linguistic meanings which frame their world view. I have explored the literature on gendered frames (for example, Shakeshaft 1989, Coates 1993, Tannen 1992), which refer to the effect on linguistic variation of the identities which men and women assume by gender. I have included references to exchange structure theory and frame and schema theory, which I use in my analyses in chapters 6 and 7 and which are useful tools with which to analyse speech events involving male and female managers. The frame and schema theory may be used to understand and gain insights into the different approaches which men and women may have towards interactions, and the exchange structure model is useful in interpreting the function or dysfunction of anticipated patterns of interaction and which may characterise gendered speech repertoires.

I have concluded by looking at a recent and useful model explored during the last few years and growing in importance over the last three or four years, the notion of the Community of Practice (Eckert 1990, Eckert and McConnell-Ginet 1992, Bergvall 1999, Holmes and Meyerhoff 1999). Advocates of this model focus on diversity as the basis of linguistic variation, rather than the difference between genders in terms of language use in any specific communicative scenario. They also focus on the diversity of language use in any individual's idiolect influenced by the membership of a number of other communities of practice, apart from that of gender. I explore the model's relevance to my own research into the linguistic strategies of middle managers in interactions with their teams, in greater detail later in chapter 8.

In the next chapter, I outline and explain the methodology I used in my fieldwork and analysis, reflecting upon the issues involved and showing how some of the work of previous researchers reviewed in chapters 1 and 2 informed my choice of methods. The issues which I carry forward from this chapter are as follows:

- the recognition of the importance of function as opposed to form in the linguistic analysis of men and women's interactions, involving a focus on the context of the organisational culture in which the speech event takes place and the context of the interaction itself

- the importance of investigating the linguistic strategies of men and women in real managerial situations with their teams and testing out the theories derived from the literature regarding the specific differences identified from previously publishedresearch
- the nature of any gender differences in the language use of the managers in my case studies
- the effect of other influences on the repertoire of managerial interaction, apart from that of gender, following the model of the community of practice, for example linguistic diversity informed by the organisational culture of the school in which the interactions take place,
- and the nature of language repertoires of middle managers, regardless of gender.

CHAPTER THREE

HOW WAS THE STUDY DESIGNED?

Introduction

In the previous two chapters, I examined the theoretical debates in the literature on gender and management style, and on gendered linguistic repertoires. Having focused on the issues arising from recent applied studies of men and women's speech patterns and begun to consider the implications of these for my own research, I now want to turn to an exploration of the ways in which the work of previous researchers has informed my choice of methods.

In this chapter, I restate the research questions and give an account of the methods used in the research and discuss some of the surrounding issues of the methodology. I outline the practical and ethical implications of this research study, and discuss issues which arose during its progress and which arise for many researchers in the fields of educational and linguistic research, where human behaviour is investigated within real, natural contexts.

The research problem

My study began as an investigation into reasons for the clear imbalance between males and females in middle and senior management posts in secondary schools in England, according to statistics published by the Department for Education and Skills (DfES). It became clear that linked with this imbalance was an awareness of the possibility of different styles, perceived or actual, of language use and management strategies, adopted by male and female managers, and a notion of a "glass ceiling effect" (Davidson and Cooper 1992), through which women are unable to proceed to senior management. There also seemed to be a pattern emerging from recent research undertaken in both management and linguistics, which supported such a gender difference, and which I discussed in chapters 1 and 2.

I aimed to investigate linguistic repertoires adopted by male and female middle managers in secondary schools as they "managed", specifically as they conducted their normal team meetings. I was therefore looking at real interaction in real situations. I chose the context of team meetings because this comprised a situation in which managers had to interact with a number of staff at the same time, make decisions and possibly handle conflicts. They would therefore be managing a range of different aspects. The aim was then to see whether I would identify similar patterns to those identified in the literature, outlined in chapters 1 and 2, which offered a hypothetical explanation for the research problem and which were as follows:

- that women use speech repertoires which suggest support, facilitation, and the empowerment of others, reflecting a feminine profile of co-operation, unity, building relationships and rapport (these corresponded with the feminine cluster of traits identified in the literature on management communication which indicated a supportive, empowering and collaborative style)\
- that men use speech repertoires which suggest authority, dominance, and status differentiation, reflecting a masculine profile of competition, striving for status and task achievement (these corresponded with the masculine cluster of traits identified in the literature on management communication which indicated a detached, rational, tough, depersonalised style)

I wished to explore the idea that these differences could be explained by the theory that men and women bring to speech situations a different frame or schema (Minsky 1975, Goffman 1974,1981, Gumperz 1982, Tannen 1994) which influence their choice of linguistic repertoire, as outlined in chapter 2.

I also aimed to explore another hypothetical explanation for the research problem, which was the idea that there are other strategies employed which raise other issues, for example, the theory that there is an identifiable repertoire associated with the role of the middle manager per se, regardless of gender and that this might also be affected by the particular organisational culture in which it occurred (as in the Community of Practice theory, discussed in chapter 2, Eckert 1990, Eckert and McConnell-Ginet 1992, Holmes and Meyerhoff 1999, Bergvall 1999).

Thus, my research problem was concerned to investigate whether there were differences and similarities between the way that male and female managers communicated to their team members in the specific context of the team meetings in my case studies of different organisational cultures; to look at the issues of gendered language involved; and to investigate whether feminine linguistic strategies might play a part in negatively valuing women as managers in secondary schools.

The research questions

The questions, therefore, which I aimed to address in my case studies of the middle managers in four schools, were:

- how does language work as part of the management process in real managerial transactions, and how does it reflect the skills and characteristics of middle managers?
- are there differences in men and women's linguistic repertoires which may reinforce senior managers' perceptions of management performance?
- do senior managers' perceptions of valued middle management skills and characteristics favour men over women?

Methodology: issues arising from the research questions; my approach

My epistemological position

My approach to the research questions was underpinned by my epistemological position, which owed much to

(1) Dell Hymes' (1977) ideas on the "ethnography of speaking", or the necessity of investigating and interpreting the functions of real speech events, within their contexts, and not only analysing "form" in linguistics in the scientific positivist tradition, discussed in chapter 1 and 2,

(2) the concept of gender as a social construct (Cameron 1992, 1997, Coates 1993, Tannen 1992, 1994, Wodak 1997) reflecting the social distinctions drawn between men and women, their socially constructed attributes and learned behaviours, as opposed to biologically defined sex categories, discussed in chapters 1 and 2, and

(3) the post-modern constructivist approach, whose advocates reject the view that there is a true knowledge "out there" and argue that "the social world is constructed and shaped by members of society" (Abbott and Wallace 1997). The emphasis is on a rejection of the scientific "positivist" approach to research methodology whose advocates profess the need for an objective discovery of the truth "out there" and claim that the researcher is not involved subjectively or personally in the research process. Adherents of the post-modern constructivist approach reject the view that the social researcher can be a dispassionate and uncritical "scientific" observer and argue that "the experiences and feelings of the subject should be at the centre of the production of all social knowledge" (p295). Arising from this underpinning was the choice of qualitative methodology as advanced by Strauss and Corbin 1990, Silverman 1993, and Bryman 1995, and discussed in the following section of this chapter.

The basis of my approach was that in social research, and more particularly in the linguistic research I was conducting, it was not a question of discovering external and objective facts, but of investigating and interpreting the meanings of events which were socially constructed, and which specifically concern the social constructs of gender. As a researcher, therefore, I could not stand outside the events which I investigated since I was also influenced by those social constructions, and in that sense was a participant in my enquiry.

As with previous researchers in sociolinguistics, I have adopted the dialectical approach to linguistic theory, using less emphasis on the coded nature of words (the "form" of pure linguistics) and more emphasis on the role of context, the pragmatic speech activity within an interaction, or "function" (exemplified by Hymes 1977, Holmes 1984, Graddol and Swann 1992, Coates 1989,1993). I argue that if men and women tend towards different world views, and may bring to speech events different agenda and frame/schema (Minsky 1975, Goffman 1974,1981, Gumperz 1982, Tannen 1994), their discourse utterances may be shaped by different functions, and this will influence the use of different linguistic repertoires which reflect these different functions (see chapter 2). The importance of "function" in this study therefore (rather than pure linguistic "form") means that I have foregrounded subjective interpretation in my analysis in which I, as researcher, could not be said to maintain a detached objective position.

However, I have used what is termed by Southerland and Katamba in O'Grady (1997) as "social network analysis", relying on examining first hand, in this case as a non-participant observer, the language use of a pre-existing social group. In order to do this, I needed to establish a rapport with the managers whose interactions I was studying, so that there was a basis of trust. However, although informed consent was needed from those under study, a **detailed** knowledge of the research questions and linguistic implications could have affected the linguistic choices made by the managers involved and therefore invalidated the research (Labov's variation studies 1972). Thus, for these reasons I had to maintain an extent of objectivity and detachment to the **proceedings** of the meetings I audio-recorded and analysed. In this way, the managers were not participants with me in a co-operative enquiry. There was also a similar interlinking of objectivity in investigation and subjectivity in interpretative analysis in the semi-structured interviews with the headteachers. These issues involved in the dynamics of the conflicting elements of the study determined my choice of research methods so that I could find the most appropriate way of addressing the research questions.

My position is also influenced by the concept of gender as a social construct. This is not to say that I am taking a feminist stance often associated with this concept. Cameron (1997) comments that most contemporary research into language and gender is feminist in orientation, but that in principle the subject matter can be treated without reference to feminism either politically or theoretically. Much of the literature outlined in chapter 2 reflects a feminist orientation, whether it be using a deficiency/dominance model (Labov 1972, Lakof 1975) or a difference model (Shakeshaft 1989, Tannen 1992). Although my starting point is an enquiry into the disparity between men and women in reaching promoted positions in secondary schools, and into the role that linguistic style and management style play in this phenomenon, nevertheless I do not approach the problem, or the interpretations of the data, on a feminist linguistic level of paradigm and dogmatics. I attempt to address the problem at a descriptive level in terms of the data found, without imposing prior assumptions of gender differences or assuming in fact that gender differences constitute the most important variable in linguistic data. Feminist linguistics tends to place male and female linguistic behaviour closely within the biological sex designations of men and women at the centre of its interpretations. Although I explore the concept of gendered frame and schema, I recognise that this is not necessarily the only frame and schema at work in any interaction. It is for this reason that I am interested in the more recent model of the Community of Practice (Eckert and McConnell-Ginet 1992). Using this approach researchers can interlink interdependent differences in orientation to other social categories with differences in gender.

My epistemological assumptions have implications on my approach to the research problem in the following ways:

- my methodology: I argue for a qualitative approach
- my choice of methods:case studies, in order to investigate contexts; observation; audio-recording and transcriptions; interviews; interpretation of documentary data
  - my language style used in the research report: I use the first person in my account of the research, with chronological narrative in my description of the fieldwork processes, and narrative in the commentaries on the transcripts in order to capture a flavour of the immediacy of spontaneous speech interactions

However, in order to address the research questions, I also employ non-participant observation in my recording of meetings and therefore a level of detachment in the observation and analysis, although the latter requires subjective interpretation. I want to turn now to look at these choices in more detail.

Qualitative research issues

Bryman (1995) outlines the view that quantitative and qualitative research methodologies are based on fundamentally opposing epistemological views about how social reality ought to be studied. The philosophical issues underlying quantitative research are that knowledge exists independently of context and hard facts can be discovered objectively, while qualitative researchers recognise a need to explore social constructs, human behaviour and functioning to gain insights which cannot be adequately known by means of quantitative methods. As Strauss and Corbin (1990) claim: "qualitative methods can be used to uncover and understand what lies behind any phenomenon about which little is yet known" (p17).

In order to investigate the question of gendered linguistic repertoires, I needed to analyse real situations as they occurred, since the basis of my research concerned testing out theories and looking at what actually happens in one area of normal day-to-day managerial work; any invented or specially created scenario would have resulted in insecure data under the terms of my study. A person's language use is easily altered when he or she becomes conscious of the investigation and makes guesses as to what is required (Labov 1972). The data collected would then become unreliable. The research was not an "experiment" in a scientific sense of testing processes under rigorously controlled conditions, but was more concerned with observing and analysing what actually happens in real life experiences (Strauss and Corbin 1990, Silverman 1993, Bryman 1995).

This work needed to take a qualitative approach, in that I was concerned to "understand individuals' perceptions of the world" and to "seek insights rather than statistical analysis" (Ball 1987). It was the "complexities of human interaction" which I was to deal with (Cohen & Manion 1989) and I needed **real** settings and **real** managerial/interactional situations. I was not looking at language in terms of the Chomskian "what it is" (its form), but following Hymes' view of language being inseparable from its use and its context (its linguistic and social function), the "ethnography of communication", in other words (Hymes 1968, 1977, Saville-Troike 1989).

Discourse analysis—a qualitative approach

I have defined discourse analysis in the linguistic use of the term in this research study, as the analysis of:

- speech events (or utterances) within interactive spoken texts (or connecting sequences),

41

- the organisation of these texts and the ways in which parts of the text are connected, and
- the devices used for achieving textual structure as part of the interactional process (Hymes 1977, Fasold 1990, Southerland and Katamba in O'Grady 1997).

Because my work foregrounded an interpretation of the way that men and women use devices to organise their speech events in interaction with others, therefore, discourse analysis in this research was closely interlinked with semantics (the study of meanings in human language) and pragmatics (the study of how the meaning that the speaker intends to communicate by using a particular utterance in a particular context is understood by the addressee). I recognise that there were problems inherent in analysing and interpreting these because of the semantics and pragmatic understandings which I, as researcher, brought to the situation. I would argue that in order to understand the function and significance of the utterances within that particular context, such interpretations are necessary. To this extent, there had to be a level of subjectivity in my analysis of the fieldwork and that in this way I, as researcher, was involved in the research process. In my analysis, I could not be "a dispassionate observer" of objective facts.

The research methods

Case Study

I chose to use case studies of four middle managers in four secondary schools in which to base my investigation into the language used by male and female middle managers. Yin (1989) describes the case study method as useful when the focus of the research is on contemporary phenomena within real-life contexts and when the study is explanatory (how or why the phenomena occur), exploratory or descriptive (p21). He identifies the case study as "a distinctive form of empirical enquiry" (p21). In my study I wished to investigate the real-life context of the team meetings but also the context of the schools in which these took place. Other methods would not have allowed me to investigate these contexts in depth or explore the focus of the study, which was the linguistic usage in pre-scheduled, pre-existing team meetings in order to give an intense analysis of the multiple phenomena at work in the data. I wanted to use multiple sources of evidence: observation, audio-recording, transcription, interviews with the headteachers, and documentary data collection.

I chose to investigate four Local Education Authority (LEA) secondary schools within one Midlands county, so that they were geographically accessible to me for fieldwork. I wanted to use two schools with male headteachers and two schools with female headteachers, so that I could investigate whether this variable created any significant differences in the data. I wanted to observe and audio-record the team meetings of four middle managers (two men and two women) in each of the four schools, in other words sixteen meetings in all. However, first of all, I wanted to interview the headteachers in order to gather data which would give insights into the organisational culture of that particular school, especially with regard to gendered status. I also wanted to gain insights into the value each headteacher assigned to a range of leadership skills a middle manager might demonstrate, in order to investigate any gender bias in preferred skills within the culture of the school. This interview stage of my investigation provides insights into the specific school context for the main body of my research study, the fieldwork involving recording and analysing the middle managers' language strategies with his/her team in formal meetings.

Issues of validity and reliability

Qualitative research, and case study in particular, has been criticised (see criticisms outlined by Silverman 1993, Bryman 1995,Yin 1989) on a number of grounds: subjectivity, bias, lack of precise quantification and therefore lack of accuracy, problems with validity and reliability. The subjectivity of the qualitative approach to the case studies has already been argued, in earlier sections of this chapter, as an advantage of this social research. An interpretative approach in order to gain insight into an event of real human communications and to understand the function and significance of the interactions was necessary. The point of the discourse analysis was to explore what was happening in a real situation, not to make a quantitative count of linguistic units without reference to their context. Holmes, as outlined in chapter 2, makes this point clearly in her analysis of gendered use of tag questions (1984).

Silverman (1993) points out that validity can be undermined by the use of data extracts which support the researcher's argument without proof that contrary evidence has been received. However, validity in qualitative case study research can be addressed by choice of design. Silverman suggests, for example, that analytic induction offers a tool for validation and argues that it can overcome the danger of "purely anecdotal field research" often found in qualitative case studies (p170). I have used a case study design based on those illustrated in Silverman, Bryman (1995) and Yin (1989) which owes much to the variation on the analytic induction design used by Bloor (1978). I have used what Yin refers to as "multiple-case replication design", in which I have used case studies of four managers, two men and two women, in which the discourse analysis produced replications of discovered phenomena. These fitted the hypothetical explanation of the research problem as defined at the start of the chapter. I then provided two more from a different organisational culture in which to test my emerging hypothesis and this resulted in a minor reformulation of the hypothesis, shifting the emphasis further onto variation between different organisational cultures. The next set of four case studies from a further organisational culture, with a female headteacher, tested my hypothesis. A final check from the last school with a female head confirmed the hypothesis. In this way I have used a variation of the analytic induction method of theory construction and validation. The process follows Bloor's approach to checking validity by means of procedural stages in which a definition of the problem is produced, a hypothetical explanation is offered, an examination of cases is used to determine the fit with the hypothesis, further cases are used if a variation emerges, the hypothesis is reformulated, further cases are examined to confirm the reformulated hypothesis.

Bryman points out that generalisation from case studies is a problem for qualitative research. I had only four case studies of schools and sixteen case studies of individual managers. This was not intended to represent large scale sampling, but an investigation into what was happening in these managerial interactions. However, in following the processes outlined above, hypotheses could be tested and comparisons made across multiple case studies. Yin claims that the issue is not the generalisability of the case study to the population but to the theoretical proposition.

I discuss issues of validity and reliability of the processes of discourse analysis specifically in a subsequent section of this chapter. However, regarding the reliability of the analysis of both the discourse, the documentary data and the interviews with the headteachers, I have in all cases attempted to provide enough detail for this to be checked (Stokoe 1997). However, triangulation or checking by the participants, whether headteachers or middle managers, would not have been feasible; after all, I was not investigating the participants' interpretations of their own interactions.

Sampling

Issues of practicalities of sampling, if we take that to mean the selection of the four schools to use as case studies, are outlined in the last part of this chapter, where I provide a chronological narrative of the methodological processes. The selection, apart from my requirement that I used two schools with male headteachers and two schools with female heads, became entirely pragmatic. It became a question of which schools provided me with access. I needed to restrict the field to a geographical area which was accessible to me. In the case of schools with women as headteachers the choice was limited by the fact that there were few within the chosen county.

As far as the sample of middle managers whose meetings I was to observe was concerned, the headteachers, apart from one case where the head delegated the task to a deputy, all selected the middle managers themselves. My criteria were, firstly, that I wanted two males and two females from each school, then the practicalities of availability and willingness. I had to accept that in ethnographic research everyday considerations of the calendar/other commitments had to prevail and that of course agreement / willingness to participate must be sought. In some cases the willingness factor was already predicted by the Head, but permission was sought from all participants. The heads themselves were unaware of **exactly** what traits I was investigating and therefore this did not affect, or constitute a factor, in the selection or non-selection of any individual. This basis of sampling was advantageous to the research design, as in many cases I had no prior knowledge of the individuals, and was therefore able to remain distanced. The alternative (a random selection) may have produced an unwilling or impractical sample. In the case of the female middle managers, there were often few to select from anyway and therefore little scope for choice.

Non-participant observation

My method of observation needed to be non-participant because of the observational setting chosen, team meetings in which I was not a member of the team. I needed to be detached from the group itself so that my presence altered the situation as little as possible and so that the event remained as close as possible to the pre-existing social group whose meetings took place on a regular basis. The research setting was therefore unstructured by me as observer, but structured by the participants themselves, by means of the set agenda and of the communicative utterances of the participants in response to the agenda items. The research setting was therefore composed of people for whom the setting was individually meaningful and subjective. My technique as a non-participant observer meant that I was able to audio-record a group interaction, focusing on the team leader, the middle manager, with a degree of detachment and objectivity to the interactions I was investigating.

My presence needed to be explained and I needed to gain the trust and confidence of the team members, so that they might be able to conduct their interactions with each other as they would in my absence. This was not unlike the process of incorporation and acceptance into the group for a participant observer. I established credibility as a researcher at the access to field stage through my introductory advances and again during initial interviews with the headteachers, by emphasising my fellow-teacher status. In most cases I was able to speak with the middle managers before the meetings and share common experiences which helped to establish a rapport. This was not always the case; it depended on practical considerations within the field such as the availability of the manager. I requested in each case that the manager advised their team members prior to the meeting I attended, gave a brief explanation of my presence and obtained their consent to my recording of the meeting. Issues of informed consent and confidentiality are discussed in a later section of this chapter. In no case was there any objection to my presence and recording.

Audio-recording/transcription

From my initial review of the recordings, I selected key areas of the meetings which demonstrated the managers' transactional language within their interactions with their team, in other words the speech events in which business was negotiated and navigated towards a conclusion. I therefore focused on the sequences which showed how the individual manager used language in order to:

- establish their status
- deal with critical incidents and handle team members in the course of reaching the objectives of their meeting
- handle/resolve conflicts
- make decisions

I decided that the opening and closing of the meeting were key areas, and any other part of the meeting where the criteria above were demonstrated.

I am aware that in many ways this process was subjective as it was selective and interpretative. However, to transcribe and analyse the whole of each meeting would have been unwieldy and without focus on the area under study, and not consistent with my own chosen discipline of sociolinguistics. I refer to Wolcott's (1995) discussion of ethnography in which he argues that a fieldwork methodology may be ethnographic but the analysis / interpretation has to be consistent with the researcher's particular disciplinary field. Mine was a focused and specific ethnography common to educational research, which Wolcott refers to as "microethnography". Silverman (1993) claims that ethnography often depends on generalisations made on the basis of "truncated data extracts" (p52) and that a solution to this is the transcription, a methodology and topic in its own right, which forms concrete data and which can be tested for reliability.

I have attempted to transcribe speech sequences of other team members prior to and following the middle manager's utterance wherever relevant, in order to indicate enough detail about the context of the conversation (for example, membership of the meeting, agenda items) and of the utterances (for example, items in an exchange structure), so that the significance of the manager's utterance is clarified and the reliability of my interpretation is enhanced. I have used traditional transcription conventions as they may be useful to the topic, although I have not normally indicated non-linguistic or para-linguistic features. I am aware that this is selective and subjective, but justify the decision by the need to concentrate the attention on the focus of the enquiry.

Dr Julia Helene Ibbotson PhD, FHEA

Analysis

Stokoe (1997) clearly outlines one of the problems inherent in analysing transcript data in studies of gender and language in educational contexts. She argues that there is a danger of assigning interpretations to men and women's utterances which are, themselves, based on gender stereotypes. She offers an example of a study in which one specific male speaker's contribution which had been analysed as interrupting, topic-changing, floor dominating (stereotypical masculine characteristics), but which could, on the other hand, have equally been analysed as supportive, building on others' contributions, building rapport (stereotypical feminine characteristics). In my analysis I have taken into account the context of an utterance in order to reduce the effects of this subjectivity of interpretation. I would argue that where the basis of a research study is to identify gender differences in speech, there is more likelihood of the interpretation of analytical items being subject to preconceived assumptions of gender. The basis of my analysis is not to highlight gender differences but to also seek out gender similarities within the context of managerial interactions.

Semi-structured interviews

For my investigation into the organisational culture of the schools in which the meetings took place, and into the assessment by the headteachers of those skills and characteristics valued by them in their middle managers, I chose to conduct semi-structured interviews with the headteachers (that which Yin 1989 refers to as an "open-ended but focused interview"). I wanted, for reasons of reliability and validity, to be able to standardise the skills areas of the exercise, so that I could conduct a content analysis and categorisation exercise, which could then be compared across schools. However, I also wanted to allow the heads room to discuss their reasons and philosophies, give their insights, and to elaborate upon their points if they wished to clarify or justify choices. This provided me with data for my interpretation of the organisational structure of the school. Some of the skills used necessarily required linguistic interpretation; an individual head might interpret a word in a different pragmatic context from another head and validity necessitated clarification of the pragmatic understanding used by the head. Lexis such as "tough", "democratic" and "compliant" need further explanation: how was the head interpreting this word when he/

she valued it as a middle manager's leadership skill? It has to be accepted that different people might have different pragmatic understandings of some lexis which they identify as emotive because of their own personal experiences. This issue is explored further in chapter 5 where I outline this part of the investigation in detail.

Ethical issues

There are a number of ethical issues arising from my choice of methods. Woods (1986) argues that negotiating access for ethnographic research into educational settings is not just "about getting into an institution but proceeding across several thresholds that mark the way to the heart of the culture." He talks of the "honest project", that is, one that is "designed for the purposes of the advancement of knowledge that might improve . . . the conditions of others." The suggestion is that participants might be more ready to cooperate if they see a research project as in this sense "worthy", or rather if the researcher can persuade them that this is the case. Certainly, Woods sees the first stage of access as the generating of trust and the establishing of rapport. This is commensurate with the notion that the researcher is the "primary research tool" and that the researcher's **self** (interpersonal/ interactive skills, ability to enlist support) is the one most important explanatory factor in the successful entry to field. I found that in my research it was important to predict the heads' anxieties about the method and usage of the research. I needed to reassure the heads (the gate-keepers) that there would be no additional commitment/workload required from their staff, that confidentiality and anonymity would be respected (and to outline the methods I would use to ensure this), and that the research purpose was not to undertake surveillance or monitoring of the school's performance or policies, but to investigate issues of gendered talk.

Nevertheless, Troman (1996) argues that a concentration on the researcher's self and the micro-context of the particular fieldwork may obscure the real influence of the macro-context on research relationships. Issues such as Local Management of Schools (LMS), National Curriculum, inspections by the Office for Standards in Education (OFSTED), and so on following the 1988 Education Reform Act (ERA), have all changed schools as institutions tremendously, and have necessarily influenced headteachers' attitudes to researchers. Troman (1996) identifies nine explanatory factors for unsuccessful attempts to gain entry. They include the perceived intensification of teachers' workload, fear of surveillance from external "experts" (for example, policing of externally imposed curriculum and assessment by OFSTED), and financial considerations (what's in it for the school?). Troman claims that "headteachers and teachers, deskilled in the sense that they no longer engage in critical reflection on the very measures which disempower them, are the ones most likely to exhibit no entry signs when engaged in negotiations with ethnographers" (p85). My own attempts to gain access to field tended, where they were unsuccessful, to be blocked at the first stage, either by the gate-keeper's gate-keeper (the head's secretary) or by the gate-keeper (the head herself), before the proposal could be properly explained, other than the (necessarily) brief outline in the initial letter of introduction. Assumptions of workload or demands on staff were made without a proper consideration of the proposals. It is also probable that other fears and anxieties by heads about the presence of a researcher in the workplace, and in actual work situations, prompted refusals. However, where attempts to gain access were successful, the reaction of heads and staff to my work was that it was a "worthy and honest project" and they were very accommodating and supportive.

In terms of a "pay-back" for the school, I offered feedback, individual interview and In-service Training (INSET) to the participants although in only one case was this taken up, where feedback was useful for the National Vocational Qualification (NVQ) (Management) which some of the participants were undertaking.

I gained informed consent from the heads and all the managers, giving information about the area of research, that is, into linguistic strategies used by middle managers in interaction with their teams in meetings, and into whether this varied between the genders. As with the heads, there was a varied level of understanding as to what this meant. I did not give details of the traits which I was investigating or of issues of gendered linguistics. As discussed earlier on page 55, in linguistic research this can be counterproductive to explain exactly what features you are looking at, since this in itself can make the participant more aware of their own speech features and that very consciousness (and self-consciousness) can affect the naturalness of the interaction. This would then have affected the research results. I asked each manager to request confirmation from their team members about my presence as a researcher prior to the meeting. In asking managers to relay information about my research to their team members, before the meetings took place, I also sought permission from them and assured them that withdrawal at any point from the research situation would be respected.

Although the team members were aware in advance of my visit and purpose, I did not wish to be too obtrusive during the course of the meeting and thus affect the interaction to any greater extent than necessary. Usually, the participants forgot the presence of the recorder once the matter of the meeting was underway. I wanted to have as little influence on the conversation as possible, although I am aware of course that my very presence itself necessarily alters and affects the situation to an extent. I felt that the alternative situation, where I set up the recording without being present and without participants' knowledge (apart from the manager) was ethically flawed even if the consent was obtained later, as the recording itself would encroach on individual privacy. Yet I did not have a practical situation in which I could "acclimatise" the participants over time to become so used to my recording that they could forget I was there. However, it seemed to me as an observer that after the first few minutes of the meeting, as people became engrossed with the issues under discussion, they became less aware of my presence. This is still a problematical area for sociolinguistic research methodology.

The members of the teams were in some cases interested in my research project and in no case did anyone object to the recording taking place. In one meeting, however, one of the team requested the recorder to be turned off while she criticised a senior member of staff not present, and I conceded her request for privacy. I did not note what was said nor use it in my analysis, except to give a brief indication of the reason for the request. This is shown in chapter 6. I had assured the participants that the report would be anonymous both in terms of the school and the individuals, and that therefore identification protected: I felt that respecting privacy and protecting confidential material in this way was the ethically sound course to take here. I also felt that this must be respected in order to retain my integrity as a research and the confidence and trust of the participants. In fact, of course, I was focusing on the speech strategies of the middle manager and not on the conversational discourse of the other participants per se.

Dr Julia Helene Ibbotson PhD, FHEA

Summary

I have outlined the position I adopted in terms of the research problem and the choices I have made in addressing it. I have outlined my approach to the methods chosen and to ethical considerations. I now want to explore the process of the research method as a chronological narrative.

The process: access to field

Table 1 on p. 69 shows that the process of gaining access to field took 14 months and that 8 schools were negotiated in order to achieve the required 4. The first audio-recordings were already taking place, therefore, while access to other schools was being negotiated. My particular difficulty was gaining access to female-headed schools in the county, of which there were far fewer than male. In fact, towards the end I was in danger of running out of female headteachers altogether. However, it shows the difficulty of gaining access even to the initial interview with the "gate-keeper" with whom I would negotiate the fieldwork and select the participants.

In the interests of confidentiality and anonymity, all school names and identities have been changed. I have used the designation ANO 1/2/3/4 for schools to which access was denied either immediately or eventually, but have used pseudonyms for the four schools to which I gained access and which became my case studies.

Table 1: chronology of process—access to field

Activity	Notes
Begin to obtain access to field: letters to 4 schools (Broadmarsh, High Ridge, Droverslea, + ANO 1)	2 female heads
	2 male heads
	Midlands county secondary comprehensive schools
Telephone follow-up to arrange initial meeting with heads to discuss proposal (Broadmarsh, High Ridge, Droverslea successfully gained access)	1 female head
	2 male heads

Interview with head of High Ridge, gathering data re organisational culture & skills assessment task, request for access to fieldwork with middle managers, both genders being represented	male head
Interview with head of Broadmarsh, as above	female head
Organisation of fieldwork subjects and dates at Broadmarsh complete	female head
Interview with head of Droverslea, as above, organise specific fieldwork	male head
Begin organisation of fieldwork at High Ridge, but awaiting contact	male head
Need another female-headed school, so letter requesting access to field to ANO 2	female head
Contact with ANO 2 by phone, fax, letter, claim that my letters & faxes "lost"	
Letter requesting access to field to ANO 3	female head
Telephone ANO 3, no access allowed to head, no messages returned.	
Refusal from ANO 2	
Head of High Ridge now allows access to field and to deputy who will organise subjects and dates	
Send fax confirming arrangements to High Ridge	
Redraft letter requesting access to field, pertinent alterations assuring heads that recordings are of existing meetings, not requiring additional workload	
Letters requesting access to field to Beckfield and ANO4. Running out of female heads within the county.	female heads
Phone contact with deputy from High Ridge to organise specific fieldwork	

Phone contact with head's secretary at Beckfield, refusing access when head takes over call and responds positively and enthusiastically to proposal, arranges interview date.	
Refusal from ANO 4	
Interview with head of Beckfield, as above, gain access to field, organise subjects and dates for recording. Finally gain access to four schools, with 2 male and 2 female heads, fieldwork organised.	female head

My research involved accessing four secondary schools and in order to achieve that field I found that I in fact negotiated twice that number, four being unsuccessful. The first two were relatively easy: they were two schools with which I already had close working contact and where I had direct access to the (male) heads' decision. These were schools in which I was personally known and trusted, my professionalism as a fellow teacher respected and therefore anxieties of the head overcome easily. In High Ridge, however, having successfully negotiated access to the head, I found that the practical arrangements were delegated by him to a deputy with whom I had less easy contact, and over the following year of research found difficulties with the organisation of appropriate dates and staff. Clearly, this teacher did not share the head's enthusiasm for the project, and was already facing a heavy workload himself. I found that I needed to take a somewhat "bureaucratic" stance here, as negotiations required much exchange of paperwork, as well as much patience, and I found it helpful to keep liaison in written form, and to take copies of all faxes and letters, which stated my requirements and confirmed decisions taken.

At the first school to which I attempted to gain access (designated on table 1 as ANO 1), negotiations took nearly three months to even acquire a decision. After a number of letters which were not answered, and phone calls where access to the head was denied by her secretary ("she's in a meeting/on the phone/she'll ring you back"), I eventually gained access to the head who sounded very "rushed" and assured me that although she was interested she would need to consult with the Curriculum Coordinators the following week. Nearly two months later, I wrote asking for a decision.

The immediate reply was that the request had been discussed with the Curriculum Coordinators, but that entry was denied due to "too many commitments to take on additional activities"—this despite the fact that I had assured the head that my recording/observing existing meetings which were already on the calendar would not involve any extra commitments in time from staff. Was the head suffering herself from educational changes creating extra stress? Was she shielding her staff? Certainly her secretary had shielded her and there were therefore at least two stages of "gate-keeping" in ANO 1.

In Broadmarsh school, again a female head, access was granted readily, both to the head and to the research field, and interest expressed in the nature and subject matter of the project. This head ran a school where many researchers were clearly welcomed and even valued; there seemed to be a pride taken in the research/media interest that the school inspired.

Another school to which I attempted unsuccessfully to gain access (ANO 2) was approached by letter and follow-up phone calls but access to the (female) head not gained in the three phone calls made during the next three weeks. Eventually, the head's secretary claimed not to have any knowledge of the original letter and I faxed a copy that same day. That, also, was "lost". Details were again taken by the secretary and I was promised an early response from the head. It was four months before I made direct contact with the head, at my instigation, but access to the field was denied as the head was retiring at the end of the year and felt that there might be continuity difficulties with her successor: she also claimed not to have seen the letters or faxes sent over the previous months.

There continued a very similar process with ANO 3 (the third unsuccessful attempt) over a span of about four months, when direct access to the head (female) was denied by the secretary: she was constantly "unavailable" and although she eventually offered me access to a deputy, he did not return my call.

At this point I redrafted my original letter requesting access in order to make it even more explicit in writing that I did not anticipate that the research would increase participants' workload (see Appendix 4). I could not allay any other fears, other than via the outline of the research purpose and method already contained in the letter. I was beginning to become concerned that there were few female heads left to contact in the county. I approached two further schools, my last two chances, Beckfield and ANO 4. ANO 4 was helpful but informed me that the female head had recently left and had been replaced by a male head who was willing to speak with me. However, since at this stage I needed access to a female head I declined.

I was beginning to wonder whether there was any significance in the problems I was experiencing in gaining access specifically to female heads when I gained entry to my final school, Beckfield. Within a week of sending my access letter, I rang the school to be told by the school secretary that she was in a meeting. I asked to speak with her personal secretary who seemed helpful but cautious. Suddenly, the head herself took over the call and expressed enthusiasm for the project and a pleasure in helping in any way she could.

It transpired that my two female heads with whom I successfully gained access were people who knew of me professionally and/or had previously had some personal connection, either directly or indirectly through a mutual contact. All my four successful bids, then, were characterised by a common element of personal connection and knowledge of my work. Perhaps this constitutes a significant factor in overcoming prejudice or misconceptions of a researcher's validity. Certainly, my experiences of unsuccessful attempts seem to support some of Troman's arguments: the increasing workload of teachers was a strong factor, even where a head had granted access this reservation was expressed. It seemed that secretaries were shielding heads and that heads were shielding their staff. I did come across the request to produce a specific benefit/outcome for the school in return for acceptance into the field ("what's in it for the school?"), but not as widely as I had expected. I would surmise that the fact that I was a serving full-time teacher myself helped the achievement of trust and acceptance.

During my semi-structured interviews with the headteachers, I discussed, as fully as they individually required, my purposes and methods, reassuring them on issues outlined earlier in this chapter. I collected third party data, such as staffing/management structures and equal opportunities policy documents, which would provide evidence for an assessment of the organisational culture of the school. All headteachers were happy to provide this information and documentation, and no sensitive material was required. This evidence is outlined in chapter 4. I also conducted a skills assessment exercise with the heads in order to gain an insight into the value headteachers placed upon skills and characteristics associated with the leadership role of the middle manager. This exercise added to the data collected on the organisational culture of the school and provided me with comparison between male and female headteachers of their evaluations and an idea of those evaluations which might reflect a gender variable. These are outlined and discussed further in chapter 5.

The process: fieldwork

The chronology of the main part of the research process, the fieldwork, consisting of audio-recordings and observation of team meetings of middle managers, is set out in the table below. In the interests of confidentiality and anonymity, pseudonyms are used for all participants.

Table 2: chronology of process—fieldwork recording and observation

Name	Male/female	School
Ivan: Head of Humanities	m	Broadmarsh
Cheryl: Head of Upper School	f	"
Gertie: H of Learning Support	f	"
Patrick: Head of English	m	"
Clive: Head of English	m	Droverslea
Isabel: Head of Humanities	f	"
Kath: Head of Modern Languages	f	Beckfield
Gladys: Head of Year	f	"
Keith: Head of Technology	m	"
Joe: Head of Science	m	"
Horace: Head of Modern Languages	m	Droverslea
Sally: Head of Year	f	High Ridge
Liz: Head of Year	f	Droverslea
Chris: Head of Science	m	High Ridge
ANO 1: Head of Year	m	High Ridge
ANO 2: Head of English	f	High Ridge

I contacted all managers individually after their selection by the Head, in order to organise the visits and to establish trust and rapport. I was observing meetings which were already scheduled by the schools and which were a normal and regular occurrence in the teachers' work schedule. They tended to be mainly organised after the end of the school day and to last for about an hour. The agenda was in all cases set by the manager and was in response to needs arising naturally from issues of the time, either set externally by senior management or internally by the demands of the department/pastoral work. I did not want a situation where I had any input into this, nor any participation in the meetings themselves. I was clearly a non-participant observer and I tried to place myself and my audio-recorder in as unobtrusive position as practically possible in each case.

My field notes from my observations mainly consisted of diagrams to indicate where participants were sitting and an identification of gender and name (pseudonym). I noted down an indication of contributions from different individuals in the meeting so that I was more able to identify the speakers when I listened to the recordings, as in many cases I did not know the people involved. Information was given to me by managers in my meeting with them beforehand. I noted the timings of the meetings, the agenda, the ratio of male to female team members, whether they had any management role outside of that particular team, (for example, a deputy Head in an English department team), any events during the meeting (interrupted recording, papers given out, use of overhead projector), any asides or off-task conversations between members of the team, in case any of these had a bearing on the manager's discourse. I noted down any incidents which might be interesting for me to use in my subsequent analysis.

The process: transcription and analysis of fieldwork

The audio-recordings themselves were undertaken as and when the schedule of meetings in schools permitted, whenever selected participants were available, and to an extent in accordance with the chronology of gaining access to a particular school. However, I rearranged the chronology of transcriptions, commentaries and analyses, first of all in groups of schools, then by gender alternately. This enabled me to make a more effective comparison of data, both between genders and between schools. I began with the two schools with male headteachers to reflect the fact that the majority of secondary schools have male heads.

The chronology of the transcription and analysis process is set out in the table below:

Table 3: chronology of process—fieldwork transcription and analysis

Subject	Activity, post—audio recording	Notes
Clive (Droverslea)	• reviewed cassette, selected key areas for transcription establishing status; • dealing with critical incidents/handling conflict; making decisions) • transcribed key areas of meeting • annotated transcript / analysis • wrote up analysis—commentary form • wrote conclusion, focusing on gender linguistic issues	
Liz (Droverslea)	Process as above	
Horace (Droverslea)	Process as above	
Isabel (Droverslea)	Process as above	Patterns beginning to emerge re management similarities & gender similarities and differences
Chris (High Ridge)	Process as above	Chris chosen next in order to test emerging patterns
Sally (High Ridge)	Process as above	Female chosen here to test emerging gender patterns.

Joe (Beckfield)	"dipstick testing" within key areas	Interrogating rest of data in the light of emerging patterns and hypothesis
Keith (Beckfield)	"	"
Kath & Gladys (Beckfield)	Review of recordings / "dipstick testing"	"
Cheryl & Gertie (Broadmarsh)	"	Interrogating data in the light of emerging patterns and hypothesis.
Patrick & Ivan (Broadmarsh)	"	"

Having recorded the meetings, I then reviewed the tapes and selected key areas for my transcription, using the following criteria. I focused on the interactions directly involving the managers, since I was looking at the managers' speech, and I concentrated on openings and closings of meetings, management interactions, critical incidents, and managerial transactions which would indicate the manager's handling of the team and the way in which decisions were reached. It was these key areas which I transcribed and used for discourse analysis. The issues of subjectivity and interpretation in the selection process here were discussed earlier in this chapter.

The discourse analysis involved a certain amount of quantitative work in that I counted, for example, the number of interruptions of and by the manager, the number of direct imperatives used by the manager, and other speech strategies, but I then needed to interpret these within an overview of that manager's general interactional strategy. I then needed to interpret these findings in terms of a comparison between male and female managers' interactional strategies.

The criteria I used in order to investigate my data were the presence of the following speech features: tag questions, politeness forms, interruptions, use of modals/modal auxiliaries as directives, conditionals, imperatives, statives and declaratives, interrogatives, epistemic modality, qualifiers, minimal responses, and passives, amongst other linguistic forms as they arose in the data. These basic search features were those which arose as issues within the literature on gender differences, as I outlined in chapter 2.

My analysis was then written up as a commentary for each participant's transcription, including linguistic analysis and reflective description of the interactions involved. My analysis was therefore an interpretative account of the linguistic usage of each manager within the context of that particular meeting on that occasion and of the pragmatics therein. Charts and graphs of linguistic unit counts were therefore inappropriate to the purpose of the study, which focuses on function in real contexts, not pure form, and thus needed interpretation for insights into the interactions and their meanings to be gained.

I found that after the analysis of the fuller transcriptions of the first four meetings, patterns of gender similarities in linguistic usage and patterns of gender differences were becoming apparent from my data. I therefore continued the same process with a manager of each gender from the next school in order to test these emerging patterns, and found that these were confirmed. A hypothesis was beginning to be formed.

I then needed to reassess my original research design which was to transcribe and analyse in full all sixteen meetings, and to plan a new strategy for the analysis of the rest of my data. I decided instead to use a "dipstick testing" method in order to interrogate the rest of my data in the light of my emerging hypothesis. This is not unlike Yin's (1989) multiple replication case study design discussed earlier in this chapter. It also reflects the processes of analytic induction method (Robinson 1951, Lindesmith 1968, Bloor 1978) also discussed earlier in chapter 3 in the section on validity. I focused down on the key areas in which I had found clear comparative data already, and transcribed and analysed small critical sequences from the remaining meetings which demonstrated the areas of major focus of patterning. My criteria for selecting sequences were those demonstrating the way in which the manager established status, handled conflict and decision-making. The issues of validity arising from the selectivity at this stage were discussed earlier in this chapter.

I focused on the two males in the third of my schools, the first one headed by a woman, because I wished to investigate the variable of gender in the Head's influence on the manager's communication strategies. I then reviewed the tapes for the two females in the same school and for all the managers in the final fourth school. Thus, I progressively focused down more closely on the critical sequences and on gendered language, interrogating my data in the light of the emerging patterns found and the hypothesis developed. These processes are discussed in chapters 6,7 and 8.

Summary

In this chapter, I have described and discussed my methodology for addressing the research problem. I have outlined the practical and ethical issues arising from those choices.

I have argued that my epistemological position is closely linked to my choice of qualitative research methods, in that I am investigating a real social situation (middle managers' team meetings in secondary schools) in which the focus of my research is that of socially constructed items (gendered talk). I have argued that my analysis of this talk is subjective and interpretative because I wish to explore the way that language works as part of the management process in real managerial transactions within a particular context. This epistemological position also underpins the choice of semi-structured interviews with the headteachers of the four schools in which interpretation is used both by the heads in their responses to my questions and by myself as researcher in exploring these responses in order to gain insights into the organisational cultures of the schools.

I have also outlined the implications of these epistemological assumptions on the language used in this thesis: the use of the first person in the report, the use of chronological narrative in the outline of the investigative processes, and the use of narrative for the analytical commentaries on the transcripts.

I have outlined my chosen methods: case studies of four schools, in which I use semi-structured interviews with headteachers and the collection of documentary data in order to investigate the organisational culture for the contextualisation of the study, and, for the main body of the fieldwork, non-participant observation and audio-recording of team meetings, followed by discourse analysis of the managerial linguistic strategies used.

I have discussed the issues arising from my choice of research position and from the methods used to address the research problem. These issues concern validity, reliability and ethics. I have argued that as far as possible I have addressed these through the research design, the approach to transcription, the use of informed consent, the right of withdrawal, anonymity and confidentiality. I have indicated that my research design followed a variation of the analytic induction method of theory construction and validation.

I have charted the chronology of my investigation in order to clarify the processes involved in access to field, in the fieldwork (observation and recording of meetings), and in the data analysis (transcription and analysis of the recordings).

In the following two chapters, I explore the organisational culture of the four schools in my study; firstly outlining the content and issues of interpretation arising from the collection of secondary sources from each school, and in the following chapter outlining the subjective interpretation of the semi-structured interviews with the heads.

CHAPTER FOUR

WHAT WAS THE ORGANISATIONAL CULTURE OF THE SCHOOLS UNDER STUDY? (FOCUS ON GENDER ISSUES OF MANAGEMENT STRUCTURE)

Introduction

In the previous chapter, I outlined my approach to the methodology of the research and discussed in detail the practical and ethical issues arising from my chosen methods. I argued that my epistemological position owed much to the post-modern constructivist approach which underpinned my choice of qualitative methods using case studies, non-participant observation, audio-recording and discourse analysis of transcripts, as well as semi-structured interviews with headteachers and the interpretation of documentary evidence on gender policy and management structure of the schools.

It seemed increasingly clear that, in order to investigate sociolinguistic dimensions to management and communication within secondary schools, it was important to explore the organisational culture of the institutions in which the investigations were taking place, especially with regard to the cultural assumptions on gender issues.

The arguments in the literature outlined in chapter 1 (for example Shakeshaft 1989 and Evetts 1994) identified the effect on women's roles of the organisational culture of the workplace; and Hargreaves 1998 focused on the effects of current changes in the organisational culture of secondary schools on all staff. Davidson and Cooper (1992) argued the existence of a "glass ceiling" effect which inhibits women from higher management positions and which tends to constrain women in the type of management roles associated with their assumed role in society.

The argument throughout chapter 2 focused on the importance of analysing language use within the context of its usage, that is, both the immediate context of the interaction itself (in my study, the meetings), and the wider context of the setting in which that interaction takes place (the school in which the meeting occurs). It is therefore reasonable to suppose that an ethos which promotes and indeed positively values gender equality of contribution and opportunity would tend to make it easier and even desirable for more feminine styles of management to succeed. In such institutions we might therefore see a valuing of stereotypically feminine style characteristics, such as consensus-seeking techniques, interpersonal emphasis, and colleague supportiveness, as opposed to the more masculine characteristics of depersonalisation, distance and competitiveness traditionally valued in secondary school management (see Loden 1985, Shakeshaft 1989, Darking 1991).

In this chapter, I explore the content of documentary sources collected in each of the four schools used in my study and the issues arising from an interpretation of them. These sources included the school prospectus, Equal Opportunities (EO) documents/ policy statements where they were available, and documents on the staffing (management) structure.

All the schools and staff have been given pseudonyms to preserve confidentiality and anonymity.

School 1—Droverslea

The School background

Droverslea had a male head and was a large mixed 11-18 comprehensive school of 1800 pupils and 112.6 (fte) staff. At the time of the study, it had local authority Voluntary Controlled status. It had a large sixth form, with examination results well above the national and county average. It served a mixed geographical and social area, but with a weighting towards the middle class commuter groups.

In 1990, the school reopened as a split site all-through 11-18 comprehensive school, amalgamating two local junior highs on the site of one of the previous schools to form the new Lower School. The existing senior high remained on its own site, becoming the new Upper School.

The pupils moved to Upper School after Year 9. This was previously the practice with the junior highs. Most staff taught on both sites and travelled between them. During this reorganisation in 1990, the decision was made by governors and LEA to keep the existing senior management team (all male) in their respective base sites. The headteacher was based at the Upper School site and a deputy head (previously the deputy at one of the junior highs) was appointed to act as the manager in charge of the Lower School site. Middle managers of all three previous schools had to apply for the equivalent jobs in the new organisation, as did junior managers. The result of this, according to the present head, was a certain amount of rivalry and discontent, aggravated when most of the middle management posts went to the incumbents of the senior high. The head's comments on this are discussed in the next chapter.

Staffing structure (management)

Table 4 shows the management structure at Droverslea and indicates the distribution by sex of the management posts. The whole of the senior management team was male (the head and three deputies), although on the next level of management (senior teachers and pastoral Heads of School) three out of five were female. However, the posts held by women were Equal Opportunities (cross-curricular) and pastoral headship, both of which could be seen as caring, nurturing, supportive roles. This is in keeping with the stereotypical female role discussed in chapters 1 and 2. All four Heads of Year (pastoral) were women. However, on the academic side, there was only one female Head of Faculty out of nine, and this was at the lower level of faculty headship. Of the thirteen assistant heads of faculty, six were women, although of these three were at the lower level of management, while only one man was at this lower level.

Table 4: management structure at Droverslea,
showing distribution by sex

```
                         Head (M)
                            I
Deputy Head (M) -------- Deputy Head (M) ---------Deputy Head (M)
            I                                  I
   EO (F)----------------Resources/            I
            I           Finance (M)            I
            I                        HoS (F)----HoS (M)------HoS (F)
HoFs (5) (M)-(M)-(M)-(M)-(M) *       (lower)   (upper)    (post-16)
            I                           I          I          I
Asst. HoF(M)-(F)-(M)-(M)-(F)      HoY(F) (F)   HoY (F)    HoY (M)
HoFs (4) (M)-(F)-(M)-(M)             I          I          I
            I                           I          I          I
Asst. HoF(M)-(F)-(F)-(F)     Asst. HoY(M)       (M)        (M)
                                  (F)           (F)        (F)

* cross-curricular posts at this management level:
examinations officer (M); RoA (F); ICT (M)
```

Key: HoF= Head of Faculty; HoS= Head of School section; HoY= Head of Year; EO= Equal Opportunities; Asst. HoF/Y=assistant Head of Faculty/Year

There were a number of anomalies at Droverslea in the "responsibility points" which were awarded to managers according to their level of responsibility and were reflected in their level of salary. These were evaluated by the head and governors and awarded to post holders usually for the duration of their role. However, historically at Droverslea the major academic faculties were awarded 5 points for their heads of faculty, whilst the heads of faculties regarded as "minor" were awarded 4 points (hence the 5 and 4 designations in table 4 above). Likewise, assistant faculty heads were awarded 4 and 3 points respectively. There were new proposals were to amend this so that all faculty heads would receive 4 points and all assistants would receive 3. This was going to be phased in over a period of time, as post-holders left and new allowances could be attached to those posts. There was a similar anomaly with assistant Heads of Year. At the time of my study, there were a number of management post-holders on the lower level of allowances: of these five were women and only two were men.

However, it is clear that at the time of the study women were under-represented at both middle and senior management level at Droverslea: there were no women senior level, while upper middle female representation was weighted towards pastoral posts. Women were under-represented at middle management (faculty) level although well represented in pastoral posts, and equally represented at junior management (assistant) level, in both faculty and pastoral teams. There was a clear discrepancy here: women struggled to rise above junior management level, and those who did, tended to achieve their promotion in pastoral posts, which are associated with caring skills, rather than academic (faculty) posts which are associated with intellectual skills.

A clear outline of the responsibility points awarded is shown in Table 5. It is worth clarifying that as points were reflected in salary, they reflected not only the present career level of the post-holder but also the next likely step. In other words, women were clustered at lower management/salary levels, with less potential for promotion to higher levels.

Table 5: distribution of allowances (responsibility points) by sex at Droverslea.

Post	Points	Men	Women
Head and 3 deputies	Special scale	4	0
Head of Faculty	5	5	0
Head of Faculty	4	3	1
Head of School	5	1	2
Head of Year	4	1	3
Cross-curricular	5	1	1
Cross-curricular	4	2	1
Asst. Head of Faculty	4	3	0
Asst. Head of Faculty	3	1	5
Asst. Head of Faculty	2	0	1
Asst. Head of Year	3	1	1
Asst. Head of Year	2	2	1
Asst. Head of Year	1	0	1

The ratios of men to women at different management levels were as follows:

- management below 4 points (not including non-management posts) 4:9
- 4 points 6:5
- 5 points 7:3
- above 5 points 4:0

Of these, management head posts showed a ratio of men to women 17:8 and assistant posts 7:9. Women were well represented at assistant level but only half the management head posts were occupied by women.

Equal Opportunities policy

Nevertheless, the school's Equal Opportunities (EO) policy document indicated some commitment to the idea of acknowledging the need to avoid stereotyping roles and discriminating against groups of people on the grounds of their gender. Indeed the introduction to the document specified gender as an issue, as well as other areas of possible discrimination such as race and religion. An awareness of some of the issues in general was shown in the following examples from the document:

> "The hidden curriculum must not be ignored . . ."
> "Implementation of staff development programmes to ensure that the school Equal Opportunities policy is disseminated and actively pursued . . ." (Guidelines)
> ". . . explicit teaching programmes designed to challenge stereotyping . . ."

However, there was nothing explicitly on (a) INSET for or career development of female staff, (b) female role models, (c) staff development and staffing policy. There was also no official gender staffing/development questionnaire or research undertaken, although there was some EO working party research done by members informally in 1990-1992, which was taken to Curriculum Committee. However, the head commented that it seemed to have been disadvantaged by virtue of the fact that the body did not then have Committee status. This was not re-addressed at a later date and therefore for technical/bureaucratic reasons the issues lost their high profile.

Conclusions

Despite the stated concern about discrimination and hidden agenda in the EO policy document, the management structure at Droverslea indicated a bias towards men at the higher levels of management, and a clustering of females at the lower levels of management and in pastoral posts. It indicated that there was more opportunity for potential women middle/senior managers to gain posts through the pastoral channel, but less opportunity than men to achieve this level of management through the academic (faculty/departmental) channel. This reflects the argument of Davidson and Cooper (1992) that women tend to be given stereotyped roles in the work context which reflect the assumed female role in society (that is, the caring nurturing roles), and that where they are offered promotion at work it tends to be within these kinds of roles.

This evidence from secondary data collected from the school suggested a conflict between the stated mission of the EO policy and the reality of the actual management structure by gender. The head's comments on this are discussed in the following chapter.

School 2—High Ridge

The School background

High Ridge also had a male head and was a mixed comprehensive school with 1000+ pupils and 60 full-time staff. At the time of the study the school had Grant Maintained status, having opted out of local government control in 1993. Originally, it was an 11-16 school, but in 1995 it added a sixth form, thus becoming a single site all-through 11-18 school. The problems of communication and whole school ethos encountered by Droverslea as a reorganised split site school did not therefore arise at High Ridge. It gained examination results slightly above the county and national average. It served a mixed geographical and social area.

Until the retirement of the previous head in 1987, the school had a stable staff of higher than average age who had mainly been in post for many years. Managers were often promoted from within the school on a seniority (long service) basis. There was a high proportion of non-graduate staff and the emphasis tended to be less academic than Droverslea. Since the current (male) head was appointed in 1987, there had been a number of appointments of younger staff at most levels and far more promotions from outside the school than previously, thus bringing into the school wider experiences of management.

Staffing structure (management)

Table 6 shows the management structure at High Ridge and indicates the distribution by sex of management posts. As at Droverslea, the whole of the senior management was male, that is, the head, two deputy heads, and three senior teachers (Curriculum Directors, and Site/resources manager). Three of the nine Heads of Faculty were women, while three of the five Heads of Year were women. Only two of the six assistant Heads of Faculty were women, while four of the five assistant Heads of Year were women. As at Droverslea, managerial posts went to women in the pastoral area rather than the academic (departmental) area.

Table 6: management structure at High Ridge, showing distribution by sex

```
                          Head (M)
                             I
Deputy Head(M)---------------------------------------Deputy Head(M)
                   I
      Curriculum Director(M) (M)---------Site/Resources Manager(M)
                   I                                      I
HoF(4points) (F)-(F)-(M)-(M)-(M)-(M)    HoY(4points) (F)-(M)-(F)-(F)-(M)
                   I                                      I
             I          I                                 I
             I     HoF(3points) (F)-(M)-(M)               I
Asst HoF(F)-(F)-(M)-(M)-(M)-(M)                           I
                                  Asst HoY  (F)-(F)-(F)-(M)-(F)
```

The pattern which emerged at High Ridge was very similar to that of Droverslea. Women were clustered at junior management level, or if they achieved higher level management roles these tended to be in pastoral posts. Again, the Davidson and Cooper (1992) argument is reflected.

Tables 7 and 8 show, respectively, the distribution of responsibility points by sex and the comparative picture with regard to this distribution from 1987 (the arrival of the current head) and 1992.

Table 7: distribution of allowances (responsibility points)
by gender at High Ridge

Post	Points	Men	Women
Head and 2 deputies	Special scale	3	0
Senior teachers	5	3	0
Head of Faculty	4	4	2
Head of Faculty	3	2	1
Head of Head of Year	4	2	3
Asst. Head of Faculty	2	4	2
Asst. Head of Year	1	1	4

The ratios of men to women at different management levels are as follows:

- management below 4 points (not including non-management posts) 7:7
- 4 points 6:5
- 5 points 3:0
- above 5 points 3:0

Unlike Droverslea, there were management head posts on only 3 points. Thus, management head posts showed a ratio of males to females 14:6 and assistant posts 5:6. As at Droverslea, women were well represented at assistant level but poorly represented (fewer than half) at management head levels. This picture showed an improved distribution by sex from 1992-4 as can be seen in the following table.

Table 8: comparative distribution of responsibility allowances
by sex 1992-4

Points	Men 1992	Women 1992	% women 1992	Men 1994	Women 1994	% women 1994
Head	1	0	0	1	0	0
Deputy	2	0	0	2	0	0
5	2	0	0	3	0	0
4	5	3	38	6	5	45 *
3	4	5	56	2	1	33
2	6	3	33	7	2	29
1	1	4	80	2	6	75
Main scale	9	13	59	10	12	55
% with points	70	54	44	70	56	45

* the school's own record shows 6:6 = 50% female at 4 points for Table 8. However, this was not born out by the staffing structure grids (tables 6 and 7) and other documentation from the school. I have therefore adjusted the statistics for Table 8 as shown above.

Data from High Ridge also showed that between 1987 and 1994, 23 teachers were appointed: 17 women and 6 men. During this period, 27 internal promotions were made, 12 to men and 15 to women, taking the percentage of men on responsibility points from 61% to 70% and of women from 42% to 56%.

Clearly, the trend had been towards promotion of more women to management posts at junior level and above, and the fact that data was available from the school to demonstrate this, suggested that it had become a conscious aim by the head and governors. However, the probability of women gaining management posts on 3 points and above (management heads) was less than 1 in 4 (6 out of 27 women on the staff), whereas the probability for men was 1 in 2 (14 out of 33 men). There were still no women holding positions of 5 points and above, while 6 men had senior teacher posts (5 points) and senior management posts (head and deputies). This clearly demonstrates Davidson and Cooper's "glass ceiling": women are (for whatever reason) marginalised when it comes to senior management posts and academic (faculty/departmental) middle management posts.

Other secondary sources of relevant information

1. The school prospectus

Interestingly, in the school prospectus, the head was linguistically labelled as "Headmaster" rather than headteacher, with its value-laden pragmatics of a male-oriented organisational culture. This tended to be supported by the images in the prospectus. There was only one photograph of a female member of staff shown in a situation of authority, although there were 7 images of males in this capacity. There were, however, a number of pictures of female dinner assistants, which indicated that this was an assumed female role in the school. However, the school's Equal Opportunities (Gender) policy statement included a Sex Equality Audit, which indicated an awareness of some gender issues on the part of the head and governors, who instigated this approach.

2. Equal Opportunities(Gender) policy

The policy statement reflected an awareness of gender issues in staffing, promotion and INSET as well as in the chosen role models to present to the pupils. The latter was not entirely born out by the images in the prospectus outlined above, however. Statements included:

"Visitors to school should include a balance of positive female and male role models . . ."

"The aim of this policy is to ensure that the recruitment, selection, training and promotion of staff are based solely on the criteria of merit and ability."

"Positive action should be taken through in-service training to encourage and promote the career development of women."

These statements were by their very nature generalised and therefore suggested only a line of development rather than specific action. Much of this is open to a range of interpretations. For example, "positive role models" of women may be interpreted as involving women on a far lower level of authority than senior managers, whereas the opposite could be applied to men. Also, the clause regarding recruitment and promotion being based on "merit and ability" could still militate against women if the selectors' criteria were masculine-model oriented. In other words, if the selectors decided that the best manager for the job is one who displayed depersonalisation, distance and competitiveness, for example (masculine traits), rather than interpersonal skills and supportiveness (feminine traits), then a man would be more likely to be offered the management post as the best person for the job. The comment on training was promoting positive action, but there was no indication of the nature of such training. This could reflect Davidson and Cooper's (1992) argument that there are pressures on women to learn to adopt masculine managerial skills in order to gain promotion.

3. Sex Equality Audit

This document arose from the research instigated and undertaken by the equal opportunities working party in the school following initiatives from the LEA. The audit itself which is quoted below consisted of questions to and responses from the head and senior management (all men). Questions and answers included (answers are indicated by the use of italics):

"Are women and men to be seen in positions of authority by pupils at every stage of their school life?"

"Present: no. There is a male dominated management hierarchy and few women staff are perceived to be in positions of authority.

Future: develop and implement strategies to overcome this—eg. women fronting assemblies."

(re interviewing procedures) *"Our interviewing procedures have been well thought out and work very well. Feedback from candidates, male and female, has been very encouraging."*

"What does the staffing structure of the school indicate about the relative status of women and men and their roles?"

"School employs the most suitable person to the post regardless of sex. I do not see that staff will ever be selected according to sex bias for any reason."

"What is being done to move towards a staffing structure that reflects equality of the sexes and equal participation?"

"Answer as above"

The last two questions and answers reflected the statements in the Equal Opportunities policy document and the same comment regarding the ambiguity of the concept "most suitable/merit/ability" applies here as I have discussed above. The first answer seemed to reflect an acknowledgement of the general problem and issues of gender inequality in management at the school, but it was not clear how the school would address gender issues, nor indeed whether there was an awareness of the hidden agenda behind the issues. For example what were valued as the most suitable characteristics for a manager at the school and were these characteristics male-oriented? The comment on "interviewing procedures" left room for a hidden agenda: who thought the procedures out and on what criteria, what feedback was referred to and how was it obtained? The suggestion of women "fronting assemblies" in order to show them in positions of authority was a thin response to the problem of the marginalising of women within the formal management structure, rather in the same way as the head of Droverslea (discussed in the following chapter) spoke of females being valued within the informal networks of the school for their help and advice, while being excluded from the formal management structures.

Conclusions

As with Droverslea, there was a stated awareness of some of the issues of gender equality in posts of authority, but the awareness failed to be supported by action or even by planned future action by the head. The EO policy did indicate a commitment to training women but it opened up the question of whether the idea of the training exercise would be effectively to teach women masculine strategies for management promotion. The head's responses to the Sex Equality Audit's questions implied that he was satisfied with the current procedures. There was an indication that there was room for some development of strategies to raise the profile of women in the school, but this did not extend to reviewing areas like promotional criteria and interviewing, which are regarded as crucial in the literature (eg Shakeshaft 1989, Davidson and Cooper 1992, Evetts 1994). The discrepancy between the awareness of gender issues and the reality of the existing management structure at High Ridge was clearly shown by the sex distribution in management demonstrated in this chapter. Senior management is wholly male, faculty management is predominantly male, and women were clustered in assistant posts and in pastoral management roles. The head's comments on this discrepancy are discussed in the following chapter.

School 3—Broadmarsh

The School background

Broadmarsh Community School had a female head and was a mixed 11-16 comprehensive school built in 1974. It had 820 pupils and 60 (fte) teaching staff. It was a local authority school which draws pupils from an area on the southern outskirts of a Midlands city, an area characterised by high levels of unemployment and social disadvantage It was also an ethnically mixed area and one with a mobile population. Up to 5% of the school population moved annually. The numbers of long family visits to India and Pakistan were common enough to warrant instructions on procedure to be followed in the admissions section of the staff handbook. There was a strong language support team including bilingual support teachers. Communications with home could be translated into Punjabi, Urdu, and Hindi through appropriate staff. Examination results were markedly below the county average for students gaining grade C and above, and slightly below for students gaining grades A to G.

The school handbook notes that there was "positive pastoral care in the form of a tutorial programme and strong home/school liaison." "Support" was a word which arose frequently in the school documents and the head's comments in the staff handbook read "The aims of our Community School are based firmly on the belief that people of all ages have a right to educational experiences which answer their needs . . . learning is seen as a lifelong process" and "we believe an effective communications system is essential."

The staff handbook clearly outlined the head's values and strongly reflected her personal involvement in its production. It was clear and straightforwardly user-friendly, but also contained thoughts and epigrams from, for example, Flaubert and Plato. She asserted in interview that she was proud of the school's OFSTED report, of the gaining of the Investors in People award in 1995, and also of the attention the school had received in the media and from researchers. She and the school maintained a high profile locally; in fact, she had been awarded the OBE for her work in the community. She wrote in the handbook that "the promotion of a strong image in the community is essential." The publicity material for the school evoked a happy and inclusive image: photographs selected by the head included smiling ethnically diverse children alongside a smiling head in informal settings.

The inspectors' document from the Investors in People award used expressions such as "commitment of senior management", the Head personally . . .", "very enthusiastic", "empowered staff", "supportive (atmosphere)", "very involved (with staff issues". I also noted during my visits, interviews and observations, that the Head was clearly very involved in a "hands-on" way with the day to day running of the school as well as with its policy making. For example, on several occasions during the interview session, the Head would be asked advice about handling a specific pupil or parent (by staff via the secretary, and on one occasion by the member of staff directly).

Staffing structure (management)

Table 9 shows the management structure at Broadmarsh and indicates the distribution by sex within it. Although the head and one deputy were women, there were no female senior teachers, and of the seven Heads of Faculty ("curriculum teams") only two were women, yet eight out of the ten assistants were women. On the pastoral side the sex balance was more even, with a male and a female pastoral Head and two female and one male assistant. It should be noted that Heads of Faculty and pastoral Heads all had 4 points, but their assistants only one point.

Table 9: management structure at Broadmarsh showing distribution by sex

```
                          Head (F)
                             I
Deputy Head (M)-----------Deputy Head (M)---------Deputy Head (F)
                                                     (pastoral)
           I                                            I
Senior Teachers (M)------(M)------(M)                   I
           I                                            I
HoF (M)----(M)----(M)----(F)---(M)----(M)---(F)    Head --------Head
           I                        Upper Schl (F) Lower Schl (M)
Asst. HoF (F)-(F) (F)-(F)-(F)-(F) (M)-(M) (F)-(F)    Asst. (M) –(F)    (F)
```

Cross-curricular managers (3points):
Language support (F)
Learning support (F)
Health related fitness (F)
IT (M)
Examinations (F)
Careers (F)

As in the two previous schools outlined, the women were clustered around the junior management level, generally as assistants to men, with the exception of the pastoral area where there was an even balance. The female deputy head was in charge of pastoral matters, and of the six cross-curricular managers, who did not necessarily have a team, three focused on support roles. Of these six, five were women. Therefore, as in the other two schools women were marginalised when it came to faculty headships, with their academic/authority role. The position of women on the school management grid identified them more with the supportive role of pastoral and cross-curricular management. Even with a female head, the distribution of males in management was very strong in the senior management and curriculum leadership roles, and almost non-existent in the assistant and support roles. However, it should be noted that the pastoral roles and organisation was very highly valued in the school.

The distribution of responsibility points is outlined more clearly in the following table.

Table 10: distribution of allowances (responsibility points)
by sex at Broadmarsh

Post	Points	Men	Women
Head	Special scale	0	1
Deputies	Special scale	2	1
Senior teacher	5	3	0
Head of Faculty	4	5	2
Head of School	4	1	1
Cross-curricular	3	1	5
Asst. Head of Faculty	1	2	8
Asst. Head of School	1	1	2

The ratios of men to women at different management levels were as follows:

- management below 4 points (not including non-management posts) 4:15
- 4 points 6:3
- 5 points 3:0
- above 5 points 2:2

Of these, management head posts showed a ratio of men to women of 11:4, and assistant posts of 3:10. The statistics showed a clear trend towards men achieving leadership roles and women in support roles. This pattern does not appear to vary whether the head is male or female.

Equal opportunities policy

The policy statement was broad based, especially as a large emphasis is on racial and religious issues, given the ethnic mix of the student population. Sex equality was, however, one aspect of the policy. The statements in the staff handbook regarding staff development were gender-free, but the emphasis was on a policy that "requires us to confront racism and assumed stereotypes wherever they occur" and ensuring that "racism and sexism are always confronted and challenged." However, there was nothing specific regarding staffing and management.

Conclusions

Although Broadmarsh had a female head, nevertheless the patterns of gender distribution of management posts were very similar to the male-headed schools, Droverslea and High Ridge. Men were in higher levels of management and women were clustered in the junior assistant levels, and in pastoral posts. Again there was more opportunity for women to gain management posts through the pastoral channel although there were fewer of these posts available than faculty head posts and senior management posts. Despite the female head, women seemed to be given stereotyped roles in the work context here, just as in the two schools with male heads. The data from secondary sources indicated general equality issues rather than specific policies regarding gender equality of opportunity for career development. This reflected the ethnic and religious mix of the school, as a local community school, but was a clear omission nonetheless.

School 4—Beckfield

The School background

Beckfield Community School also had a female head and was a local authority 11-18 school on a single site with 1160 pupils and 70 (fte) teaching staff. It was a mixed comprehensive school with examination results above the county average.

It was situated in the south western suburbs of a Midlands town and served a mixed community. The Learning Support department included a specialist teacher of English as a second language (E2L). The school was involved in the town's reorganisation programme in 1991 when two junior high schools (11-14) schools and a senior high (14-18) were merged to form a new 11-18 mixed comprehensive school. There were nearly 250 students in the sixth form. The head joined the school at reorganisation.

The school prospectus stated that the school's pastoral structure and discipline "are rooted in the context of care, friendliness and good humour and great stress is placed on the partnership between school and home." This implied that there was an informal and friendly atmosphere valued in the school. The OFSTED inspection in May 1994 reported that Beckfield was "a good school with high standards of teaching, learning and behaviour."

Staffing structure (management)

Table 11 shows the management structure at Beckfield and indicates the sex distribution of management posts. Although the head and one of the two deputies were female, only one of the four senior teachers was female. The latter post was a role in charge of personal and social education (PSE) and vocational education, an area linked to the pastoral side. Of the eight Heads of Faculty, only two were women. Both pastoral heads, on 5 points, were men. There were twelve assistant Heads of Faculty, of which seven were women, although the two posts which attracted 3 points were held by men; the others were awarded 1 or 2 points. All six assistant heads of pastoral teams had 3 points and three of them were women.

Table 11: management structure at Beckfield, showing distribution by sex.

Head (F)
I
Deputy Head (F)-------------------------------------Deputy Head (M)
I
Senior teachers (F) (PSE/vocational)---------(M)---------(M)---------(M)
I   I
I   Pastoral Heads (5 points) (M)—(M)
HoF(4) (M)—(M)—(M)—(M)—(F)—(M)(3)—(M)—(F)   I
I   Asst. HoY (3) (F)-(M)-(M)-(M)-(F)-(F)
I
Asst. HoF (M)(3)-(F)(2)-(F)(2)-(M+F)(2)-(M+F+F)(1)-(F)(2)-(M+F)(2)-(M)(3)

<u>Cross-curricular</u>

IT (F) 2 points

Asst. PSE (M+F) 3 points + (F) 2 points

Learning support (M) 4 points

Asst. Learning support (F) 2 points

Staff development (F) 4 points

Examinations officer (F) 3 points

As with the other schools in the study, the pattern showed that women were under-represented at middle and senior levels of management and were marginalised at the level of faculty headship where leadership of a team is required. At this school, even pastoral headships were not occupied by women and this was different from the other schools in the study, where the pastoral area seemed to provide women with greater opportunities for promotion. Women were well represented in cross-curricular management roles although two of these roles were at assistant level and none were leading teams.

Table 12 outlines the sex distribution of responsibility points. It is clear that there was a wide discrepancy between points awarded at assistant Head of Faculty level, varying between 1 and 3 points, and at cross-curricular level, varying between 4 and 3 points. The table provides additional information on the distribution by sex of these allowances as opposed to the management roles themselves.

Table 12: distribution of allowances (responsibility points) by sex at Beckfield.

Post	Points	Men	Women
Head	Special scale	0	1
Deputy Heads	Special scale	1	1
Senior Teachers	5	3	1
Pastoral Heads	5	2	0
Head of Faculty	4	5	2
Head of Faculty	3	1	0
Asst. Pastoral Head	3	3	3
Asst. Head of Faculty	3	2	0
Asst. Head of Faculty	2	2	5
Asst. Head of Faculty	1	1	2
Cross-curricular	4	1	1
Cross-curricular	3	1	2
Cross-curricular	2	0	3

The ratios of men to women at different management levels were as follows:

- management below 4 points (not including non-management posts 10:15
- 4 points 6:3
- 5 points 5:1
- above 5 points 2:1

Of these, management headship posts showed a ratio of men to women of 12:5 and assistant posts 9:13. As with the previous schools, women were well represented at assistant level, but fewer than half the management head posts were occupied by women, despite having a female headteacher and deputy. There was a gender difference of access to pastoral management posts in this school, but in fact it is a male bias here, unlike the other schools in the study.

Equal Opportunities policy

The school had a clear statement of equal opportunities as required by the local authority. Within the context of an ethnically mixed community it concentrated on racial equality "in a pluralistic society". It looked at practical details in its "Policy for Managing Equality", such as "students should be encouraged to accept and respect names from other cultures", and included the unacceptability of "racist symbols, badges and insignia". It encouraged "positive images of all groups" and for resources to be "non-sexist" also. "Staff must be conscious of any racist or sexist connotations in the language they themselves use."

In regard to staffing, the policy document stated: "the school values diversity amongst the staff" and "in all staff appointments, the best candidate will be appointed, based upon strict professional criteria." This again, as with Droverslea and High Ridge, begged the question of a hidden agenda or of the "professional criteria" involving assumptions of a male-model of management capability. Certainly, in assessing the management structure by sex at the school, I would be left to ask if this implied that women were assumed to be less suitable professionally than men at middle and senior management levels, especially where team leadership was involved. These issues are discussed in the following chapter.

Conclusions

Despite having a female head, like Broadmarsh, Beckfield's patterns of gender distribution of management posts were very similar to those at the schools with male heads, Droverslea and High Ridge. Again, men were in higher levels of management and women were clustered in the junior assistant levels. At this school, women were not clustered in pastoral roles, and it should be noted that the pastoral headships were both occupied by men, and that all the pastoral management posts, heads and assistants, were rewarded with higher responsibility points than the equivalent academic/ faculty posts. It is interesting that this was the only school of the four in which this clear distinction was apparent and the only school in which there was not a majority of women in the pastoral management posts. In other words there seemed to be a correlation between higher points and men occupying those management roles, regardless of whether they were pastoral or academic roles. Like Broadmarsh, data from policy documents concentrated on racism rather than sexism and reflected the fact that this was a community school for an ethnically mixed population. However, there was nothing documented on staff development although there was a policy on staff appointments which begged the question of the possibility of a hidden agenda.

Comparison between schools

The proportion of women within management headship/leadership roles, whether faculty or pastoral, was fairly constant between the four schools. The proportion of women within pastoral headship roles showed a greater variation between schools, with the two male-headed schools demonstrating the highest figure. The proportion of women in assistant management roles was fairly constant between three of the schools, but Broadmarsh (a female-headed school) showed a far higher proportion than the others.

Table 13: comparative proportions of women within different management roles in the four schools.

school	% leadership roles given to women	% of these being pastoral roles	% pastoral management roles given to women	% assistant roles given to women
Droverslea	32	62.5	71	56
High Ridge	30	50	60	55
Broadmarsh	27	25	50	77
Beckfield	29	0	0	59

The issues relating to Beckfield's pastoral headship posts have already been discussed in an earlier section of this chapter. Clearly, in the schools with male heads, pastoral roles were more accessible to women as a means to management promotion than faculty roles, whereas in the schools with female heads faculty headships were more accessible. However, in all four schools the discrepancy between leadership and assistant roles was clearly marked, with only around 30% of leadership roles but 55%-77% of assistant roles going to women. Looking at the statistics the other way round, around 70% of the leadership roles went to men but only between 23% and 45% of assistant roles.

Summary

In this chapter, I have explored the sex differences in the management structures. I have presented evidence of the management structures of the schools and examined the distribution by sex of management and leadership roles and of responsibility allowances (points) associated with them in each school. To an extent the responsibility points allocated by the head and governors to different management posts reflected the valuing of that role in the school. The points also indicated the level an individual had attained in his/her career development, as they were linked to salary levels. However, the management role itself was also an important factor in career development. In other words, a post as Head of Faculty on 3 points in one school would have provided the post-holder with a greater experience of leadership and responsibility than a post as assistant on 3 points at another school. Both of these aspects need to be taken into account when assessing the opportunities (or indeed differences in opportunity) for career development accessible to men and women.

I have also reviewed the data from other documentary sources regarding policies on equal opportunities. It must be noted that all the four schools were within the same local authority and were required by that authority to produce such a policy. However, the wording of the policy was specific to each school, and the emphases varied. I found that there was little explicit detail on staff development and staffing issues in the two schools with female heads, partly possibly because they were both community schools with pupils (and staff) from mixed ethnic backgrounds and therefore the racist issue was perceived as prioritised over gender issues. Even so, it was a significant omission. The documents in the two schools with male heads showed a greater awareness and prioritisation of gender issues, especially High Ridge, although there was nothing explicitly on staff development (gender) or staffing policy in the documents from Droverslea. In two of the schools, one female-headed and one male-headed, staffing and appointment issues were included in sections on gender equal opportunities, but both indicated only a merit/ability approach, which avoids recognition of a male-model hidden agenda.

My investigations have produced the following conclusions: that in all the four schools, women were under-represented at middle and senior management levels that women managers were clustered around the junior management level, especially in support and assistant roles that women managers at middle and senior levels were more likely to be in pastoral or pastoral-related roles than academic/faculty roles that these features existed even where there was a female head, although the evidence shows that academic headship roles were somewhat more accessible to women in schools with a female head that these features existed even where EO policies and other documents indicated an awareness of sex differences in the management teams and in women's career opportunities.

In the following chapter, I explore another aspect of the organisational culture of the four schools, namely the four heads' views of the middle management role and the skills required for it. This takes the form of a review of semi-structured interviews undertaken with the heads. In the chapter, I discuss some of the issues arising from the heads' interpretations of those roles and of the management structure of their school. I also set these issues in the context of the theoretical underpinning of this thesis.

CHAPTER FIVE

WHAT WERE THE HEADTEACHERS' VIEWS OF MANAGEMENT AND GENDER IN THEIR SCHOOLS?

Introduction

In the previous chapter, I explored an aspect of the organisational culture of the schools, as it related to my study: documentary data on gender and management structures in the four schools. I compared this data across the schools to see whether there were differences between them, and in particular whether there were variations between schools with male heads and those with female heads. I found that the four schools were similar in that in all of them women were under-represented at middle and senior management level. This clearly reflected the statistics published by the DfES. I found that women in management tended to be found in assistant roles and/or in pastoral roles although academic headship roles for women were slightly more likely in the schools with female heads. I found these structures even where documentary evidence suggested an awareness of gender imbalances in promotion. In other words, I discovered very little difference between the schools with male heads and those with female heads on these issues. However, this data provided an insight into some of the values (in terms of gender) demonstrated by the head and governors in their decisions about appointments and therefore provided one angle on the school's organisational culture.

In this chapter I review the interviews which I undertook with the heads. I explore their views on the middle manager's role and on the skills they perceived as important for the job. In the chapter I discuss some of the issues which arise from these perceptions, especially in the light of the actual management structure of the particular school and in the light of the secondary data collected from the school. These explorations of both data and interpretation are inevitably more subjective than the evidence presented in the previous chapter, both in terms of the heads' views and of my interpretations of them. However, they pursue further the issues raised in the last chapter and give an insight into the policies, decisions and justifications expressed by the Heads concerned. This, therefore, adds significantly to the knowledge gained from the data outlined in chapter four.

The structure of the interviews

I chose to use semi-structured interview techniques with the heads, so that I could give similar opportunities to each one to express their views yet be flexible enough to allow the heads to elaborate on any points of interest which they might raise. I aimed to gain insights into the individual head's perceptions of gendered status in his/her school, into the value each head assigned to a range of leadership skills a middle manager might demonstrate, and into any gender bias in the head's preferred skills for the post.

Firstly, each head was asked an open question about his/her views on management style within the school. They were also asked about the school's management structure with regard to gender, and were invited to provide hard copy of the management structure and of any other documents relating to gender issues and equal opportunities in the school. This evidence was discussed in chapter four.

Then, each head was asked to undertake a skills selection exercise, in which he/she had to rate skills and characteristics in terms of their importance in the effectiveness of a middle manager. The skills and characteristics were those identified in the literature, and outlined in chapter one, as Ball's (1987) "ideal types" of management and as those associated with masculine and feminine styles of management in a number of research projects, for example Ozga (1993) and Loden (1985). Each skill or characteristic was printed onto a card and the head was asked to sort these into one of three categories: rated highly, essential to the effectiveness of a middle manager, a skill required to be demonstrated by the appointee; rated well, desirable but not essential, and rejected, an undesirable characteristic in a prospective appointee, one which would cause problems for a middle manager.

The skills/characteristics were listed in random order, as shown below, so that there were no obvious ideal type/masculine/feminine groupings for the heads to identify as a pattern, and thus "second guess" a response. However, they were presented to each head in the same order. This reduced the possibility of any bias due to word association for any one head. The skills/characteristics are listed below in the order in which they were given to the heads. I have identified beside each one the whether the skill is associated with a masculine (M) or feminine (F) style in the literature, although this information was not given to the heads.

Table 14: items in selection/sort exercise on skills/characteristics of middle managers given to headteachers

1	consensus-seeking	F
2	dominant	M
3	disciplinarian	M
4	adversorial	M
5	authoritative	M
6	rooted in "professional colleague to colleague" approach	F
7	accessible	F
8	negotiating	F
9	consultative	F
10	persuasive	F
11	manipulative	F
12	charismatic	M
13	controlling	M
14	open-minded	F
15	having sound expertise/knowledge	M/F but F tends to base authority on this
16	decisive	M
17	enabling	F

18	supportive	F
19	good listener	F
20	motivational	F
21	assertive	M
22	skilled in interpersonal relationships	F
23	democratic	F
24	competitive	M
25	tough	M
26	analytic	M
27	detached	M
28	team-focused	F
29	innovating/initiating	F
30	compliant	F
31	cooperative	F
32	organised	F

The headteachers often gave a commentary during the exercise in which they explained and justified their choices, or questioned the semantic and pragmatic implications of the word on the card. I have referred to these in my report on each head's approach to the exercise and his/her decisions within it. I was also able to use the opportunity of the semi-structured interview in order to question the head further or clarify the points raised. This exercise inevitably contained an element of subjectivity in its form as well as in its outcome, since the words would be interpreted by the heads within their own individual contexts, of background and experience. They would, as with the main part of the fieldwork, be affected by the frame and schema, and the pragmatic understandings within it, with which each person approaches the situation. However, this in itself added to the insights gained into the organisational culture of each of the four schools in which my study took place. It was important to contextualise the fieldwork, the recordings and analysis of the team meetings, by gaining insights into the schools in which these meetings took place.

I now provide a narrative commentary on the headteachers' responses and on my interpretations of them. All quotations in inverted commas are indicating the head's own words used.

Dr Julia Helene Ibbotson PhD, FHEA

School 1—Droverslea

At the start of the interview, the head of Droverslea was asked about his views on the management style within the school. He stressed the importance for him of an "open" style of management. He contrasted this with the style he perceived as characterising the regime of the previous Head on the Upper School site prior to and during reorganisation, under whom he had worked as one of three deputies. This previous regime he characterised as "authoritarian management" and a "benevolent despot" style which made use of a "small clique" or "inner circle" for decision-making. He also claimed that the previous style had been based on competitiveness within and without, which he "rejected" in his own regime. He spoke of the problems which he had inherited from the previous Head in terms of management style and "ethos". He spoke of the school failing to establish a new identity as a whole 11-18 school after reorganisation. He perceived that the "power bases" (personnel/senior management) had remained constant, and different, on each of the two sites following reorganisation, resulting in a difference of "ethos" and management style in each. He spoke of his commitment to working towards a unified ethos and style between the two sites, based on his own preferred "open" style of management and a less competitive environment.

The head spoke of his dislike of the "traditional competitiveness" which he perceived as existing between the two sections of the school and stated his preference for a movement towards a new unity. He identified the old regime, of which many features within the ethos still existed, as an approach which encouraged "toughness", "detachment", "isolationist fighting your own corner". The approach he criticised reflects the traditional masculine style, as opposed to the feminine collaborative/ unifying style, and is referred to in the literature review in chapter one (see Loden 1985, Darking 1991, for example). He referred to his own philosophy of management as "open, democratic" and as valuing teamwork and a participative approach. He discussed the importance of being flexible and being able to admit mistakes or the need to rethink policy, being open to others' views on issues and being accessible to staff "at any level" to "air their views". At the same time, he admitted to being aware of the "pragmatics militating against the institutionalisation of this philosophy."

Much of the headteacher's argument reflected the feminine style of management identified in the literature (see chapter one) and this suggested that he would favour this style amongst his middle and senior managers, and hence favour women in these posts. However, the analysis of the management structure at Droverslea outlined in chapter four (see Tables 4 and 5) did not indicate this at all; women were little represented at senior management level and at middle management level they were clustered in pastoral posts rather than faculty posts, although they were well represented as assistants to men.

The headteacher was asked to comment on the management structure with regard to gender, and specifically the lack of women in management posts in the school. He spoke of being "disappointed" that this was the case. His two points in answer were that (a) women "do not apply for the jobs": "women don't come forward" and (b) he did "not agree with positive discrimination"; it must be "the best person for the job, regardless of gender".

These answers raised a number of questions. Why do women not apply for management jobs? This is, however, not a question being dealt with in this study and is explored in other research projects and texts such as Davidson and Cooper (1992). Who exactly is the best person for the job? The problem here has already been suggested in chapter four and concerns the criteria that are used in judging this; do the selectors already have masculine traits in mind when assessing a candidate's suitability for the job so that clearly men are bound to be regarded as the best person for the job? There was clearly a potential source of conflict here, between the stated values and the actuality of the appointments. It was possible that such assessments and evaluations, or indeed, women's understanding of them prior to applying for a job, could be the reason for the head's assessment, if correct, that fewer women applied for management posts.

As a result of the headteacher's comments, I informally surveyed twelve female members of staff at the school, asking them about their views on applying for management posts. I found that every one of the twelve claimed that they would, without reservation, apply for middle or senior management posts, as applicable, should they arise. Only one woman said that she would not want to apply for a faculty post as she felt that "it would require more undissipated concentration of time" than she was prepared to expend on the same subject, since her interests were more diffuse, but that she would certainly apply for a pastoral post. All others claimed that they would apply for faculty/curriculum posts. It is clear, therefore, that women who have been applying for promotion would disagree with this particular head in his evaluation of the situation.

The headteacher of Droverslea was then asked to undertake the exercise outlined at the start of this chapter, rating skills/characteristics required for effective middle management. He rated highly the following: consultative, enabling, a good listener, cooperative, team-focused, skilled in interpersonal relationships, motivational, supportive, decisive, accessible, democratic, and consensus-seeking. He qualified some of these as follows:

- listening: "listening properly, responding to what people say, active listening, valuing what people say"
- cooperative: "with the senior management and the team"
- skilled in interpersonal relationships: "tied in with listening skills"
- motivational: "getting others to perform, not necessarily charismatic"
- decisive: "not making decisions hastily, but not wavering"
- consensus-seeking: "although at times responsibility means that there needs to be a decision of one's own"

He also added that having expertise/knowledge and being organised would be assumed to be required skills for all applicants to management posts. He felt that the manager should perform as a professional colleague with the rest of the team, although he did not speak of the approach of the manager towards the rest of the team. He rated as desirable but not essential the following: innovating/initiating, and negotiating. He rejected the following: authoritative, compliant, controlling, manipulative, adversorial, disciplinarian, dominant, tough, competitive, detached. When asked what would be meant by "authoritative", he indicated that he had assumed this meant "authoritarian" (that is, as in the Oxford English Dictionary, opposing freedom/desiring obedience, instead of having power invested in them by virtue of status and knowledge). When this was clarified, he withdrew his rejection of the characteristic.

The profile which the headteacher of Droverslea sketched incorporated many of the characteristics identified with the feminine cluster of management skills discussed in chapter one, and he rejected those associated with the masculine cluster. This further reinforced my critical analysis of the conflict between stated approach and the reality of the management structure in the school, which showed a considerable gender imbalance against women, as outlined in the previous chapter.

However, the headteacher also pointed out that the "informal structure" existing at the school was very important to the day to day running of the school, and that informal structure often included women whom he would "seek out for their opinions and advice, even though they did not necessarily have formalised senior status". He spoke of the "underpinning of the infrastructure" being just as important in terms of influence and "respected, assumed status" as actual status.

Clearly, however, that respect does not in reality extend to a recognition of the women staff's need for formal status, for a public and financial recognition of their role which would then allow them access to further promotion as it does for male managers. It is interesting to note also that the "informal structure" of which the head spoke and his examples of personnel, applied *only* to women, the men having achieved position in the formal structures anyway. There were indications here of Davidson's (1992) theories of women's assumed social roles of support and group unity extending to the expected professional roles. This also had implications for role models within the school. Women were likely to be seen as people who support and advise but who were not given formalised status within management, and therefore were less highly valued than men.

Conclusion

The headteacher's evaluations of the required skills of managers suggested a "female-friendly" working atmosphere. This was, indeed, highly valued in the informal networks, yet not reflected in the formal status structure. It was possible that the legacy of the previous regime remains a driving force behind the establishment of formal status structures. It was also possible that this was a desired status quo on the part of the head and present beneficiaries of that structure. It was also possible that there was a genuine inability to find female staff willing and able to compete successfully on the selection criteria for posts.

Data on the organisational culture of Droverslea would lead me to anticipate a less clear-cut picture of management communication styles, with both masculine and feminine strategies being accepted and employed.

However, it is also possible that the more ambitious women managers here could use masculine speech traits to a greater extent than most women, reflecting the style which is most likely to get results in terms of promotion and position in the formal status structures. There did seem to be a "glass ceiling effect" here, as explored by Davidson and Cooper (1992) and Hall (1996), that is, women managers can get so high but no higher.

School 2—High Ridge

Again, at the start of the interview, the headteacher of High Ridge was asked about his views on the management style within the school. He emphasised a "whole school ethos" of management. He spoke of "collectivity and teamwork" being particularly important in his management philosophy. He stressed that it was important that "everyone knew what was happening" in the running of the school, and as such therefore the "communication systems" operating in the school were "the key". He expressed the necessity for hierarchical responsibility within the structure's decision-making processes, the idea of "the buck stops here" concept. He also spoke of the need to make all negotiation and consultation processes clear to the participants. However, he did "not feel comfortable with the idea of 'open management'", unlike the head of Droverslea, and he spoke of the need for a "top down" approach, although he did speak of "accessibility" of senior and middle managers. He stressed the need for delegation, a recognition of authority and its responsibilities, accountability, and the need for the post holder to manage (at whatever level they held) "within the framework of a whole school basis". He spoke of this responsibility being especially pertinent to middle managers whose function was to see that this framework (originating from senior management) was operational by the staff in the team. He summed up his ideas of effective management by stressing that he thought it was achieved through (1) the ability to delegate while recognising the ultimate responsibility within the bounds of that particular post, (2) teamwork, (3) the acceptance of one's own authority and decision-making brief, (4) functioning within the whole school basis, not "fighting one's own corner", (5) interpersonal skills and the quality of communication. He claimed that these were the skills he would be looking for in applicants for middle and senior management appointments.

Like the headteacher of Droverslea, the headteacher of High Ridge also accounted for the imbalance of women to men in middle and senior management positions by claiming that they "did not apply for promotions" believing this to be because of "personal and home situations". He added that some young female potential candidates for management posts had left to have children and then returned on a part-time basis, which he considered "an unsuitable basis for management responsibilities". This, however, does not take into account older women candidates who may no longer have such personal constraints. This reflects the idea that the whole assumed career structure rests on a concept of a progression based on criteria appropriate to an essentially male life-pattern (as suggested in Shakeshaft 1989, Ozga 1993, Evetts 1994 outlined in chapter one). In other words, one which progresses step by step from one responsibility level to the next within full-time positions. Ozga, for example, suggests a redefining of the concept of "career" to include many women's experience of varying structures, often those which can accommodate their current personal/domestic responsibilities as well as professional, and where there is often a break/return, part-time/full-time pattern necessary in order to do this.

In this school also, like Droverslea, the headteacher expressed an antipathy towards "positive discrimination" as a means of achieving a balance between men and women in management. The headteacher's assumption was that this was the only alternative measure possible in order to deal with the imbalance in the management structure, despite the clear pattern of women clustered in junior assistant posts and failing to advance to leadership posts. The final two questions on the Sex Equality Audit undertaken by this school elicited the same response from the head as he gave during the interview. He re-asserted that the only criterion for appointment to a management post was "the most suitable person for the job" although he refused to be drawn on the implications of this in terms of the assessors' assumptions or in terms of any hidden agenda. These points were outlined in the previous chapter. He also refused to be drawn on pertinent issues such as INSET, career development, and existing procedures for promotion criteria and interviewing.

The headteacher of High Ridge was then asked to undertake the skills selection exercise. In rating the skills/characteristics of effective middle managers, he chose the following as highly rated/an essential requirement for a post at this level: authoritative, accessible, charismatic, consensus-seeking, open-minded, decisive, supportive, motivational, skilled in interpersonal relationships, team-focused, and innovating/ initiating. He also claimed that managers should regard themselves as professional colleagues alongside others in the team. He qualified some of these as follows:

- charismatic: "able to inspire pupils, be confident and able to communicate a love of their subject from the heart"
- open-minded: "an important quality . . . a capacity to listen to arguments and weigh up their implications and perhaps change one's own preconceived notions"
- consensus-seeking / democratic: " . . . approaches preferable where the manager is supporting or promoting the policies of the school and its culture, the whole school policies"

He rated as desirable in certain circumstances the following: dominant, competitive, tough, detached, analytic and qualified his ideas on these as follows:

- dominant, competitive, tough: "there's a place for this . . . although not adversorial—not in a macho sense!"
- detached / analytic: "in the sense of objective wouldn't be essential for a middle manager, but would be the icing on the cake"

He wanted to place negotiating and consultative skills in between categories 2 and 3 ("would not rate highly, possibly desirable, not rejected"). He added that these skills may be appropriate at times, while "at others the middle manager's role is to provide information on decisions made elsewhere, for example by the SMT, passing on and reinforcing those decisions." He rejected the following skills/characteristics: compliant, controlling, manipulative, adversorial, and disciplinarian.

To this headteacher, the middle manager was seen very much in terms of the hierarchy of the school structure where the head (and possibly the senior management team) initiated the policies and the middle management helped to drive the operation of those policies. He added: "as a middle manager, you have to recognise the head's authority delegated to you. You are therefore accountable to the head. You have some input into policy decisions, but at the end of the day you have to support the majority view." He qualified "the majority view" as that of the head and his senior team.

The profile outlined by the headteacher, as with Droverslea, embraced many characteristics of the feminine style of management, with its emphasis on interpersonal skills and team approach. However, he himself introduced concepts of managerial delegation, and objectivity, which are associated with the masculine style. His rating of the more masculine characteristics, namely dominant, competitive, tough, detached and analytic, as "desirable" and "the icing on the cake" suggested an underlying (incipient) bias towards the masculine style. These were reinforced by the language used by the head (and by other managers during the fieldwork). Linguistically, two metaphoric fields emerged here: that of "wholeness", as in whole school policies, and that of business and industry. Linguistic items used to reinforce the metaphors within the semantic field of wholeness included "ownership" (as in "the ownership of policies"), "participation", "purpose" (as in "shared purpose"), "in the best interests of the school", "the whole school", "shared responsibility with other managers", and "collaboration". These expressions implied a shared pragmatic understanding of the semantics of sharing the same ideals/goals and of working together towards that common end. They suggested a strong team spirit, unification, and consensus. Linguistic items used to create metaphors within the semantic field of business/industry included "line management", "driving policy", "shop floor", "line of communication", "marketing", "selling the product", "disseminating information", and a "PR job". These expressions implied a shared pragmatic understanding of semantic meanings associated with a dynamic, thrusting work ethos. It implied that colleagues were not only working towards a common end, but working energetically, competitively, and assertively. This language reflected an approach more commensurate with the traditional masculine style of management, characterised by dominance and competition, as outlined in chapter one. Metaphors were not used so clearly and consistently by the heads in the other schools. It should also be noted that middle managers at this school also used these metaphors, as can be seen in the transcriptions and analyses later in chapter seven in a way which did not occur in other schools. This reflection of language usage therefore implied that there was a pragmatic understanding (between the participants) of the head's ideas, and implied, at least to some extent, an acceptance of them. These helped to provide insights into the organisational culture in this school.

Conclusion

The ethos of High Ridge tended to encourage a gender-aware culture and a female-friendly working atmosphere in many ways, with its emphasis on team-building, collectivity, shared responsibilities, and its head's stress on "the team" at a whole school level. However, although this team management style emphasised a high regard for both people and task, which tends to be associated with the feminine style, nevertheless it is clear also from the head's comments (p 81) that there was in place a "top down" management approach, which therefore in practice, through the male-only structure of senior management, militated against a high-profile role of women in the school. The head's comments on five "desirable" characteristics for middle management (p 83-84) implied a bias towards a masculine style and in this it was a markedly different approach from the other heads, who all rejected those five.

I have noted two metaphoric fields used by the head during the interview, that of wholeness, associated with ownership and participation, and that of business/industry, associated with a dynamic work ethos. These led me to explore the use of similar linguistic items in the communication strategies of the middle managers in their team meetings. It is possible that the female managers as well as the male would use these forms of language in order to reflect status differentiation and to emulate those involved with the strategic policy-making. In this case it could more easily and accessibly provide a linguistic base for asserting the leadership role amongst the female managers, which otherwise could conflict with the feminine frame of avoiding tension in relationships. As with Droverslea, there seemed to be a "glass ceiling effect" here, and this could also affect the linguistic strategies used by women at middle managerial level who aspire to higher management levels. This implied that the language of management was likely to be closer to the masculine repertoire than the feminine in this school.

School 3—Broadmarsh

When asked to comment on the management style at Broadmarsh, the headteacher spoke first of all about the emphasis she laid on the "pastoral structure and operation at the school". She spoke of many systems being "underpinned by this structure" and of "staff appointments which bear in mind the importance of this ethos." She referred to the support systems for pupils which she had put in place in the school, such as pastoral tutoring and monitoring as well as accessibility of tutors and of herself for pupils experiencing problems, and the close links between parents and staff. She spoke of the "high regard for this role in school life". The head also spoke of preferring to be "personally involved with many of the aspects of school life" and wishing matters to be "referred to (her) rather than to be delegated." She talked about "a need to know what is going on, rather than being a figurehead," and that her style was "hands-on leadership."

When asked to comment on the gender distribution of management posts in the school, the headteacher said that she "believe(d) that (her) female staff were well-placed in pastoral and cross-curricular management" and that "this (was) the more popular area than faculty management for (her) female managers to enter". She again emphasised the high value she placed upon the pastoral area of school life and the importance of this area of management. She said that she saw this as an channel to senior management for women in no less a way than the faculty area. She refused to be drawn on the implications of the high proportion of women in assistant posts.

At the start of the skills selection exercise, the head commented that "effective communication" was "very important to the running of the school" and that she tried to "ensure that effective systems are in place". She rated highly as skills/characteristics required for effective middle management the following: listening skills, consensus-seeking, supportive, accessible, negotiating, decisive, and motivational. She qualified some of these as follows:

- consensus-seeking: "with the emphasis on the seeking, not necessarily getting" and "this should underpin exchanges with the team"
- decisiveness: "after negotiation there (was) a place for decisiveness" motivational: "but not necessarily involving a charismatic personality, not necessarily ebullient"

She chose the following as desirable but not essential: having expertise/knowledge ("expertise in general issues of education, not only in one's own subject area"), cooperative, team-focused, skilled in interpersonal relationships, analytic, organised, professional colleague approach, innovating/initiating, open-minded, assertive, persuasive, authoritative, consultative, and enabling ("they need to empower the staff on the team").

She rejected the following:

- democratic: "not appropriate in some situations and for some decisions, as certain issues are imposed on the organisation, and middle managers need to work within this framework
- charismatic: "can be motivational without charisma—what is it anyway?"
- compliant: "I would like managers to agree to suggestions in some situations, but they need also to make their own decisions"
- controlling
- manipulative: "it depends on the moral framework and intention—manipulating a situation could be OK"
- adversorial: "no, no!"
- disciplinarian: "only *aware* of discipline"
- dominant
- competitive: "only in terms of own individual competitiveness—with self"
- detached: "only on certain occasions"
- tough: "I'd hesitate, I like a manager who is resilient, able to bounce back, but not tough in the sense of a disciplinarian"

It was interesting that she independently identified skills and characteristics as associated with masculine and feminine styles. She identified the feminine style with the following: supportive, accessible, professional colleague, negotiating, assertive, enabling, and listening. She identified the masculine style with the following: competitive, dominant, tough, controlling, manipulative, adversorial, and disciplinarian. She added that she thought that cooperativeness was a characteristic of both masculine and feminine styles. Without prompting, she pointed out that she had chosen characteristics on the feminine side for the majority of her high-value requirements for middle managers, and had rejected those on the masculine side.

Conclusion

The headteacher's rating of skills required for middle managers suggested (as she herself analysed) a female-friendly working atmosphere in the school. However, although there were women in faculty management at Broadmarsh, there was more of a chance of gaining a pastoral post (50-50) or cross-curricular (especially support roles). There was a high incidence of women in assistant roles to men. The situation with regards to women's actual access to management posts was therefore not markedly dissimilar to that of the schools with male heads. A "glass ceiling effect" could be identified here as well. The difference lay in the clearly stated attachment of the head to pastoral issues, which tend to be identified with the feminine style, and to skills which she herself identified as "feminine".

This implied that the language of management was likely to be closer to the feminine repertoire than the masculine. I did not identify in the school's literature examined in chapter 4 a particularly gender-aware culture; in fact much seemed gender-free, although the headteacher herself explicitly outlined a view that was gender-aware.

School 4—Beckfield

At the start of the interview, the headteacher was asked to comment on the management style she encouraged at Beckfield. She spoke of the importance of a "positive" and "colleague to colleague" relationship. She felt that "appreciation and feedback staff to staff as well as to pupils (was) crucial" and commented that she thought that "women managers tended to be able to do this better than men". She spoke of disliking a "disciplinary relationship between staff" and preferred any monitoring and appraisal of other staff to be based on an "Action Research level of observation", in other words that line managers "observe and work with their team members" in a "spirit of research and progress".

She expressed a great interest in the current research study and claimed a "personal involvement with the difficulties women face in the workplace and especially in gaining management positions." When asked about the sex distribution in the management structure at Beckfield, she said that "women tend(ed) not to apply for middle and senior management posts as much as men did" and that "the field (was) therefore restricted". The conflict here between value/interest and actual management structure implied that somehow unencouraging messages were emerging for women which deterred them from applying for such positions.

During the skills selection exercise, the head chose the following skills/characteristics as essential for effective middle managers: accessible, enabling, listening, professional colleague, supportive, negotiating, consultative, open-minded, persuasive, organised, decisive, motivational, and skilled in interpersonal relationships. She also commented that the following were especially relevant: interpersonal relationships, the ability to motivate, and being supportive. She added that persuasion and negotiation were also high on her priorities. She said that a manager "has to occasionally take a decision and stick with it, but there should be a build-up of trust over time." She concluded that "therefore, listening skills are very important and being sensitive to the needs of the group and individuals—a professional trust".

The headteacher chose the following as desirable but not essential: assertive, authoritative, consensus-seeking, analytic, having expertise/ knowledge, being team-focused, co-operative, detached, and innovating/ initiating.

She rejected the following as not important for a middle manager:

- charismatic: "not as a personal image, although motivational is essential—giving some kind of inspiration somehow"
- disciplinarian
- adversorial: "no!"
- manipulative: "smacks of cliques, could be destructive"
- controlling
- tough
- dominant
- competitive
- democratic
- compliant: "implies lack of thinking or initiative"

She chose skills and characteristics associated with the feminine style of management and rejected many of those associated with the masculine style. Overall, her choices were similar to those of the female head of Broadmarsh, although their distribution between high rating (1) and desirable but not essential (2) varied.

Conclusion

There was again an emphasis at Beckfield on the supportive pastoral side of interpersonal relationships. A high status was given by the head to support structure management, such as personal and social education (PSE), Learning Support for pupils and professional development for staff. However, although this ethos, underlined by the head's stated values and her choice of skills for effective management, implied a female-friendly environment, this was not borne out by the staffing structure itself. Women were still largely represented in support and assistant roles and in fact, unusually, in this school, not represented at all in pastoral management.

Therefore, data on the organisational culture of Beckfield implied that feminine linguistic repertoires would be accepted and employed, but it also led me to anticipate that masculine speech traits could be used to reflect the style which was most likely to attract promotion within the management structure.

Comparative data—conclusions

A comparison of the choices made by the heads in the skills selection exercise revealed some interesting patterns of evaluation of skills and characteristics associated with the feminine or masculine cluster in each case. Rating 1 are those deemed essential; rating 2 are desirable although not essential; rating 3 are those rejected or undesirable. The actual number of skills chosen for each category associated with each gender cluster are given first on the table, and then the ratio of feminine to masculine traits chosen is given as a percentage. In this way, the weightings given to masculine or feminine traits in each category given by each head is clarified.

Table 15: the Headteachers' skills selection exercise—comparative data

Ratings	Droverslea	High Ridge	Broadmarsh	Beckfield
Rating 1: no of skills in feminine cluster	11	8	6	12

Rating 1: no of skills in masculine cluster	1 (decisive—qualified)	3 (decisive + authoritative, charismatic)	1 (decisive—qualified)	1 (decisive)
Rating 1: ratio of feminine to masculine choices as %	92%	73%	86%	92%
Rating 2: no of skills in feminine cluster	2	0	11	6
Rating 2; no of skills in masculine cluster	0	5	3	4
Rating 2: ratio of feminine to masculine choices as %	100%	0%	79%	60%
Rating 3: no of skills in feminine cluster	2	2	3	3
Rating 3: no of skills in masculine cluster	8	3	8	7
Rating 3: ratio of feminine to masculine choices as %	20%	40%	27%	30%
Ratio of masculine characteristics rejected as %	80%	60%	73%	70%

All the headteachers rated highly, as essential, skills and characteristics associated with the feminine style but the male headteacher of High Ridge demonstrated a markedly different profile of evaluation from the other headteachers. He showed an underlying valuing of masculine characteristics (dominant, competitive, tough, detached, and analytical) regarding these as "the icing on the cake", although he added "not in a macho sense". This reflects an unwillingness to accept or acknowledge a valuing of the "macho culture" as defined in the Oxford English Dictionary as "exhibiting virility or manly courage", with its pragmatic association with a non-politically correct elevating of masculine stereotypical characteristics above the feminine. Nevertheless, his choice of these five characteristics as desirable indicated an incipient leaning towards the masculine style, whereas the other headteachers demonstrated a more consistent leaning towards characteristics of the feminine style of management, at least in their ostensible evaluations. The male headteacher of Droverslea can be seen to veer most clearly and consistently towards a valuing (high rating) of feminine characteristics with the highest ratio of these in categories 1 and 2 and with the highest ratio of masculine characteristics in category 3, the rejected traits. The two female headteachers showed a similar profile to each other, with relatively high ratings of feminine characteristics in categories 1 and 2, and with high rating of masculine characteristics in category 3, the rejected traits.

My investigations produced the following conclusions:

- that all headteachers claimed it was essential for effective middle managers to be: supportive, accessible, motivational (all associated with the feminine cluster of management style) and decisive (masculine, although qualified by two heads as having to make the ultimate decisions)

- that three out of the four headteachers rated at either 1 or 2 that middle managers were: skilled in interpersonal relationships, consensus-seeking, professional colleague, negotiating, consultative, open-minded, having expertise/knowledge, enabling, having good listening skills, organised, cooperative, innovating/initiating, team-focused (13 feminine traits), analytic and authoritative (2 masculine traits)

- that both female headteachers chose the above, along with at least one of the male heads (most usually the head of Droverslea) in each case. that all the headteachers rejected the following characteristics: disciplinarian, adversorial, controlling (3 masculine traits), manipulative and compliant (2 feminine), although the two feminine characteristics were seen as value-laden words (emotive terms) with undesirable semantic implications: manipulative as underhand or dishonest, compliant as lacking initiative or independent thought.

Therefore, the most highly valued skills and characteristics required by these headteachers for their middle managers were in the main those associated with the feminine management style identified in the literature. The only dissenter was the headteacher of High Ridge who demonstrated an incipient valuing of the masculine style of management. The two women headteachers demonstrated similar feminine-valuing profiles, the male headteacher of Droverslea tended towards a feminine-valuing profile the most of all four, and the male head of High Ridge the least. It might therefore be expected that three of these schools promoted an organisational culture which valued feminine characteristics and therefore favoured women as middle managers. For High Ridge whose male headteacher seemed to value the masculine style more than the other heads, the picture was not as clear. However, clearly the management structures in all four schools, outlined in chapter four, did not reflect a valuing of a feminine management style

Setting the observations into a theoretical context

One of the most interesting features to emerge from this study of the organisational cultures across the four schools, is the fact that, whatever the management "ethos" of the school, the staffing structures revealed a very unequal distribution of management status by gender. Women in all four schools tended to remain at junior management level, largely in supportive roles, often as assistants to men. These findings parallel those of the DfS surveys (1992 to 2001) discussed in the Introductory chapter. It is, however, even more interesting that this phenomenon occurred even where there was a female headteacher and even where the organisational culture seemed geared to a female-friendly style.

If we look at Ball's "ideal types" of leadership outlined in chapter one, we see that they contained no reference to gender differences in style, as if all were subsumed under a masculine model. Yet women seem to have assumed, or been sided into, a quite different professional role from men (see Mills 1988). This raises the question of the close relationship between the professional and social role of women: that which in our sociocultural context is concerned with supporting, nurturing and caring, as opposed to leading, dominating and enforcing discipline and control (Mills 1988, Davidson and Cooper 1992, Ozga 1993). This was reflected in the largely pastoral management role given to the women in this study. In the USA, too, similar trends have been found. Shakeshaft (1989) raised the question of barriers to women's professional promotion and suggested that concepts of, among others, a type of meritocracy (the best person for a management job), and male dominance (male characteristics being the best for a management job) contribute to this effect. This was not borne out in the present study by the heads' stated preferences in assessment criteria in the form of evaluation of skills and characteristics.

The headteachers in this study all claimed to base appointments on the idea of "the best person for the job". But the fact that few women are promoted to higher management posts suggests that therefore women are either not competent/suitable or that they are at least *less* competent/ suitable than men. Either (a) this is not true, or (b) the judgements of competence/suitability are based on assessment criteria which tend to exclude women. Discrimination where one group excludes the participation of another can be founded on such a case. The idea that women cannot meet the assessment criteria for managerial promotion can either be consciously perpetuated by the interested party (the excluding group, in this case assessors who belong to the senior management, largely a male group) or is self-perpetuating through the internalisation of the judgements of the dominating group. Yet this explanation conflicts with the heads' ostensible evaluations of required skills in my study.

One possible explanation comes from Shakeshaft who suggested that the greatest barrier was male dominance where other models were subsumed under this, the male model, and where, for example, internal barriers (socialisation, lack of self confidence, self doubt) were, in fact, external barriers arising from a "sex-structured society" which generated the belief in women that they lack ability. This would account for the reluctance, claimed by the four heads, of women to apply for top promoted posts. But, as Shakeshaft claimed, this is to view the world through the "male lens" and women "experience a different reality from men". Within the theory of male dominance (the feminist "patriarchy" theory) lies not only the deficiency model for women, outlined with reference to linguistic theory in chapter two, but also the danger of the desire to perpetuate one group's vested interests at the expense of another's in upholding the status quo. The inherent conflict between philosophical values and actuality is clearly demonstrated in this study. Clearly, heads, male and female, used the discourse of one set of values (associated with the feminine management style) but in practice employed another discourse (that associated with the masculine style) when it came to applying promotional criteria in making appointments.

Speaking and listening skills, most commonly associated with the feminine style, are those most valued in schools. All the heads discussed the importance of these within the context of interpersonal relationships and communication. Therefore it would seem that the trend would be towards encouraging men to emulate these skills. In some ways I would argue that this is happening, but without the overt recognition that female potential in management is based on these very skills, and that therefore women managers should logically be valued for this aspect of their management style. This does not appear to be the case from the evidence of the management structures of the schools in this study.

Unlike Ball's gender-free ideal types of leadership, Loden (1985) looked at masculine and feminine leadership models and devised a model based on approaches to conflict resolution: the masculine style being that which goes for the "quick fix" solution, while the feminine style is geared to "long haul" solutions. The latter fits with the feminine stress on the build-up of interpersonal relationships within the workplace, the team focus, and the consensus aim. Strachan (1993) also acknowledged women's preferred style of management, which she (after Court 1992) called "affiliative" and which stressed the importance of relationships, shared decision-making processes and empowerment of others. Loden claimed that studies in the USA have shown that those companies utilising feminine styles and approaches have gained greater productivity, employee commitment and greater cooperation with management's aims. This is an interesting reflection on Statham's (1987) identification of the feminine style as more task/people oriented and the masculine style as more image-engrossed.

Additionally, a number of researchers have suggested that this feminine style is the one especially appropriate to educational management (Shakeshaft 1989, Strachan 1993, Evetts 1994), in the light of the importance of interpersonal relationships and the nurturing role of schools. Yet this current study shows that this is not being translated into actual management positions for women.

Ozga (1993) suggested that the concept of "good management practice" needed redefining, as women's experience "inclines them towards a management practice which is not recognised as appropriate by males"—or by their, usually male, assessors. Davidson and Cooper (1992) discussed the potential stress on female managers to adopt masculine managerial attributes and skills, where often this is based on a model of management which may no longer be entirely appropriate. They referred to the discrepancy between the desired managerial qualities perceived by women and those proposed by their employers.

Pessimistically, Ozga saw a "step back" from any movement towards accepting the feminine styles as valid and desirable, with the post-ERA (Education Reform Act) environment encouraging the masculine style again, as in the LMS (Local Management of Schools) manager—business style. It is interesting here to refer to the linguistic style of the head of High Ridge outlined earlier in this chapter, with its business/industrial metaphors. Ozga suggested three factors which influence women's promotional opportunities:

- that the areas in which women have advanced tend to be in keeping with female "social roles"
- that the lack of role models deters women
- that the "masculinisation of management" deters women

The differences in feminine and masculine management style and language underpin and perpetuate these discrepancies. The question remains: how do women break through this barrier to show that their style and repertoire is as valid in management as men's? Loden's (1987) "holistic approach" to management where the necessity for both styles in a management team is recognised as essential, seems a long way off yet.

As Mills suggested in 1988, organisations are a key aspect of a given culture, hence organisational analysis needs to take account of the relationship between gender and organisational life. "Gender" and its semantic and pragmatic associations is shaped by the expectations and assumptions within the sociocultural context. This includes issues of dominance, difference and diversity. I discuss these issues further in chapters 8 and 9 with reference to the findings from my fieldwork which are examined in the next two chapters (6 and 7).

Summary

In this chapter, I have explored the organisational cultures of the four schools in the study, using data from semi-structured interviews with the heads. My investigations have produced the following conclusions:

- that all the four headteachers claimed that it was essential for effective middle management that the manager should be: supportive, accessible, motivational (all feminine traits)
- that three of the four headteachers claimed that it was essential or desirable that middle managers were: skilled in interpersonal relationships, consensus-seeking, authoritative, professional colleague, negotiating, consultative, open-minded, having expertise/knowledge, enabling, supportive, having good listening skills, motivational, organised, cooperative, innovating/initiating, team-focused, analytic (2 masculine traits, 13 feminine)
- that both female headteachers chose the above, along with at least one of the male heads (most usually the Head of Droverslea) in each case
- that all headteachers rejected the following characteristics: disciplinarian, adversorial, manipulative, controlling, compliant (3 masculine, 2 feminine)
- that the most highly valued skills/characteristics for effective middle management were in the main those associated with the feminine style as identified in the literature, and it could be expected that these schools were therefore promoting a female-friendly ethos
- that, nevertheless, the interview responses from the headteacher of High Ridge suggested an incipient valuing of masculine characteristics, and that this reflected a different organisational culture from that of the other three schools, which may be reflected in the linguistic strategies chosen by middle managers at High Ridge
- that, however, women's access to managerial posts is restricted as outlined in chapter four, even where the head's stated values

and requirements for effective middle management reflects a female-friendly ethos in the workplace

I have also referred to the theoretical debates which relate professional to social roles for women and which suggests that leadership role models are still based on male-model assumptions of management style and language. In some ways this is self-perpetuating since those in senior management roles tend to be male and therefore assessment criteria are likely to be within a masculine framework. Because of this, women may be perceived as falling short of requirements or they may themselves create internal barriers to perceiving themselves as suitable for higher management.

Where there is a high profile accorded to pastoral and support systems in a school, women may gain management roles within this context. Their style and language may be seen as appropriate to the management ethos in this area. Here it is clear that the difference rather than the deficiency model is operating. Within all the schools there was a marked shortfall of women in curriculum and senior management roles. The research question is; do women's style and language repertoires reflect characteristics associated in the literature with an essentially feminine management style, and do they contribute to militating against women's appointment to curriculum and senior management positions?

In chapters six and seven, I transcribe and analyse the meetings I observed. I explore the way that men and women managers in the four schools use language in order to manage their teams during those meetings. I analyse the comparative linguistic usage between men and women, and between schools, in order to ascertain whether differences occur between men and women and between different organisational cultures.

CHAPTER SIX

HOW DID THE COMMUNICATION REPERTOIRES OF MANAGEMENT TEAMS COMPARE?

Introduction

In this chapter, I transcribe and analyse, in commentary form, the four meetings from the first school in my study, Droverslea. The middle managers whose linguistic strategies I focus upon are: Clive (Head of English), Elizabeth (Liz) (Head of post-16 pastoral team), Horace (Head of Modern Languages), and Isabel (Head of Humanities). I draw conclusions based on my interpretations of the strategies used, at the end of each commentary.

I was investigating whether there were gender differences in the way that language was used by middle managers in this school in the course of communicating to their teams in meetings. I was analysing the nature of any differences found and comparing patterns with those identified in the literature. I wanted to investigate the hypothetical explanation that gender differences mark different frame or schema which each gender brings to their interactions. I also wanted to investigate whether there were gender similarities which indicated other linguistic frames being brought to the situation. I then, in the following chapter, wanted to compare my findings with those in different schools with different organisational cultures.

As I have outlined in my chapter on methodology, I audio—recorded meetings of the appropriate team or faculty, making fieldnotes at the same time. These meetings tended to be of between one to one and a half hours duration and usually took place after normal school hours at the end of the afternoon session.

I then reviewed the whole cassette tape several times and made note of areas to select for the transcriptions. My chosen focus was on the speech events in which the manager's transactions with the team were evident. I wanted data on the way that he or she was conveying his or her own assessments/evaluations of an issue, and the way he or she led the course of the discussion/information-giving/ decision-making process of the meeting. In short, I was focusing on the way that the managers used language in order to: establish their status deal with critical incidents; handle team members in the course of reaching the objectives of their meeting handle / resolve conflicts make decisions

I therefore searched the tape recording for such "key" events to select areas for transcription. Speech events by other members of the team which did not involve the manager in any direct transaction were not required. I wanted the opening, closing and any points at which managerial interactions or critical incidents revealed the manager's handling of the team or reaching of a decision. Any interesting features here were noted.

Having transcribed these areas of the meeting, I then analysed my data for the features of speech used by each manager in the context of the interactions within his or her team meeting. I reported these in the form of a commentary in which I tried to give the flavour of the spontaneous speech event by using the present tense, followed by an account of my interpretations of my findings. I analysed the data for patterns of gender differences in strategies between the managers and compared these with those identified in the literature. I looked at similarities between men and women and investigated whether there were other linguistic frames influencing the language of the managers.

A chronology of the analysis process is shown in the table below.

Table 16: the chronology of the analysis process

subject	activity
Clive (Droverslea)	* audio-recorded meeting + fieldnotes
	* reviewed cassette, selected key areas for transcription (establishing status; dealing with critical incidents; handling conflict; making decisions)
	* transcribed key areas of meeting
	* annotated transcript /analysis
	* wrote analysis—commentary form
	* wrote conclusion, focusing on gender linguistic issues
Liz	recording—process as above transcription/ analysis—process as above
Horace	process as above
Isabel	process as above

Transcription conventions used

The use of verb tense

Following common linguistic practice, I have used the present verb tense throughout the analytical commentaries, in order to capture the flavour of the immediacy of the spontaneous speech interactions which I was studying. In this way, I feel that the commentaries link more closely to the transcripts immediately before them.

The use of pseudonyms

All the names used in the transcriptions are pseudonyms in order to guard the confidentiality of the respndents.

Key to transcription symbols used

] overlapping speech / interruption/ closely abutting
. . . pause

(3) length of pause in seconds where the pause is significantly long **bold** intonational stress where clearly marked in speech

(345-354) tape counter reference to original recording

DC1 indicates turn numbering to identify position in transcript for use in prose analysis (initial of school, followed by manager's initial, followed by number of the speech item.)

DROVERSLEA SCHOOL

Droverslea—Head of English—Clive

This faculty meeting took place after the end of the school day as usual and was preceded by general chat amongst the members of the team as people arrived, some from the other school site. There were five female staff and two male staff, including the Head of Faculty, present. It was the Head of Faculty's policy at this time to circulate the role of Chair. On this occasion it fell to the only other man present (Tony). This meant that Clive's role as Head was not directly reinforced from the chair as the other managers' roles were, with the exception of Isabel.

The agenda included items on redesigning the reading recommendation sheets, library resources and stock, collecting GCSE texts (all of which were matters arising from the minutes of the last meeting), the faculty policy statement, boys' achievement, and a questionnaire from SMT on differentiation.

TRANSCRIPTION

C—Clive   T—Tony
A—Angela   F—Felicity
J—Jackie   JO—Josie
JA—Janet

[general informal chat as people came in to room]

DC1 *C : Right, there are two or three things that—that come out . . . um . . . one is we talked about redesigning the reading recommendations sheets . . . um . . . and I sort of spent ten minutes on the fancy computer over there and knocked this one out . . . I just wondered what people thought]*

DC2 *J:] it was on the (unclear comment)*

DC3 *C:] have you seen it . . . yes . . . did I give—give you copies of it (unclear responses) yes here right . . . um. the only thing I was really thinking of was could—could we actually make this simpler for us to fill in and if we can get the kids to fill in the top bit then we just put the recommendations in at the bottom . . . um would this actually make the process easier and more manageable cause we'd just hand these out and they could fill in the top bit for themselves rather than us having to ask them and then us write them down , that was the only thing I was thinking of]*

DC4 *J:] it saves us time doesn't it*

DC5 *C:]I was thinking of*

DC6 *J:] I mean actually all of the things you put in the profile are things we tend to do when we look at their records with them don't you and you know see how many books they've been reading over the months and I mean they can easily do that]*

DC7 *C:]yeh and from the things I read they tend to say how many books people read on average , they note books they have read and you know which newspapers and magazines perhaps, so that's what people tend to write down for themselves anyway.So if you're happy to do that right then we can switch—use that one]*

DC8 *J:] the only thing I did wonder was whether to put the dates in by the names then they can fill in the date when they did it so we knew . . . whether they'd done it early on in the year or not . . . or . . .*

DC9 *C: yeah . . .*

DC10 *J: whether they'd done it]*

DC11 *C:] yeah and then start off]*

DC12 *J:] at the end of the year*

DC13 *C:]yeah right*

DC14 *J:]or we could see how it went*

DC15 *C: all right I . . . I*

DC16 *J: I mean I find it a nuisance having to date it but if they don't do it . . .*

DC17 *C: Right, yeah, OK . . . er, anything that saves us time I think has got . . . got . . . er . . . to be there. Right, and the second thing is Angela suggested that we talk to the librarian about this problem of all the kids chasing the same texts . . . er I've done that and she's aware of it and she does feel she'll be able to supply the demand at least for theclassics from those er pound um classics that er are available now (minimal supportive* *responses from A & J). Another thing that I thought of is er this one's a difficult one because sometimes people send students down who can't get a book in the library , they know it's a book the student wants to read and they ask me if I can have one from here—if they can have one from here. Now that presents two problems, erm, one it depletes the sets and secondly it can lead to a breakdown in the recording of what they've actually got, you know they a a am I'm responsible for chasing them up or are you responsible for chasing them up, I don't know , I'm concerned that books get lost that way and so I'm a bit reluctant to take books certainly from sets which are used. On the other hand we have got sets of books which we don't very often use now . . . erm . . . (supportive minimal responses from J) you know like Im the King of the Castle and It's my Life and things like that and it might well be worth pushing a few of those into the library to make them available . . . and . . . I don't know what people think about that . . . but I'm certainly reluctant to with the ones that are used as sets to give individual copies out because otherwise you know what it's like you come and get a cop—especially with groups going up next year er you know even more sets likely to be (fades)*

DC18 *T: well you see if you took six of It's my Life out then you've say got twenty four ish left now that's probably not going to be a great deal of use as a set is it]*

DC19 *C:]that's the problem]*

DC20 *T:] if you put six in the library,say]*

DC21 *C:] that that what I'm thinking of Tony is (a) sets which are depleted anyway which we wouldn't top up like I'm the King of the Castle]*

DC22 *T:] oh yes yeah*

DC23 *C: and put a few of those , and things like It's my Life which we perhaps used when we had CSE sets but don't tend to be used much anyway*

(12-76)

DC24 *JO: Perhaps if I could identify which texts came into that um area and then perhaps circulate that so that people could say I mean it might be that we put a title on the list and somebody says well I actually do it]*

DC25 *C:] right um generally speaking I do know which ones are used because they tend to come in and out of here so I have a fair idea of what's er what is used . . . um . . . so we could perhaps look at that anyway.*

DC26 *A: It might be possible that we don't all know what what's available because some might stay in people's rooms—stock rooms—year after year*

DC27 *C: that shouldn't happen [general laughter] and it is very much part of our policy that this shouldn't be private stocks er having said that I remember (B) and (S) used to have a set of Inspector Calls which they passed between each other and they never saw the light of day elsewhere um but generally speaking I don't think that that does happen er too much I think most of them do come back and people are pretty fair actually on that er but (laughs) I'm trusting human nature here when I say that but I think that they do generally come back and we are generally (fades)*

DC28 *C: OK that was the second thing so hopefully that will get better. (a brief item) um the GCSE texts um I have collected a lot of books from a lot of students and a lot of lists are written down there er I know generally people have been checking to see which ones of theirs have come in I think the majority are probably in now but there are still quite a few that are . . . (mumble) that haven't come back . . . but if you can check the lists but it might be better if I'm there to explain it to you because they're a bit complicated it's not as straight forward as it er er as it seems I'm sorry about all this hassle um it it's one of those things*

(82-130)

[discussion of changes needed to faculty policy statement}

DC29 *C: that's a continuous thing without necessarily having to be er formalised in that way er I would agree er I'm quite happy to make those changes certainly*

DC30 *A: There's no mention in it anywhere of the SATs testing and the changes in the GCSE I mean we're now in more of an exam system aren't we rather than um a hundred per cent coursework and I don't know exactly where that it it just seems a little bit]*

DC31 *C:] dated*

DC32 *A:] out of date*

DC33 *C: so you think the assessment area needs looking at and perhaps . . . re . . .]*

DC34 *J:] yes because it's geared towards coursework this one isn't it]*

DC35 *A:] yes it is really]*

DC36 *C:] yeah I mean I did think that at the time when I wrote it . . . it was very much a record of what we where we were at at the time again it rather stands out that one . . . all right . . .*

DC37 *T: Any other suggestions?*

DC38 *C: I wondered if we should have something on differentiation? (pause 2) . . . There's not actually . . . we've got SEN . . . (indistinguishable comment from other) . . . yeah . . . I wonder if something separate on differentiation may be useful.]*

DC39 *J:]there's nothing about differentiation is there under special needs*

DC40 *C: Not as such, no. (continues with anecdote about ILEA advisory group and OFSTED)*

DC41 *C: Just one thing of a general nature er which is important and it does say in the faculty policy it it's important we actually know what it is and I think in broad terms we do, I don't think there's a problem, but one of the things I've always said is whenever we get complaints from parents, if you're carrying out faculty policy there's no problem—that's my problem—um, it's a bit like when (T) does this monitoring and takes in your books, you know if you're carrying out faculty policy and he comes to me and says you know such and such is doing this, this and this, then if I can say well it's faculty policy you know if it's wrong you know if you don't like faculty policy then come and argue with me about faculty policy—it makes it very very easy to for me to support you. On the other hand if you're doing something which is not faculty policy it makes it more difficult you know—so so—it is an important thing I think that we have got a broad sort of idea of where we are and we'll stick with that—it's important—to me it's important and er you know hopefully it is to you as well . . .*

(200-255)

DC42 *C: Right, I tried to sum up . . . (L) passed me this um document um on on which she got on a course on on er gender or (mumble) um at my annual review which I have with the Head and (C) one of the things which he asked me was what are we doing about trying to redress the inbalance of boys and girls achievement in English and I said well I'd really quite like people who keep highlighting these inbalances statistically and drawing up figures of boys and girls' achievement to stop doing that—we know all that—and start giving us some ideas about what we can actually do about it um so whether it was a result of that or whether it was of general interest (L) passed this onto me and it's a review of a period covering 1988 to 1991 by HMIs as they were before they became OFSTED—um—(draws breath) I've got some reservations about it—(JO)'s read it in full as well and perhaps has something to say about that—I've got some reservations* *about it as a piece of research because it seems to me it doesn't er in many ways er actually have any kind of rigorous or objective basis—I picked this up even from the summary . . .*

(257-274)

(long turns by JA and JO discussing strategies for boys' reading including the suggestion that boys work together with girls more rather than segregating themselves in all-male friendship groups)

DC43 *JO: But we tend to make the decision don't we most of us to actually formulate the groups ourselves]*

DC44 *C:] yeah I mean again it's subjective but again it's quite interesting isn't it that what it comes down to so often in these things is the quality of the teacher is the biggest single factor always you know—if you're enthusiastic about reading and encouraging children to read you know that that's really going to matter whatever else you do that's the most crucial thing isn't it you know in whatever way . . . if you're enthusiastic and an expert on what you're doing and keen that's . . . it seems to cry out for specialist teachers doesn't it (mumble and fades)*

(350-360)

(C requests responses to questionnaire originating from SMT for faculty discussion)

(team is discussing responses to section on differentiation)

DC45 *C: Any other ways we differentiate—I still say it's—it's not fashionable and HMI will crucify you in OFSTED—but I still think that differentiation by outcome is a valuable aspect of English you know and I think we've got to fight the Inspectors on that one and say look you know you **can** differentiate by outcome—not **totally**—but to some extent you can]*

] (several interruptions together)

DC46 *JA]If we use differentiation all the way through then I think we're doing them a grave disservice because if we then present them with SATs and we present them with GCSEs then they're not prepared for it and we've differentiated them out of any achievement haven't we—I think there is a problem with it—I'm not saying we don't **do** it but I do think that unless they—we start to differentiate on the exam papers much more then I think it makes a nonsense of differentiation]*

DC47 *C:] that's right*

DC48 *JA:] all the way through their school careers doesn't it]*

DC49 *C:] and in any case we would presumably would argue for exam papers which aren't that differentiated because]*

DC50 *JA:] yeah*

DC51 *C:] we don't need to differentiate that much in English do we you know which proves that you can differentiate by outcome . . . er I mean what Inspectors are saying at the moment . . . (reported speech by Adviser and OFSTED Inspector)*

(530-541)

DC52 *C: Just one other thing which won't apply to all of you but we've got the er pre sixth form course coming up next week and we are assigne d to the Friday afternoon—that's me, (JA) , (JO) and (S) so we'll have to briefly get together and decide exactly what we're going to do on that er sometime er I know what I er (mumble) possibly showing videos or something like that but I'll catch up er and we'll talk about that (fades) . . . Right (looks to Chair)*

DC53 *T: End of meeting?*

DC54 *C: Thank you*

(704-715)

ANALYSIS

In examining the linguistic data we can see that the management transactions fall into three stages through the meeting; managerial strategies signalled by linguistic strategies change somewhat as the meeting progresses. I have used references to "turn" numbers in my commentary in order to more easily identify the position of the speech item in the transcript (for example, the **first** speech at **D**roverslea in **C**live's transcript would be identified as DC1).

1. The manager begins the meeting with an assertive but informal opening, "Right" (DC1), which, after the general chat taking place as people came into the room, marks the opening of a new section of discourse. He begins with two statives, "there are two or three things" and "one is . . .", but the following discourse (DC3) is marked with hesitations and pause fillers and with qualifying weakeners such as "the only thing I was really thinking of" and "we just put" in order to make his suggestions about a redesign of reading record sheets seem more palatable. He also uses a question form of syntax in "would this

actually make . . ." when in fact the function of this utterance is stative. The use of modals, "would" and "could", are addressee-orientated and there is a direct request for opinion /response in "I just wondered what people thought"(DC1). Epistemic modality, such as "just", "sort of", or hedging devices, suggest hesitancy or a desire to moderate the utterance's directive function.

There are many supportive signals in this first section where Clive is using "yeah"/"right" to the utterances from Jackie (DC7,9,13), although these were at times, and clearly in the first "yeh and from the things I read", anaphoric references in fact to the theme of his own previous utterance in DC3 about his ideas for a new design. Clive eventually uses no less than three supportive responses together in "right, yeah, OK" (DC17), although this also signals a winding up of this topic and a moving on to the next topic, introduced by the use of "right" here as an assertive opener to indicate a topic shift beginning a new section of discourse, this time concerning library resources. Clive completes the decision on the first topic with a causal and conditional "So if you're happy to do that . . ." (DC7) which has the effect of softening the decision and making it sound democratic and a summation of colleagues' opinions.

The long turn which Clive has in this opening section of the meeting (DC17) indicates that he holds the floor for a considerably longer time than any of his colleagues during the course of the meeting. Having built up a climate of support, he is able to use the minimal responses, firstly (responses by Angela and Jackie) to enable him to signal a new topic and begin a new section of discourse, and secondly (by Jackie) to gain encouragement to continue his point with examples. However, he expresses some tentativeness and even anxiety where he talks through a problem ("I don't know", "I'm concerned", "I'm a bit reluctant.") and uses the interrogative when indicating policy ("am I responsible . . ."). The effect of this might of course be that he gains empathy from the listeners. He then uses lexical repetition but with a structural change of intensifying adverbial ("I'm **certainly** reluctant . . .") which strengthens his point and uses a statement as an indirect request for response to his idea ("I don't know what people think about that"). Clive also uses a direct address to the audience with the second person pronoun "you" in "you know what it's like" which has the effect of reflecting a common experience and encourages unity in the group. By the end of this relatively long turn (DC17), however, he loses momentum and fades.

Tony then is able to step in and use a conditional "if you took . . ." in order to continue and thus support Clive's point with an example, whereupon Clive in return supports Tony with a strong stative "that's the problem"(DC19) which is in effect supporting his own previous argument in DC17. He continues this with a direct statement of his own opinion ("what I'm thinking of ") and a modal ("we wouldn't top up") used as an assertive declarative (DC21). It seems that in this section of the meeting Clive has created an atmosphere of mutual support and is now able to move on more assertively in his expression of his needs/desires.

2.   In the second phase, as the meeting progresses, Clive uses fewer conditionals, modals, weakeners and hedges (epistemic modality) and fewer qualifiers and disclaimers. He still uses supportive minimal responses such as "right" and "yeah", He also uses personal example, anecdote and reported speech which has the effect of personalising his points and gaining sympathy for his intended directives, as in those regarding ILEA , Advisers and OFSTED as he argues for differentiation by outcome (DC 40, 41, 42). He uses interruption but this tends to be supportive as he is helping the other person to express their point and agreeing with it , as with Angela's point about the assessment section in the faculty policy statement, and where he sums up her idea with "so you think . . ."(DC33) and ends with an agreement, "all right" (DC36).

There is a greater use of statives and strong declaratives here, for example "I do know . . . because . . ."(DC25), "that shouldn't happen"(DC27), "it is very much part of our policy"(DC27), where Clive is more clearly and directly stating his opinions on strategies for the storing and sharing of stock. He also makes statements of his own responsibility, and therefore by implication his status, as in "I'm trusting human nature here", "it might be better if I'm there to explain it to you"(DC28 regarding a point of administration), and "I'm quite happy to make those changes certainly"(DC29 regarding changes to the faculty policy statement). "That's **my** problem" (DC41) is a clear and direct statement of that responsibility and status. This is emphasised in "if you don't like faculty policy then come and argue with me". Again, his own opinion is clarified in the use of intonational stress, "to **me** it's important".

Directives and commands tend to occur in the form of conditionals, as in "if you can check the lists", rather than "check the lists", and "if you're carrying out faculty policy there's no problem",

Clive has control over the topic in most of the items partly because he controls the agenda and because he has had preparation time and opportunity for familiarisation before the meeting : "Just one thing of a general nature"(DC41 which introduces an item on following faculty policy and individual responsibility), and so does "I wondered if we should have something on differentiation?"(DC38) although this takes the form of a weakened interrogative by the lexis "wondered" and the modal "should". He also controls the topic where there is a response requested from the faculty to a document and, in the third section of the meeting, a questionnaire, both of which he has had access to prior to the meeting.

Professional lexis has already been used such as "differentiation" and "OFSTED" but towards the end of this section this tends to be developed into longer more formalised authoritative phrases, such as "at my annual review", "trying to redress the inbalance of boys' and girls' achievement in English", "a review of a period covering 1988 to 1991 by HMIs", "the quality of the teacher is the biggest single factor"(DC42,44), which has the effect of raising the discussion to the level of a report , and this is continued in the ensuing discussion of strategies amongst the members of the faculty team. Here Clive is enabling the colleagues to air their views, but he makes his own feelings clear in "I've got some reservations about it"(DC42) which he then reinforces with appeal to JO and J's responses to it.

3. The final phase of the meeting continues the emotive language Clive uses to reinforce his opinions on teaching strategies for reading at the end of the second phase, "enthusiatic", "keen", "encouraging", "expert"(DC44), where again he is commenting on differentiation. Here he is establishing an argument and asserting it in his leadership role, "not fashionable", "crucify you", "fight", "valuable", "proves"(DC45,51).

He tries to unify and spur on the team in the use of the pronoun and imperative "we've got to fight"(DC45). Intonational stress also operates to emphasise this. He also agrees with Janet's emotive "nonsense" with the supportive interruption "that's right"(DC47) which is of course anaphorically referring to his own expression of opinion in DC45. Clive structures his argument and marks it with "I think", "and in any case, we would . . . because" and "we don't need", "which proves . . ."(DC49,51)

He ends the meeting with the introduction of a final item which applies to only some of the team but fades on this with an unfinished phrase, hesitancy and uncertainty, "sometime", "something like that" and pause fillers "er"(DC52), although he ends the meeting with a look towards the Chair and a more assertive "right" and "thank you"(DC54).

Conclusions

There were five females present and it was interesting to note the extensive use of supportive minimal responses used by the females to each other and to Clive, often murmuring and "mmm", suggesting Tannen's (1992) signalling of "carry on", while the two males only used "yeah"/"yes" responses often followed by fuller statements signalling "I agree with you".

This mutually supportive atmosphere does seem to be encouraged by Clive's own use of language, even to the extent of using the supportive "right" to Josie as if in agreement when in fact he then argued against the point made. He makes a point of responding to individuals' contributions much of the time and that is done positively rather than negatively. He uses a number of strategies for control, such as introducing topics and "speaking to" items on the agenda, for example reading out the questionnaire in order to elicit responses, and this is mainly because, despite not having the role of Chair, he is the only one to have information about the agenda items. He also requests suggestions from colleagues on, for example, teaching strategies, while making his own philosophical position clear with statives and declaratives. ("I've got some reservations", "I think"). He encourages interaction between members of the team and allows discussion for a number of "turns" without interruption or intervention, for example in the discussion about boys' underachievement. He often develops the responses of others and incorporates them into his own contribution, as in the topic on differentiation. At the same time, he often makes his own feelings plain either by directly referring to them in his introduction to the topic, by use of emotive language, or in an appeal to authority in reporting comments by authoritative bodies/quotations/anecdotes. He uses a clear IRF (initiation, response, feedback) discourse structure as outlined in the exchange structure theory of Sinclair and Coulthard (1975, 1992) with a three-part exchange and his feedback to the team is made strongly.

In many ways the interactions of the meeting seem cooperative and supportive, and the mangement technique facilitative, empowering and team-building. However, direction and focus suggests Ball's (1987) paradox of the use of language implying consensus/consideration yet disguising an incipient domination function, that which he terms as "within the rhetoric of control". It is interesting to look more closely at the progress of the meeting and the detail of the speech events in evidence.

While the meeting seems to reveal three sections marked by differing linguistic strategies, the meeting as a whole is characterised by stategies which seem to suggest functions of cooperation, empowerment, and consensus. Many of the linguistic traits used by Clive, such as the modals, conditionals, qualifiers, weakeners and minimal responses, suggest this. However, there is also evidence, especially as the meeting progresses, of strong declaratives, strengtheners, imperatives and statements of authority which show Clive's status in leadership and authority and which suggest an incipient domination function beneath the establishing of a cooperative and supportive interactional context. This reflects the masculine frame/schema brought to conversations, which focuses on personal control, status and domination, but also indicates an awareness of the feminine frame/schema pragmatically in this context of a team meeting.

Droverslea—Head of Post-16 Pastoral team—Elizabeth (Liz)

Unusually, this meeting occurred during normal lesson time. Meetings generally take place after the end of the school day. On this occasion arrangements were made to cover the classes of those who would normally be teaching at that time. More time was devoted to it than normal and a more relaxed atmosphere was possible than the meetings after school where there might be a "guillotine" at the end of an hour session. It was a review and planning meeting called by the Head of Post-16, Liz. There were two men and two women present, including Liz.

The agenda included items on the application process for entrants to the sixth form, numbers of students, changes in structure in post-16, the pastoral process, and the diploma of achievement.

TRANSCRIPTION

E—Elizabeth (Liz)
M—Mark
K—Keith
J—Janet

[general discussion as people settled down.]

DE1 *E: Right, if we look at the agenda, er I've put it into this order,er starting off with the application process, going through the numbers, changes in structure in post-16, pastoral process, diploma of achievement—those are the first four things. I think if we get as far as that,um, by perhaps a late lunch we'll have done well (laughs) all right? Is that OK? . . . Right Keith can you then take us through the application process this year please—so far?*

DE2 *K: All right. First of all, probably, is that I feel as though I haven't actually been involved so much as I should have been because I think it's one of those classic things you can't actually be in two places at once but I think one of the things it perhaps has done its given me quite a critical eye on what is done um um the applications were quite interesting in the sense that they threw up something that I think Liz has highlighted already is basically working to be a bit more efficient. I think the application process didn't work as well as it should have done because the forms were basically filled in very very badly and very poorly—all that they really indicated to us was that the child wanted to stay on—it didn't have for example—estimated grades for example weren't on , children were writing down multiple and I don't think necessarily terribly well thought out choices of courses, they were just writing down lots of subjects—whole sections were not completed and so basically I don't think—as far as the kids were concerned that their thoughts were as well organised as they could be but I think that perhaps is an area we need to address—I don't think there's anything particularly wrong with the form]*

DE3 *M:] I—I don't think there's anything wrong with the form]*

DE4 *K:] But I think there's something wrong with how it's done]*

DE5 *M:] No no I don't*

DE6 *E:]Are you suggesting that—sorry, Mark go ahead]*

DE7 *M:] no no I was going to say I mean what the students are—I think what this is it's just a starting point and and and to be honest I don't think a lot of students really know what to do and I don't think they properly know what the difference is between GNVQ and A level and I think they've got all sorts of ideas in their head and I think they ought to have the (unclear) to put down generally what they want and then it's for us in the interviewing process to actually make sense of that.*

DE8 *E: Did you detect that they filled this form in in a sort of sloppy way compared to how they would fill in say perhaps]*

DE9 *K:]an external one*

DE10 *E:]an external one, yes*

DE11 *K: There's no comparison—these are just filled in just to do it—I agree Mark that you know what we really want is that we want them to put down their ideas but to a great extent when these are filled in is that quite a lot of the work is in theory done*

[continues his contribution making suggestions for tutor involvement,E making minimal responses in support and comments "Right" and "I totally agree with you"]

DE12 *E: I actually think that we do need the estimated grades and I think it's part of their job to encourage high level of performance and you do that through discussing the estimated grades—but I do take your point about office staff. So, really, you don't think there's too much wrong with the form?*

DE13 *K: I don't think there's anything wrong with the form itself*

DE14 *E: So we're looking at timing*

DE15 *K: er yeah*

DE16 *E: and the actual process of filling in the form*

DE17 *K: mmm, because the form's good and the form focuses but I don't think the form focuses as well as it]could do*

DE18 *E:] could do—and you're suggesting perhaps the process—we should dovetail the processes together]*

DE19 *M:] what do you want it to focus on?*

DE20 *K: I want it basically that you get the impression that when you're looking look at them that the kids have actually taken the application to school seriously* **DE21** *E:mmm*

DE22 *K: which I don't think they do cos I think they just think well I'm staying on at school]*

DE23 *E:] or take school yes]*

DE24 *K:] or take school as a second choice if I don't get what I want]*

DE25 *M:]no I don't think so—in fact the fact that—I agree a lot of them don't fill in large sections—I think it's still a serious application I don't think its just (mumble) or second best I think most of them want to come back and to be quite honest the main thing I want from them is I suppose basically their name*

DE26 *K: well I was going to say]*

DE27 *M:] and a general indication of what they want to do so so that we can pick them up later in the system or if they don't turn up we've got an indication that they may be interested so that we can pull them up if]*

DE28 *K:] well, in which case if that actually is a suggestion then what we're actually doing is that this is ultimately a complete waste of time and is actually generating nothing useful at all because this]*

DE29 *M:] no I didn't say that no I didn't say that at all*

DE30 *E: We need more information than that because we have to be able to inform the timetabling process. So if we could get the application forms er done er with more thought we could actually inform the timetabling process and make sure that we have the right number of groups on at the right time]*

DE31 *M:] well right but can]*

DE32 *E:] So there is an important element there]*

DE33 *M:]yeah it's important but what I'm saying is this is only a first thing er er it's a big big decision for these kids to make I have every sympathy*

DE34 *J:]yes yes mmm*

[M has long turn following this line of argument, J gives minimal responses in support throughout]

DE35 *E: [interrupting] I thoroughly agree with what you're saying Mark um um I think you're right—**but** if there's anything we can do to improve the process we might as well do it so we can get perhaps more accurate information—the most accurate information so that we feel that the form's been filled in carefully]*

DE36 *M:] But that's not what I'm objecting to—it's not the quality of information I want it's the quality of them thinking about it and I think they fill in an application form which is basically yes I've got a commitment* *to the school and I want to come back—we can follow them up and then what we want is an indication of what they want to do*

DE37 *E: But we need that to be as accurate as we can]*

DE38 *J:] well I don't think you can make it as accurate as that Liz I don't think you can put old heads on young shoulders not at year 11]*

DE39 *M:] and if you want to make it accurate I think you're going to find you're going to force them to make a decision—it doesn't necessarily mean it's going to be the right decision*

[general interruption unclear followed by suggestion about forms being given via PSE]

DE40 *E: We have been allowed in this year—there was one year when we weren't but we have been allowed back this year but it was later rather than earlier. Let's just look at the timing of this. The information pack with the prospectus, application form, invitation to the post-16 evening goes out just before the Christmas holiday—right—immediately after Route 16—yes—exhibition. OK now I think that's quite good timing from my point of view—now are we saynig that we try to negotiate a PSE slot between January and March? (murmurs, identifying M's dissention) sorry Mark, what?*

DE41 *M: no no it its its nothing to do with you Liz I mean I find it completely I always try to negotiate I mean if if if PSE [indistinguishable comment of dissention from E here] can't contribute to our own school and our own kids staying on I think it ought to be you know its like a programme for teachers to turn up on time no its fundamental surely?*

DE42 *E: So . . . between January and March we will have a slot in PSE, OK?*

DE43 *K: I was going to say if you take that in its widest sense is that if PSE time has been a problem and next year it's going to be even more of a problem . . .]*

DE44 *E:] I don't think—sorry—I don't think it will be a problem because I think it was made quite clear that it was out of line so don't [unclear]*

DE45 *K: No. I was just going to say that one of the things that's so untapped in the school is the use of the tutor in the whole process and I don't think that tutors are reluctant to do things—they're reluctant to do things when they're not well planned, well thought out*

1-300

DE46 *K: I was just saying, if PSE time isn't available . . . it's caused a problem in the past , instead of just jetisoning it as an idea, is that we have a huge amount of potential to actually get it done*

DE47 *E: Well, should we agree that we would go to PSE groups—am I right in thinking that you would like two prongs of attack—one, a PSE talk, and another slot to fill in the form—yes? At the same time if [M. background murmurings] that isn't a—sorry Mark?*

DE48 *M: um I I take it that we will do the slot to actually explain what the what goes on but I mean I take it that the person will only just be PSE not us er*

DE49 *E: Yes yes PSE teacher yes. At the same time to try and encourage more involvement in the tutors perhaps—by the tutors—perhaps we should give them a package a pack. When we give the pack to the students give the tutors a pack and encourage them to discuss what is in the booklet during registration and perhaps have a series of questions to go through.*

[comments from K]

DE50 *E: Right. So let me just try to sum up. So in the er Christmas term we have the Route 16 exhibition right?]*

DE51 *K:]I'd just like to say that I thought that was a very good idea*

DE52 *E: Well, a lot of people weren't happy with it but in actual fact a lot of people came back to me afterwards and said how they'd enjoyed it so fortunately it worked . . . So . . . Route 16 exhibition followed by the giving out of the pack in December followed by er the team going into PSE in their slot, followed by the PSE staff filling in the form, at the same time we have the post-16 information evening—yeah?—and we ask for the form to be in—when?—after the post-16? which if we look at the calendar next year is er er . . . March the fifth so]*

DE53 *M:]an auspicious day*

DE54 *E: Why? Is it your birthday (laughs) it's your birthday. Right. Information evening March fifth so if we try and gather momentum should we say that it's in either Friday—er goodness I don't know about this—Friday the seventh or Friday the fifteenth—what do you think? The Friday after the post-16 evening or the]*

DE55 *J:]I think straight after that post-16 evening because then it's immediate and it still gives you sweeping up time doesn't it? I mean if you leave it a fortnight they'll have forgotten about it]*

DE56 *E:] that's right we've got two weeks to sweep up and just go through and do a little . . . right . . . Right I think that's quite a neat little package*

[some discussion of dates]

DE57 *E: Right , OK, super. Any other comment about that?*

[comments by M then K back to previous points about the nature of the form]

DE58 *E: Do you think a Helpline manned by the Student Council, say, every Tuesday lunchtime, in the information area of post-16—actually manned by the students—would be helpful?*

[discussion general]

340—375

[E leads K through a report of the process of post-16 application, prompted at intervals by E's direct questions]

DE59 *E: Did anyone have any difficulties with this piece of paper, the interview record sheet, filling it in?*

DE60 *J: I mean, as I say, my only difficulty was the fact that some of the kiddies were not satisfied with their estimated grades and then they'd be sitting there saying well that's not right*

500-505

[general comments and discussion]

DE61 *E: Moving along. Have you any idea of numbers?*

DE62 *K: Any idea of numbers? Off the top of my head, no, but probably I'll be able to give you a good idea of that er after lunch.*

DE63 *E: Oh all right. You received 230 didn't you—round about—round about 230.*

[K explains numbers, during which minimal responses from E]

DE64 *E: In actual fact the effect of our marketing is actually coming home—it was—I felt really great because when we were in Sheffield last year we actually had a student from (names other school) who was seriously thinking about coming to us because she had picked up the Faculty leaflet at the Sheffield Route 16—which actually made me feel rather pleased because we put in a lot of time for it and we are beginning to get some reward from that. Er she was a student who didn't like the formality of . . . (school) er and was looking for somewhere more informal for post-16. But from past experience I would think that that would probably come down to around 210.*

540-570

[comments on timing of infromation to Careers Service]

DE65 *E: You're quite right and Pam would like it earlier I know. The point is that the problem for us is that we don't produce new literature until we* *know or we have a good idea of the courses that we're going to run. The college produce all this wonderful literature [general agreement responses from others] yes, and its not necessarily going to be their curriculum package. I think we're going to move ahead a little bit on that in that (name) is at this moment producing a glossy flier you know like we see at Sheffield—it's to link in with the opening of the new building and he's got photographs I understand it's going to be rather nice so that will take the place of our simple school leaflet. But what I can do and what I gave them last year I don't know whether I brought them down with me or not either oh yes I have—I can give Pam these.*

573-8

[the researcher was unable to record the rest of the meeting because of teaching commitments]

ANALYSIS

After a casual discussion as people settled down, Liz opens the formal meeting with the assertive but informal "Right"(DE1) which marks the opening of a new section of discourse. She then uses the conditional "if we look at the agenda" rather than an imperative, and direct interrogatives "all right?" "is that OK?" as a request for support. She uses a direct interrogative again to Keith instead of an imperative (requesting his contribution on the application process) and also adds the politeness marker "please"(DE1).

This enables Keith to take the floor and in fact he has a long turn to introduce the topic of concern (the nature and purpose of the forms for application to the sixth form) although he is interrupted by Mark who disagrees with his point. Mark is happy with the forms as they are and has previously been closely involved with their design and use. Keith, a newcomer to the team, is critical and wants a tightening up. Both Mark and Liz interrupt Keith at one point, but Liz apologises ("sorry" DE6) and gives Mark the floor for his objection with an imperative "go ahead".

It seems that Liz is operating within a facilitating, enabling framework here, by giving the floor to Keith in requesting his report and to Mark in allowing his interruptions to succeed. She seems to be empowering Keith by giving him the space and time to report on a concern and also Mark by according status to his objections. She appears to be supportive, even to interruptions, and her whole discourse is marked by many politeness features, despite Mark's interruptions, objections, and the clear uneasiness in the relationship between Mark and Keith.

The number and nature of the interruptions which mark this discourse are interesting. Liz herself interrupts seven times during this transcribed section, three times each to Mark and Keith and once to Janet. However, of those seven, there is only one where she gives an opposing view, and even this is preceded by a supportive "I thoroughly agree"(DE35) although modified with the dysjunction "but" before raising the objection. One is where she apologises then gives Mark the floor, but the other five are all supportive positive interruptions where she helps the other person's turn or gives reassurance. Twice the interruptions could perhaps be regarded more as overlaps than true interruptions, as Liz repeats or speaks simultaneously and identically to Keith reflecting his own lexical or syntactical patterning as encouragement. ("*could do*—and you're suggesting . . ." DC18, and "or take *school* yes" DE23 which Keith reflects back again as "*or take school* as a second choice"). In one case, Liz interrupts Mark in order to continue her own turn after Mark has interrupted her: "So there is an important element there"(DE32), marking the argument process with "so" indicating the summative "therefore" and concluding the argument with a stative verb and complement. This also marks Liz's command of this section of the discourse in disallowing the interruption to succeed and rounding off her own argument despite it.

The interruptions from Keith and Mark are of a somewhat different nature and indicate the unease between the two males present. Keith interrupts five times, but three are to Liz and are supportive, two of these being overlap continuers, while two are to Mark and are disagreements. Of Mark's eleven interruptions, nine are challenges/disagreements and only one is supportive (to Janet) and one is a lighthearted comment to Liz concerning the date of his own birthday. These interruptions are therefore competitive and mark an attempt at dominance and function as negative in this situation, militating against the atmosphere of support which Liz seems to be trying to create here.

Her treatment of this type of interruption and challenge from a member of her team was interesting to analyse as critical incidents within the context of managerial interaction. Of the nine negative challenges/disagreements, five are directed towards Keith and four towards Liz herself. Yet, she uses politeness forms, apologises, and allows the floor when Mark challenges.She doggedly continues her own turn with the next stage of her argument after one of Mark's interruptions; she uses the dysjunction "but" to indicate an alternative argument. We see her supporting Keith's argument directly by the use of minimal responses and by disagreeing with Mark's interruption of Keith with a counter stative "we need more information than that" (DE30) followed by a reason and a conditional used as a directive, "so if we could get the application forms done with more thought . . ." Liz makes her support of Keith's ideas clear by the use of minimal responses as he talks and by comments such as "right" and "I totally agree with you". She follows this up with strong declaratives, auxiliary and verb strengthener "I actually think that we do need . . .", "I think . . .", "you do that through . . ."(DE12) and then she uses summing-up indicators "so really, you don't think there's too much wrong with the form?" (interrogative summation DE12) and "so we're looking at timing" (declarative summation DE14). Additionally she uses the supportive overlaps already indicated above. Liz also, after one supportive overlap, tentatively sums up Keith's argument at one point by using a weakener "perhaps"(DE18), a hesitation and self correction, and a modal "should" which might suggest hesitancy in her summation "-and you're suggesting perhaps the process—we should dovetail the processes together"(DE18).

At this point the discourse suggests a polarising of 'sides' : Liz and Keith versus Mark and Janet. Mark repeatedly reverts to the same argument and finally Liz, not managing to persuade Mark and Janet , allows the argument about the purpose and efficiency of the application form to drop. She then moves the discussion on by introducing a new issue: the timing of the application stages and the avenues to use for the conducting of the process. This indicates an interesting strategy in crisis management. Liz, unable to resolve the issue and apparently perceiving that continuing the argument is fruitlessly leading to an impasse, drops the issue in order to enable the meeting to move on, and continues on the safer ground of practical arrangements. However, the underlying conflict remains unresolved, and Mark continues to maintain the tension. Liz does not use her authority to make a decision ultimately, but to try to avoid or avert conflict.

Liz begins by giving information, leading the team through the process, yet using a direct interrogative to empower them in decision-making: "now are we saying that . . . ?"(DE40). Again she must deal with a challenge from Mark, although initially he does not make this challenge openly and clearly. Liz in fact identifies his dissention from his murmurings as she speaks and allows him to interrupt her with an apology and a direct interrogative, "sorry Mark, what?"(DE40).

Mark's agitation is implied in the number of incompleted clauses he uses which signal his discontent and unease, but having allowed Mark the floor to express this Liz then signals the need to move on to a decision with the summative and declarative "So . . . between January and March we will have a slot in PSE" followed with the assertive interrogative which is acting almost as a rhetorical "OK?"(DE42). Liz reinforces the declarative with a statement of reassurance "I don't think it will be a problem . . ." and the impersonalising passive "it was made quite clear that it was out of line."(DE44).

Although Liz retains the politeness markers throughout the meeting, and allows Mark to interrupt again, even identifying and foregrounding murmurings of dissent from him, she becomes more terse in her responses to him. For example she replies briefly with a confirmation "yes, yes PSE teacher yes"(DE49) and then repeats the adverbial phrase she used before the interruption "At the same time . . ." after which she continues her point. She is then able to recap the timetable of procedure, introducing with the seeming weakener "So let me just try to sum up"(DE50) but continuing with directing the team through the stages of the process, checking that they have the information clear. She marks the conclusion with "Right" and a positive opinion statement, "I think that's quite a neat little package"(DE56). She reinforces this with three agreement/decision markers, "Right, OK, super"(DE57) and although she invites comments and opinions, opening up the discussion, she maintains a control by direct interrogatives and prompts, by short phrases to direct procedure as in "moving along"(DE61), by the use of assertive statives marking her own insider knowledge "the point is that the problem for us is . . ." and by the use of anecdotal evidence (DE64,65). She is able to provide information which she has access to and clarify action which is being undertaken on the production of advertising material for the sixth form marketing. She uses emotive modifiers to suggest her own opinions here "glossy flier", "rather nice", "simple"(DE65).

The recording did not include the ending of the meeting because of practical difficulties: the meeting took place in lesson time and the researcher was not released from normal timetable commitments that day.

Conclusions

Liz, like Clive, used strategies of topic control, and support, using first person statives, declaratives, softeners, and professional jargon. However, there were also other features which shaped this meeting. The meeting as a whole seemed to be characterised by strategies which implied functions of empowerment and, despite potential disruptions, cooperation and team-building. Liz employed techniques in order to defuse and deflect conflicts between members of the team and handled critical incidents by allowing certain issues to drop and moving the meeting on. The underlying focus of the leadership was facilitating and enabling: see the way in which Liz gives the floor to Keith and Mark, to Keith in requesting his reporting and to Mark in allowing his interruptions to succeed. She empowers Keith in her encouragement for his reports and her supportive responses to them. Even though Janet contributes little in this section of the discourse and tends to form a "faction" with Mark, Liz remains supportive in her responses by the use of agreement markers and repetition of Janet's own phrases. In this way, the IRF discourse structure is followed but with the greater emphasis on response.

Liz establishes an example of courtesy and uses many politeness markers, even where Mark is interrupting her with a challenge. She calls upon members of the team by name in order to include them and encourages rapport, for example by lightening the atmosphere when Mark hints at his birthday date. She uses conditionals and interrogatives rather than imperatives which have the effect of softening commands.

However, she becomes more clearly assertive in her control of the meeting as it progresses and the IRF structure becomes more even, with Liz stressing the initiation and feedback more now. Having failed to persuade Mark and Janet of the need for changes to the sixth form application form she allows the matter to drop on this occasion without a firm resolution to the problem but having allowed the team members to air their views. She is then able to direct the progress of the meeting with direct interrogatives and the use of linguistic markers to develop and conclude her arguments. She signals her authority in this way and also by using her insider knowledge of events and actions. She gives information and leads the team through the task, checking the organisation carefully and in some detail. Nevertheless, the underlying conflict is unresolved, as indicated by Mark's further tension, and this indicates that Liz is more concerned with conflict avoidance than conflict resolution. She does not use a domination role to deal with this but a peacemaking, soothing role in order to deflect the conflict. This reflects the feminine frame/ schema brought to conversations, which focuses on the importance of relationship-building and unity.

Droverslea—Head of Modern Languages—Horace

The Faculty meeting took place on the regular afternoon following the school day, with a few minutes break for staff to travel from the other site and to get a cup of tea. Horace, the Head of Faculty, provided biscuits for the team. There were nine members present, seven women and two men, including Horace. The other man present, Arnold, held a promoted post on a similar level to Horace but as Deputy Head of Year.

The agenda included Induction week, Induction days, Phoenix Building opening, Open Day, tests, NPRA names, and cover for Brittany trip.

TRANSCRIPTION

H—Horace
A—Arnold
M—Margaret
C—Celia
N—Nony
F—Felicity
D—Debbie
E—Helen

[general informal chat as people settle down in which Horace takes part, as he writes up an agenda on the board behind the table, then continues . . .]

DH1 *H: Er, an approximate agenda is on the board, starting with induction to Year 12 . . . er, this is er (name)'s brainchild and um er unfortunately it coincides with the Brittany visit so um everybody's going to be on their own resources to some extent er during that. Nony that's your timetable of events for years one and two Celia that's yours it's identical it's just that you want your own copies of it, yours Felicity and you Margaret* *that's for you . . . um (name) has arranged it so that er . . . sorry with the result that Lorna Forman isn't in on on a Thursday and as a result of her not being in the Spanish input cannot go ahead with her because er she's in Brittany with us so not necessarily third choice by any means but Margaret you've been asked to do that because you're familiar with the er er A level coursework system that we have and you're currently assisting with the Spanish etc etc . . . er (name) did say (unclear) it could actually be anybody couldn't it? I said well yes you know it could be er . . .*

DH2 *N: Basil Brush*

DH3 *H: Basil Brush I won't say who I thought it could be . . . but anyway er . . . she said it could be anybody I said well no I think it couldn't be anybody because I think even not having a (unclear) there in some ways devalues the whole exercise and she said oh well er you might not get candidates that turn up in any case and the next obvious course is well why are we doing it*

DH4 *N:] doing it*

DH5 *H: but please er if you're involved in that um you will be liberated from the class that you would otherwise be working with um and if that involves you being liberated from Year 10 classes and you're unhappy about it then er you might want to renegotiate with (name) as to when you are going to be released er she hasn't used um er has she used you Felicity?*

DH6 *F: Yes*

DH7 *H: oh she has . . . she hasn't used you for period one because she said she has to leave some people free for (name) to use on the cover system, not the least to cover my 8E class, period one on Thursday]*

DH8 *N:] Can I just ask where the materials are ? In the filing cabinet under pre-sixth?*

DH9 *H: er French materials will be in the filing cabinet under pre-sixth and if you find me tomorrow morning preferably er er then I can show you through those er er Monday morning in desperation if we don't see each other . . .]*

DH10 *M:] Monday morning? I thought you were going Sunday night?*

DH11 *H: No Monday night*

DH12 *M: oh all right*

DH13 *H: so . . .*

DH14 *C: What kind of timetable is it? Is it all morning?*

DH15 *H: no no you have um a formal session . . . errrr (2) . . . 9.30 till 10.30 as it says on my (unclear) Formal session period one and an informal session* er the drop—in zone as (name) keeps calling it—it's a very (unclear critical adjective) phrase of hers er for pupils to come back and talk to you er assiduously about post-sixteen asperations er how you operate your time in the formal and informal sessions is entirely up to you.

DH16 *C: But I mean I should be teaching all that morning so will I be covered for]*

DH17 *H:] You will be covered for whatever has got a circle round it in my writing—that's the cover you're put in for.*

1-66

DH18 *H: Year 10 Induction Day]*

DH19 *M:] Hang on, hang on before we move on, can I ask two questions on this?*

DH20 *H:]Yes*

DH21 *M:]First of all, how was it decided that there should be classes of up to 33?*

DH22 *H: Erm, I don't know but I can only assume that it its because]*

DH23 *M:] and why hasn't the staff been consulted about having to take yet larger classes?*

DH24 *H: Er . . . pass on both counts er I I've (unclear) as a Head of Faculty I've been told by (name) that class sizes are going to be 33. Er I've been told by]*

DH25 *M:] Once again here is a major thing that's happening that's going to affect us all seriously which is yet again going to whittle away at our effectiveness and efficiency as teachers and you know [H attempts to interrupt but unsuccessfully] we don't even have a say in it.*

DH26 *H: Er there was talk of um that (name) might try and timetable another tutor group in Year 7 but his ability to find another 20 periods on the school timetable er would seem to be very limited so his the possibility of finding even 3 Languages teaching periods on er the contracts as they are at the moment is at zero. We have 165 lessons available and we need 164 teaching lessons. He has a flexibility of one.*

DH27 *M: My second question is what about the the split up of the languages—5 French 3 German 1 Spanish. How does that (unclear)*

DH28 *H: erm erm there's been (.4) there's been no debate about that]*

DH29 *M:] I thought there was going to be some move towards having 2 Spanish groups to make life]*

DH30 *H:] Earlier on in the year . . . can you turn that off please? (the tape recorder)*

164-190

(discussion on Year10 Induction Day—H gives information about arrangements)

DH31 *H: You shouldn't be asked to transfer sites. But as soon as something comes through I'll let you know about it. (further discussion about how it will personally affect staff) Any more on Year 10? Year 10 is a non-story.*

200-220

(Discussion about an Open Day and Evening for the new building and H declares that he does not know if this is under Directed Time, ie. that the staff are required by contract to spend the time there)

DH32 *A: That would mean that we'd already done our quota.*

DH33 *N: So they can't make us come in that evening?*

DH34 *H: I'm sure that if you've got a theatre visit already arranged as I have]*

DH35 *N:] oooh me too*

DH36 *C: But could you are you saying that maybe we could operate a rota system ?*

DH37 *H: I think that would be an excellent idea Celia and you have jumped two sentences ahead of me (M laughs) And I'll take 9 o clock till midday*

DH38 *H: It's a normal working day at school. They'll be allowed to walk around and possibly guided by Year12 students during school hours. Nobody as far as I'm aware has thought of the er post—Dunblane security implications of this but we're just allowing any Tom Dick or Harry to walk around the school site and let them]*

DH39 *N:] Can we say no?*

DH40 *H: I dunno. Dunno.*

DH41 *N: We have no say in this?*

DH42 *H: I don't think so*

235-275

(continue discussion on the Open Day with dissention about the arragements)

DH43 *H: If you have the classroom door open then let them come in. If you don't want them in, have the classroom door closed and have a notice on the door saying there is an exam going on in this room and please keep away. That should frighten most people. If you don't want people in, do that. (Further discussion) Right let's move on. Is there anything else on the Open Day?*

340

DH44 *M: It seems crazy to me spending money on sugar paper when we haven't got any exercise books.*

DH45 *H: Er the exercise book order is being followed up because it should have arrived a month ago and I've been in to see the Bursar today and he's following that up because he said they should have arrived a month ago.*

391-396

(One member relates an incident with another senior member of staff and M becomes very worked up about this requesting "you'd better turn this bloody thing off"—the tape recorder)

DH46 *H: I have some names (unclear) NPRA list which have been updated. I have received the following names (reads list of names and forms) Do you all want to (unclear) that?*

DH47 *C: I'm very surprised by Stuart Caldwell]*

DH48 *H:] It was hang on hang on (background noises) Right I'll rewind. NPRA is the er revolver for the er non GCSE um (background murmurs) hang on non GCSE languages course er people for er Year 9 into Year 10 er people who are unlikely to cope well with er GCSE course um its going to be a group which has one lesson of language per week and one lesson of basic skills per week basic skills being taught by er (name) er who is also going to ensure that the National Curriculum delivery is being met er legally by the er languages section um at the moment its the proposal is that we're aiming at about um two groups of eight so that on a Tuesday for example um 1 to 8 will do language and 9 to 16 will do er basic skills and on a Thursday 9 to 16 will do language and 1 to 8 will do basic skills.*

DH49 *C: Stuart Caldwell is in my second English group and I]*

DH50 *H:] He was recommended to me by (name of Year Staff) who didn't know the group terribly well]*

DH51 *C:] But he is a higher candidate]*

DH52 *H:] OK. Right. I'll make a note on this . . . to be removed um um all I said was . . . I'll read on (reads list) Teachers of 9J have not yet been consulted about any further names to be added to the list . . . as soon as I have details on that I'll submit this memo again can we have suggestions]*

DH53 *N:] Can we have a look at 9J then]*

DH54 *H:] can we have a look at*

DH55 *N:] Jane and I haven't even seen*

DH56 *H:]Are there any suggestions]*

DH57 *D:] I don't think there are any children in 9J who need]*

DH58 *H:] Are there any suggestions of people who taught 9J last year um who can]*

(a number of overlaps and interruptions as staff discuss relative merits of various pupils)

DH59 *H: I will update this now and I'll do a reprint of this this evening and date it er whatever date it is today er OK?*

440-470

(discussion of Exchange visit and its viability, members of staff not happy about continuing to run it because of understaffing)

DH60 *M: So we thought we might stand back from it for a year and just see]*

DH61 *H:] I would be inclined for you to stand back from it and just say look we just can't do it, end of story.*

(a long discussion continues about the need to pull out of the arrangements)

DH62 *H: Right. (signals the end of the meeting—general discussion breaking out again as people leave.)*

620

ANALYSIS

The meeting is preceded by a general informal chat as people arrive and settle down. Horace takes part in this as he writes up the agenda on the board behind the table and begins the more formal part of the meeting itself with "er, an approximate agenda is on the board, starting with induction to Year 12" , (DH 1) thus drawing the group's attention together. There is no linguistic opener to the discourse, but only the hesitancy feature "er" which is repeated throughout this part of the discourse usually as pause—fillers within a delivery which is marked by rapid speech with few pause gaps. There are few pauses between relatively long compound-complex syntactical units here and this seemed characteristic of Horace's ideolect. He also uses subordinate clauses within the long syntactical units with a reliance on subordinating conjunctions which do not always convey the intended meaning , for example when he self-corrects "so that" with "sorry with the result that" (DH1), where the first would semantically convey the idea that the subject intended cause and effect, while the revised version recognised that the subject did not.

In this opening discourse, Horace uses statives "is", "coincides", "that's" "everybody's going to be" to give information to the team and this also reinforces his own status within the group. He also achieves this by using a series of proper nouns to name colleagues individually, where simply pronouns or even one collective "you" might otherwise have been used: "Nony that's your timetable . . . Celia that's yours . . . yours Felicity . . . you Margaret" This redundant repetition can give the effect of either establishing a closer link by direct personalised address, or a tone of valuing exactness and detail.

Later in the same speech item, Horace names a third party and gives an anecdote involving direct speech, a report of a previous conversation between himself and the third party about finding a substitute for an absent colleague to deliver part of the Year 12 induction session. His own reported response to the third party contains the strong declarative "devalues" (DH3) which acts emotively here. Nony shows her support by using a simultaneous overlap "doing it" which marks her agreement with his response on the issue (DH3 &4). He is then able to return to the second person pronoun "you" in DH5 where he is giving instructions about being released from classes in order to take part in the induction sessions. Here he uses the conditionals "if you're . . ." and "if that . . ." and the modal "might" instead of imperatives. These less assertive politeness forms are reinforced at the end of this speech item where Horace uses self-correction from the declarative "she hasn't used (you)" to the interrogative "er has she used you Felicity?" (DH5) which suggests doubt and uncertainty.

When Nony interrupts Horace (DH8) with a request for information, he repeats the wording of her question as an affirmative reply. This could be as a stalling procedure, buying time, rather than leaving an indecisive pause, or again it could represent a desire to appear exacting. He uses double pause fillers "er er" twice after this in the same speech item (DH9). However, he also uses the conditional "if you find me tomorrow" functioning as an imperative.

He is interrupted by Margaret five times during this transcript, the first of which is in order to clarify information (DH10). Horace replies with a declarative giving the required information but his next hesitant "so . . ." (DH13) is cut across by Celia with another request for information. He uses statives to provide this and makes a comment aside, critical of a third party, which distances him from the arrangements he is explaining to the team. He directly addresses his colleagues with the second person pronoun and uses a declarative "how you operate your time . . . is entirely up to you" as an instruction. He interrupts Celia's question with a reply which repeats her wording, as he had done with Nony in DH9, but he also repeats his own idea in a syntically different way in DH17.

There follows a section which contains a number of critical incidents involving Margaret, who is shortly to take early retirement. As Horace introduces the next item on the agenda, Year 10 Induction Day, Margaret interrupts him with "Hang on, hang on before we move on", the repetition of the phrase signalling her anxiety at the speed of Horace's movement to another agenda item. She uses an interrogative and politeness modal to interrupt, "can I ask two questions on this?" but it is interesting that Horace gives an affirmative "yes" to what seems to be intended as a rhetorical question (because she in fact continues with her question at the same time) and thus effectively gives her permission to speak presumably acknowledging his right to do this. Margaret further interrupts his reply with another question on class sizes and the lack of consultation with staff, and her anxiety suggests a threat of confrontation (DH23). Horace deals with this challenge by using the passive construction of the verb "I've been told" which he repeats syntactically thus distancing himself from the received information. But Margaret again interrupts his repetition with an assertive declarative and deictic "Once again here is a major thing that's happening . . ." during which Horace attempts unsuccessfully to interrupt her and regain the topic(DH25).

Horace explains the timetabling situation which has resulted in the large class sizes, using statives and figures to illustrate his point (DH26), but also, in referring to the senior manager in charge of the timetable, his collocation of "his ability" and "very limited" distances himself from the decision to use larger classes to deal with the staffing shortfall. He is again challenged by Margaret on the topic of the number of Spanish groups timetabled and he uses pause fillers "erm erm" followed by a lengthy hesitational pause before again using the passive construction "there's been no debate" which also has a distancing effect.(DH28). Margaret's continued interruptions and challenging interrogatives lead to Horace handling the crisis by removing the recording (DH30).

During the discussion of the agenda item on Year 10 Induction Day, which had been interrupted by Margaret's concerns, Horace gives out information and he cuts short further discussion on how this will personally affect staff with the assertive "Year 10 is a non-story" which acts as a decisive judgement which prevents further discussion. Horace also makes his feelings clear during the following item on Open Day for the new building. He declares that he does not know whether this is under Directed Time, ie. that the staff are required by contract to spend the time there. When Nony asks directly "So they can't make us come in that evening?" Horace replies with the comment "I'm sure that if you've got a theatre visit already arranged as I have" suggesting a shared understanding of Horace's underlying meaning rather than his surface syntactical implication (DH34). Nony's supportive interruption in response indicates that this hidden meaning has been received. Both are aware that they are suggesting "bucking the system". It also suggests that there are tensions for Horace in his perception of his role in the system and that in this case he identifies with the managees rather than the managers.

However when Celia suggests a way of coping with the situation (a rota system) and expresses this as if it had been Horace's own idea ("are you saying that . . . ?" (DH36), Horace responds positively ("an excellent idea Celia") and then implies that he was about to say the same, "you have jumped two sentences ahead of me." (DH37) Again the semantic implications here suggest a shared understanding of the participants in the discourse over and above the syntactical and surface meaning. When Margaret laughs at the implication Horace confronts the second level understanding and adds a humorous comment perhaps to lighten the atmosphere.

Horace uses declaratives as he informs the team of the proposals for the Open Day but then uses emotive expressions which convey his own feelings, "post-Dunblane security implications" and "allowing any Tom Dick or Harry to walk around the school" (DH38). His distancing comment "Nobody as far as I'm aware has thought of . . ." is continued in the shared acceptance that a third party makes the decisions here when he responds to Nony's question as to whether they can veto the decision with "I dunno" and "I don't think so" (DH39-42)

The discussion continues with dissention about the arrangements for the day and the consensus seems to be in accord with Horace's views. He makes suggestions about how they might cope with the situation using conditionals "if you don't want" and modals "that should" rather than instructional imperatives or statives. He is also implying disagreement with the senior management's decisions in consensus with his team. He then uses the assertive "Right let's move on" to halt the quite heated discussion and mark a new section of discourse.

When Margaret again makes a critical comment, this time on the absence of exercise books in stock, Horace deals with this by using the passive construction again, "the exercise book order is being followed up" which distances himself from the critical situation and he then uses reported speech "he said they should have . . ." (DH45) which involves the third party in that situation and thus takes some of the heat off himself.

At this point Margaret again becomes agitated about an incident with a senior member of staff and uses the imperative, "you'd better turn this bloody thing off" referring to the tape recorder. Horace indicates agreement with her demand and during this critical incident the tape recorder was not running, while confidential comments are made off the record. Again there seems to be a tension here for Horace in his role as middle manager.

Horace then returns to the agenda item on the NPRA list. He uses declaratives as he conveys the information about the pupils named on the list. He is the only one with access to this information. The interrogative at the end (DH46) uses "all" and therefore implies that he expects a unity of reaction. However, there is some querying of names on the list and colleagues begin to speak together and Horace uses an imperative to restore order, "hang on hang on", which is repeated as he tries to explain the nature and origins of the list, with some hesitancy features apparent (DH48). He uses statives and subordinate clauses within a complex sentence structure as he explains this and then gives a detailed example of how the principle would work. He is interrupted by Celia who is questioning the inclusion of one pupil and Horace responds by referring to a third party who had recommended the pupil for the list. When Celia insists, Horace concedes with "OK. Right." and accepts the objection with a stative "I'll make a note on this" although he adds a defensive "all I said was". He then continues with a declarative assertion about his future action "I'll submit this memo". The overlaps and interruption which follow are dealt with by Horace returning to a syntactical repetition of his previous interrogative requesting suggestions, and again with a declarative which asserts his future action "I will update this" and the request for confirmation "OK?" (DH59)

Horace draws the meeting to a close with an assertive declaration of his response to a concern expressed with regard to the continuing of the exchange visits, "I would be inclined for you to stand back . . ." (DH61) which is also a syntactical and lexical repetition of the comment from Margaret ("we thought we might stand back"). He signals the end of the meeting with "Right" although general informal discussion of the issues breaks out again as people leave.

Conclusions

This meeting is characterised by many "aside" discussions involving arguments and dissent, marked linguistically by overlaps and interruptions, mostly off the record of this transcript. The transcript shows a number of critical incidents mainly involving Margaret and we can see a clear pattern of technique in Horace's crisis management.

One line he takes is that of distancing himself from the decision at the heart of the crisis. For instance when Margaret questions decisions on class sizes and the number of Spanish groups and is clearly concerned about lack of consultation with staff on issues which will have a direct and practical implication for staff, he uses passive constructions such as "I've been told . . ." and "there's been no debate about that." The use of the passive has the effect of removing the onus of responsibility from the speaker.

He also at times names a third party and gives a report of the indirect and direct speech of the exchanges. This also tends to convey a distancing from the decision and an implication of disapproval, as in the items about the Year 12 Induction arrangements and the missing exercise books. During the discussion of the Open Day both the direct use of emotive language and the use of shared implicit understanding conveys an acceptance of the role of a third party in the decision-making and of a feeling of detachment from, indeed exclusion from, the decision-making process.

Twice during critical incidents, the tape recorder is turned off, thus marking the tension which has arisen and the threat felt by the recording of clearly critical and potentially damaging remarks. There is an identified tension between the strategic and the operational policy-makers here. Horace, as a middle manager, is caught in the tension of needing to convey information from the strategic policy-makers to those who will be carrying out those policies in practice and to try to supervise the operation of those policies which he sometimes does not agree with. During the discussion on the Open Day his comments implied that he placed his allegience with the team members rather than with the SMT policy decision.

At the same time, he asserts his authority over the team by using linguistic strategies such as statives where he is conveying information to which only he has access, assertive declaratives where he is indicating his approach or future actions. He also has to restore order when the aside discussions among members of the Faculty become intrusive and disruptive to the continuance of the meeting. His ideolect which seems marked by rapid speech with few pauses, pause fillers, and long compound-complex syntactical units, creates an atmosphere of tension which is exacerbated by the emotive content of a number of speech items. Horace tends to respond to most of the comments of the staff himself, as the key person present, and there are few occasions where others hold the floor. Consensus is apparent mainly where the staff are agreeing with Horace's disapproval of arrangements for the Open Day.

Strategies used by Horace imply a domination function, but with the additional element of competitiveness which is seen in the tension arising from the conflict between strategic and operational management. There are few examples of supportive or facilitating linguistic features, nor a sense of encouraging rapport among the team except where Horace is identifying himself with the Faculty members as opposed to the SMT. The structure of the discourse is characterised by question and answer two-part exchange format rather than expounding and discursive, as with a full IRF structure, and this suggests a control strategy where a more open forum is less well tolerated. This reflects the masculine frame/schema which is being brought to this context.

Droverslea—Head of Humanities—Isabel

This faculty meeting took place after the end of the school day as usual, and began after a general informal chat as members of the team arrived, some of them having had to travel from the other site. There were ten members of staff present, seven women, including the Head of Faculty, Isabel, and three men, who comprised two Heads of Year and a Deputy Head. There was a policy of rotation of Chair as with the English faculty at this school, and in this case it fell to Mark, the Deputy Head to chair the meeting.

A full printed agenda was issued before the day and included items on the following: a report from the Staff Development Committee, Year 7 merit certificates—a working party report, Year 7 field trip—final arrangements and information, Key Stage 4 INSET days—arranging dates, and the allocation of a Faculty A allowance.

TRANSCRIPTION

I—Isabel
JA—Jackie
JE—Jenny
L—Lynda
C—Carol
H—Heather
CE—Celia
M—Mark
ME—Melvyn
K—Keith

DI1 *M: Isabel invited me to chair the meeting so I will oblige . . . Right, we'll try to keep to some kind of time. The first item on the agenda should be apologies. Do we have any apologies?]*

DI2 *I:] Can somebody do the Minutes please because er Judith's on camp, so there's no-one to do the Minutes?*

(murmur)

DI3 *I: Thank you Carol*

(Mark continues with the Apologies)

DI4 *M: OK, so the Minutes of the last meeting. You've all read them. So they are a true record, yes?*

DI5 *I:] Matters arising?*

DI6 *M: Matters arising. (continues with these items) Any matters on there? So everybody OK? All approved?*

DI7 *I: Just a point of information on Key Stage 4 er the Finance Committee has agreed to give Humanities £3000 to fund Key Stage 4 courses. I asked for double that but I was very grateful to get 3000 because nobody else got anything at all.*

(JA gives a long report on Year 7 merit certificates and feedback on processes, discussion of layout of cards—whether there are to be separate columns for effort and attainment)

DI8 *I: But why is there an argument? I think it encourages them to be more self reflective about their own ability. I'm happy with it as it is.*

(Mark calls for feeling of the meeting and concludes that it will stay as it is.)

DI9 *I: And once they—can I just ask a question—once they've—if they go off to the left, the three subject certificates, they can't then go back and do the other one, can they?*

DI10 *JA: It was an either/ or situation really.*

DI11 *I: Right. Right. OK.*

(The discussion then continues with the agenda item on Year 7 Field Trips)

DI12 *I: I still need to know which are the free places. (goes through the list of classes and names and requests information from the staff about names) Right, that's OK, I'm now able to start booking. Coaches are booked anyway. Um I set out a provisional day for it. I still recommend that we go to the church first because that's the shorter visit. That gets that over and done with—I've booked the church to arrive by ten and to be out by eleven. Um I've also booked T . . . Cavern so that we're there round about quarter past eleven and so that we go down the cavern and out again before lunch. Then it's up to us where we have lunch—we could either get the coach, go back down into C . . . , walk the kids up to P . . . Castle, get them in the castle before one o' clock and then be locked in . . . or . . . take our time and arrive at P . . . Castle at two after having had lunch probably around T . . . Cavern actually—they could be doing their panoramic view—there's a cafe there]*

DI13 *H:] There's quite a bit of space there]*

DI14 *I:] There's quite a bit isn't there there.*

DI15 *H: And if its raining]*

DI16 *I:] yeah there's a bit of cover, there's a cafe. I thought the T would be easiest actually to have lunch, have a wonder, have a wander round then a field sketch, then come back down to the castle for two, round the castle, back on the coach for quarter past three, back here by quarter to four. Same as last year but reverse order because I think the church in the afternoon was the difficult bit last year . . . (2) Is that alright, does that sound OK to everybody? I'm going to try to make sure that—now, Lynda and Mark, you didn't go last year—but I'm going to try to put people with their own form that they teach, same as last year, try and get Year*

12 helpers, same as last year . . . and everything else is basically the same. Anybody got anything to say—please don't do this or please can we do this? (follows some comments about dates and various pupils who cannot make certain dates)

DI17 *I: Right, well write them down then for me and say]*

DI18 *M:] What's the fifth of July then?*

DI19 *I: Nothing they'll be on holiday. If they give you advance warning—you see the trouble is basically if you slot them in with another tutor group they don't like it—they're Year 7s so they get all mardy about being on their own.*

DI20 *M: OK? All right about those arrangements then?*

DI21 *I: That alright?*

DI22 *M: Any questions? OK? Nobody else? Fine. Move on then please.*

(organising dates for Key Stage 4 INSETs)

DI23 *I: OK. Take the Historians first then. Haven't got Jane here. Days when we don't need cover. Haven't got Liz here either.*

DI24 *K: Am I an RE person?*

DI25 *I: Er er if you've agreed to do, which I think you have, I've been told that you have. Yes you are. Right so you're arranging with Celia then . . . (3)*

DI26 *JA: It might be easier to do this with the timetables and we haven't got them at the moment and then we can sit down and work it out from that]*

DI27 *I:] Well, can we just arrange to do that informally then because I think Lynda would I be wrong in saying that we are entitled to if we can to have a day if it doesn't cost us much cover?*

DI28 *L: Yes OK.*

DI29 *I: That OK? . . . So we can all find a mutual day that can be used to er can we do that informally?*

(discussion with Lynda, who is in charge of arranging cover, about the advisability of selecting two half days rather than a whole day)

DI30 *I: So could we look for two half days then within the next three—well within three weeks after whitsun—do that informally.*

(discussion about convenors)

DI31 *I: (to Lynda) I'm letting you know the History days two days, two half days, Jackie will let you know the Geography, and er Celia will let you know the RE. OK?*

DI32 *M: All happy? All sorted? Before we get bogged down. Item 7—discussion of faculty A allowance released by Jenny since Easter.* **DI33** *JE: I wasn't paid up to Easter, so it was released before that.*

DI34 *I: It was released in September. But it now falls—it would have come back to you, but it hasn't come back to you so there is a Faculty A allowance. Right, if you remember at the very beginning when the Faculty was set up there were two A allowances, were there not? A B allowance which is Celia's, yes, well, two B's cause one was Ian's, there's the C allowance which is Jane's and there was the D allowance which was Muriel's. Now the . . . one A allowance has been incorporated into Jane's protected B, OK? er and there's one A allowance which Jenny has rescinded, so in theory there is a Faculty A allowance which the original job description was a cross-curricular one, or a cross—Faculty one, but which in reality when Jenny held it was essentially Geography, was it not?*

DI35 *JE: Yes*

DI36 *I: Now according to (Headteacher) all Faculty allowances have to be distributed according to discussion with the Faculty, therefore I'm raising the issue of how people would like to see the Faculty allowance distributed or allocated or what we would want to do with it. If we don't do something with it it will disappear, it will be snapped up, quickly, um . . .*

(Discussion of responsibilities in the Faculty, Keith suggests a temporary allowance for specific projects)

DI37 *L: (to Isabel) Do you feel there are any gaps other than that you've just mentioned?*

DI38 *I: I feel that . . . displays? is an area, IT is an area, I think the card system is an area which becomes more onerous each term, does it not? Recording is an area um there are an awful lot which at the moment, you know are just being done generally by Jackie or by or not being done. I think there are a whole host—IT—I think one of the things that I would like to see is that because I end up being based so much on the other site because of Sociology because of A level would be somebody to take responsibility for the block as it were, this block—as in take on all kinds of um . . . areas when I'm not here, when Jackie's not here, which to a large extent is already being done . . . I think the problem of looking after the IT room when it's completed, which should be by September, is another issue and resources in general on the lower site . . . I'm also aware of RE but it's problematic because of Jane being (unclear). I'm also aware of Carol being on a protected allowance now for cross-curricular, which in effect ceases to* *exist . . . And I'm also frightened that that allowance will get eaten up if it doesn't get allocated.*

DI39 *M: What I would suggest as there doesn't seem to be an overwhelming feeling of um an ageement so could I suggest that we actually ask Isabel to prepare a short but clearly driven report on where she thinks the priorities for spending that money should be (suggestion basically summing up previous idea from Keith.) So is that a suggestion which is generally approved?*

DI40 *I: I'm in a bit of a quandry about it , I mean to a certain extent there are a whole host of administrative things which I can put on the job description. I'm also keenly aware of the fact that the whole thing because of the need to discuss it and put it open for you know someone to apply for makes it necessary for people to discuss it , but at the end of the day there are many many jobs that need to get done which are at the moment getting done by one or two people—um—and as such I'd like to move it on but I don't want anyone to say or think it's been done behind people's backs, that it's being done by allocating it to—the easiest thing is simply to incorporate it into someone else's already protected allowance er which keeps it there and then see what that person is willing to do and shunt everyone else's job description round . . . that would be the easiest thing or to get everybody round a table who holds a faculty responsibility and reissue them every year—that would be the most democratic way of working—it isn't always the easiest though.*

(discussion of ideas)

DI41 *I: It sounds like people are in agreement then with the job description put together around lower school site. Can I do that then? Put it round for discussion and then if there are no objections then can I just take it that the job description just goes up and people apply for it.*

(a number of information items from Isabel to the faculty members from other people)

DI42 *I: Anyway, thank you for the hard work that goes into the reports. Any other business? Can everybody please notice the reminder on there the faculty end of year er] do*

DI43 *M:] eh eh*

DI44 *I: Oh I'm sorry.*

DI45 *M: Any other business ?*

DI46 *I: Oh er numbers—provisional numbers for Key Stage 4. We appear to be having a very depressing 233 I was given out of the year group of 265.*

Now you had 9 forms coming in, didn't you, so that's 25 pupils that have not opted to do History or Geography or Humanities. (information about numbers in groups) 31 is unacceptable at GCSE.
(discussion of numbers and other items from Mark)
DI47 *M: Thank you very much then. Meeting closed at 14 minutes past 5.*
DI48 *I: Thank you.*

ANALYSIS

Mark, in fact, opens the meeting as he is chairing this time, rather than Isabel. However, Isabel abuts his request for Apologies with an interrogative used as an implied imperative to the general audience requesting someone to do the minutes (DI 2). Her interruption there indicates her role as Head, in the sense of the one most responsible for the smooth-running of the meeting despite Mark being in the Chair. She also is the one to thank the volunteer. Isabel then seems to prompt Mark about "matters arising" (DI 5) and Mark repeats this before continuing to outline the items. The prompt could either represent a "control prompt" which checks that Mark includes this item, or it could be an attempt to hurry the agenda along. It marks the control function of Isabel's management strategy.

One characteristic of this meeting is that Isabel provides a large amount of information to the others. She begins this by conveying information about funding for Key Stage 4 Humanities from the Finance Committee. She has access to this information but she also has clearly had an input into the securing of that funding. She uses the first person pronoun and active verbs "I asked for", "I was very grateful" to show her involvement and this, especially as she compares this with the lack of funding to other faculties, gives the impression of an active and successful leader (DI 7).

After the long report from Jackie on Year 7 merit certificates and a detailed discussion on the design of the cards, whether there are to be separate columns for effort and attainment, Isabel makes her standpoint clear with firstly an interrogative headed by a dysjunction indicating disagreement, "But why is there an argument?" Then using statives and declaratives she asserts her opinion, "I think it encourages them", "I'm happy with it". At this point, when Mark calls for the feeling of the meeting, the members of the team make supportive minimal responses, agreeing with Isabel.

Isabel clarifies the procedure with the merit certificates with Jackie (DI 9) using a politeness insert and weakener ("can I just ask a question?") interrupting her own interrogative, and then uses a conditional to set a scenario, after which she adds a tag question ("can they?") for the confirmation of her own interpretation. Jackie confirms it and Isabel uses affirmative minimal responses "Right. Right. OK" to signal that confirmation and to end this section of discourse.

As the agenda is moved on to the Year 7 field trips, Isabel uses a number of strong active declaratives, starting with one which in fact has an implied imperative function, "I still need to know" (DI 12) and continuing with verbs which state her actions, "I'm now able", "I've set out", "I've booked". She continues with the issuing of information by outlining the sequence of events which make up the day's programme. Although she declares her opinion in "I still recommend that we go to the church first", which implies an opportunity for discussion on this point, she then negates that by declaring "I've booked the church to arrive by ten". She does give some opportunity for discussion of arrangements where she uses the modal "we could either get the coach" and provides an alternative "or . . . (we could) take our time", and Heather takes the opportunity to comment with an interruption although that interruption in fact adds supportively to Isabel's own comment. Isabel interrupts back again albeit supportively with syntactical repetition and then again in answer to Heather's second comment, a conditional, where she continues the idea begun by Heather, "And if it's raining . . ."] "yeah there's a bit of cover, there's a cafe" (DI 16)

As Isabel sketches out the day's programme, she uses abbreviated clauses without pronouns, in telegraphic style, "have a wander round, then a field sketch", apart from occasions when she expresses her own opinion such as "because I think the church . . ." After a pause she then uses a direct interrogative informally to confirm the arrangements with her colleagues, "Is that alright, does that sound OK to everybody?" She then continues with a series of active stative verbs which indicate her actions, "I'm going to try . . ." which she repeats. After this, she requests feedback with suggested questions using politeness forms, "please don't do this . . ."

Mark interrupts with a request for clarification and Isabel gives a brief direct reply "Nothing, they'll be on holiday" before continuing her outlining of arrangements. Her speech again is in telegraphic style when she is organising dates for INSETs. There is an absence of pronouns which again sounds abrupt but gives the impression of decisiveness, "Haven't got Jane here" (DI 23) She responds to a request for information with firstly an opinion which rapidly becomes confirmed with a passive construction and then with an affirmative, " . . . which I think you have, I've been told that you have. Yes you are. Right so . . ." DI 25)

Isabel accepts a suggestion from Jackie that arrangements for INSET dates are done informally and concludes this part of the discourse with a modal interrogative which functions as an imperative and contains the inclusive pronoun "we" which creates a feeling of unity, "So could we look for two half days then . . ." (DI 30) She uses a stative to inform of her actions, "I'm letting you know", then statives which function as imperatives to the people concerned, "Jackie will let you know . . .", "Celia will let you know . . ." (DI 31)

The next item on the agenda, the released faculty A allowance, is introduced by Isabel and an explanation of the situation is signalled by her with "Right" (DI 34) She uses expressions here as affective tag questions, albeit rhetorical, in order to check that staff are following the explanation, "were there not?", "OK?" and "was it not?" This type of expression also suggests an idiom in Isabel's idiolect as she uses a similar construction in DI 38 "does it not?" Within this explanation, and in the discussion which ensues, Isabel uses many statives, typical of informative language, but she also uses first person declaratives to express her own actions and thoughts and feelings, "I'm raising the issue", I feel", "I think" (DI 38), and she repeats the phrase "I'm also aware of" which shows her perception of problems and suggests a pro-active approach. She appears to be brainstorming ideas here and exploring the possibilities for the use of the faculty A allowance, but there is a strength of lexical and syntactical patterning here which has the effect of creating a decisive rhythm while she puts forward a large number of ideas for consideration. She uses a number of professional jargon terms, such as "an area", "recording", "protected allowance", "cross-curricular", and more formal lexis such as "an issue", "problematic", "allocated". This lends weight to her explorations and is picked up by Mark in his summative comment requesting that Isabel prepares a "short but clearly driven report" on priorities. But Isabel returns to the subject even then with a declaration of her difficulty in decision making here, "I'm in a bit of a quandry about it" (DI 40) She expresses a concern, "I don't want anyone to say or think it's been done behind people's backs", which suggests both her own hesitancy with the decision and also her desire for unity and consensus. She uses emotive lexis which indicate her own feelings, "easiest" and "most democratic" and reflect judgements, then opens it up to discussion again having clearly not accepted Mark's summation and suggestion. Again, the control function is apparent.

Her own summation, "It sounds like people are in agreement with . . ." (DI 41) reflects her desire for a consensus as she sums up the feeling of the meeting. She uses the interrogative to clarify and reinforce her future action, "Can I do that then?" repeated syntactically in "can I just take it that . . ." where the function is in fact declarative.

Isabel passes on a number of items of information towards the close of the meeting and then uses the politeness marker "thank you for the hard work . . ." where this also reasserts her own status. She immediately assumes the role of the Chair by asking "Any other business?" but Mark interrupts her with "eh eh" to take back the role assigned to him, and she apologises showing an implicit understanding of the semantic implication here, whereupon he repeats her phrase in his role as Chair.

As the meeting draws to a close, Isabel uses the decisive stative "31 is unacceptable at GCSE" when discussing numbers in Humanities groups. It is Mark who closes the meeting but Isabel adds the politeness marker "thank you" to signal the ending of the meeting.

Conclusions

An important facet of this meeting is that Isabel is providing a great deal of information to her colleagues. This means that she is likely to use statives and declaratives as she outlines these agenda items and reinforces her role as middle manager, one of whose functions is to gain access to information and to disseminate it to others. She is also able to explain items in full to the rest of the faculty (as in DI 34).

She therefore uses topic control, first person statives, declaratives, as with the previous managers. She also uses softeners, professional jargon and supportive strategies as seen before, especially with Clive and Liz. These features are emerging as similarities between managers regardless of sex.

However, Isabel is also aware of her role as leader by the way she at times takes over Mark's role as Chair (DI 2, 5, 42). She prompts him too which could indicate "control prompts" in which she is not letting go of the role of the one in charge of the progress of the meeting, even though it is her own policy to circulate the job of chairing the meetings.

She uses statives to assert her feelings and opinions, "I think that", "I feel", "I'm happy with it as it is" and there is frequent use of the first person pronoun "I" throughout her speech items. There is notably no opposition and no evidence of critical incident and therefore no examples of Isabel's crisis management. There are few minimal responses "Right", "OK", but there are supportive interruptions both to and from Isabel, for example in DI 13-16. The tone of the proceedings is purposeful and businesslike. This is reflected in the telegraphic style of speech which Isabel sometimes assumes (DI 16).

Isabel uses active verbs with the first person pronoun frequently, as in "I asked for", "I set out", "I've booked", which indicate her actions and demands as a faculty head. This reflects a role as a manager who is active in organising faculty work, on this occasion field trips, where this is not delegated to another member of the team, and who is active in making demands on behalf of the faculty, in this case for resources. This appears to be a "hands-on", involved middle manager, who controls the day-to-day processes of the faculty and monitors different aspects of its running. This reflects the feminine frame/schema brought to conversations, where the participation in team work and the relationship-building which this entails are of paramount importance.

Isabel reflects a management functioning as organiser, spokesperson, intermediary between the team and senior management, director of tasks within the faculty and controlling the process of those tasks. In terms of Mintzberg's (1973) managerial roles, Isabel shows in this meeting that she fulfills all the informational roles as monitor, disseminator, and spokesperson, some of the interpersonal roles as leader and liaison operator, and some of the decisional roles as resource allocator and negotiator.

Linguistically she uses speech strategies which reflect all of these. She also shows that she is concerned to achieve a consensus and unity in the way that she employs politeness forms, interrogatives and statives functioning as imperatives, and direct questions to appeal for support, "Is that alright?" "OK?" "It sounds like people are in agreement", "can I do that then?" and "were there not?" Isabel's linguistic strategies imply a control function, although not overtly a domination function since there are empowering and cooperation strategies apparent also. These findings can be compared to Clive (Droverslea); for both, the use of strong declaratives and statements of opinion reinforce the authority status of the manager. Like Clive, Isabel seems concerned to achieve consensus but marks the authority status strongly, thus suggesting an incipient domination function. Isabel displays a number of masculine linguistic traits, which suggests a more masculine frame/schema, but clearly there is evidence of a strong feminine frame also in the empowering and cooperation strategies she manifests.

Summary

In this chapter, I have transcribed key areas of four meetings in the first school studied (Droverslea), focusing on events which demonstrate the middle manager's use of linguistic strategies in order to: establish status, deal with critical incidents / handle conflicts, and make decisions. I have analysed these linguistic events in commentary form for each manager, then drawn conclusions about that manager's linguistic usage at the end of each commentary. I have begun to identify emerging themes which I explore, analyse and develop further in chapter 8.

The patterns which I am identifying in my first four transcripts are as follows:

- that there are patterns of similarity, regardless of sex, in topic control, use of statives/declaratives, use of first person statives, use of softeners, use of professional jargon, use of supportive interruptions.
- that although managers were themselves interrupted, regardless of sex, these interruptions were handled differently by men and women.
- in establishing status, male managers tended to hold the floor, use imperatives, use the passive voice and retain tensions.
- in establishing status, female managers tended to use empowerment of others, supportive strategies, organisational strategies, business-like register, and the active voice.
- in handling conflict, male managers tended to use imperatives, distancing strategies, dismissive tone.
- in handling conflict, female managers tended to deflect conflicts rather than resolve them, use apologies, accept correction. in decision-making, male managers tended to use imperatives and floor dominance.
- in decision-making, female managers tended to use cooperation and consensus strategies, summarising and inclusive pronouns.

There was a high level of empowerment shown by both men and women towards their team members, but there were additional masculine strategies of domination and control for both men. It is interesting to note the incipient domination function of both Clive **and** Isabel, despite the focus on empowerment in both cases. Horace manifested fewer supportive and empowerment strategies, and more tension in crisis management, revealing his own conflicts between strategic and operational management positions. Liz, on the other hand, demonstrated a high level of empowerment strategies, softeners and politeness forms, and a focus on defusing conflict. All used the basic IRF discourse structure but with differing emphases which reflected the gendered frame/schema brought to the situation: Clive and Horace focused on the personal feedback, and Isabel on both response and feedback, while Liz for much of the time focused on the response from others.

The research question was whether there are gender differences in the way that middle managers speak to their team in meetings and whether there are gender similarities which might indicate other linguistic frames. The emerging patterns in my data indicate that there are linguistic strategies common to middle managers, whether men or women: the "middle manager-speak", or sociolect, associated with the role and expectations both of and towards the middle manager in a team meeting context. The "Community of Practice" operating here shapes the pragmatic understandings of the "core members" at this level, the managers, and is acknowledged by the "peripheral members", the team members at the meeting. However, the managers are also participants in another group or community of practice, the gender group, and this cues in other linguistic strategies, those associated with that particular gender and could be said to be shaped by the frame or schema which exists outside of the meeting but which is also brought to it. In these case studies of four managers, two male and two female, patterns indicate replications of the discovered phenomena in terms of similarities and differences between men and women in one school.

Chapters 6, 7 and 8 now develop chronologically as I test the emerging patterns and the hypothesis in a different organisational culture.

CHAPTER SEVEN

HOW DID THESE FINDINGS COMPARE WITH OTHER SCHOOLS?

Introduction

In chapter 6, I looked at one school (Droverslea) and identified a number of patterns emerging from an analysis of the data. I found that there were gender differences in linguistic strategies used but also similarities in the way in which managers of both sexes approached their meetings linguistically, in other words a common language of management. In this chapter, in order to test these, I transcribe and analyse in the same way two meetings from the second school (High Ridge), using a male and a female manager: Chris (Head of Science) and Sally (Head of Year 8 pastoral team). The process is set out in the table below.

Table 17: chronology of the analysis process for the second school
(High Ridge)

subject	activity	
Chris (High Ridge)	*	audio-recorded meeting + fieldnotes
	*	reviewed cassette, selected key areas for transcription (establishing status; dealing with critical incidents; handling conflict; making decisions)
	*	transcribed key areas of meeting
	*	annotated transcript /analysis
	*	wrote analysis—commentary form
	*	wrote conclusion, focusing on gender linguistic issues

Sally (High Ridge)	recording—process as above transcription/analysis—process as above
Chris	testing patterns emerging for linguistic traits—gender differences and similarities
Sally	testing of comparative patterns emerging for linguistic traits—gender differences and similarities assessing linguistic effects of different organisational cultures of Droverslea and High Ridge

HIGH RIDGE SCHOOL

High Ridge—Head of Science—Chris

This faculty meeting took place as usual after the end of the school day and was preceded by general informal chat as people arrived and made themselves a cup of coffee. There were nine members of the team present, two men including the Head of Faculty, and seven women. Eddie, the only other male member of staff other than the Head, was a young fairly new member of staff. Deirdre, Barbara and Judith were long-standing members of the team.

The agenda, which was not published in advance, included examination results, problem pupils, tackling a new syllabus, and INSET arrangements.

TRANSCRIPTION

C—Chris
E—Eddie
G—Glenda
F—Fiona
H—Heather
D—Deirdre
B—Barbara
J—Judith
A—Andrea

(As people arrive and settle down with informal chat, Chris gives out papers to each person round the table.)

HC1 *C: All right . . . (name) sends her apologies. (indistinct asides) OK. I haven't told you before but . . . (introduces researcher) and part of her research involves research into faculty meetings. (indistinct on recording) Right, the second apology. I'm sorry none of this stuff went out to you before today um that wasn't part of our design, that happened and I felt that if I gave you an awful lot of stuff without spending time going through some of the most important details of the stuff it would be (indistinct) The third point I have to make is probably to you people like (names) in that I want to spend a fair bit of the meeting time going through the process whereby we arrive at estimated grades. I think it really is a very important feature it's something that's certainly at the top of my mind and I've just been asked by (name) for estimated grades for our Year 11. I'd like to start by doing just that by examining the process, we can (indistinct). The first set of papers you have . . . briefly, reminds us of our er wonderful wonderful success at GCSE—of course it's some time—yes? (interrupted by an indistinct question from Barbara) I don't really want to dwell on that um I don't want to dwell on that having done it already um we don't get any satisfaction going through it again but er the thing is if you match estimated grade performance against real performance this is real performance here, the two were very very close and er I say that to add some considerable weight and strength ability to this er process of going through estimated grades I would worry if the real performance didn't match the estimated performance, on this occasion it did.*

(Chris continues a long turn amounting to another 15 minutes where he illustrates his points using the overhead projector (OHP) showing the results and statistics, and expounds them, without interruption from any of the staff, except where Judith asks, during one of Chris' pauses, "Could I just ask a question please?" to which Chris answers "By all means" and answers with factual information. This long turn consists of informational statives and deictics, such as "This column shows", "on this sheet you find", "you'll see from these figures", "one result of this is . . .")

1-256

(Chris passes out lists of students "to show you the process")

HC2 *C: There are two sheets the same in that one. The group you see now are D4—it's the group that will undoubtedly make or break our exam results. They are the students that Deirdre and Judith drive.*

(Chris continues with demonstration and exposition)

HC3 *C: I've done it as the worst case scenario. It's the sheet that's labelled. I've drawn the line in making the estimates at 25? 26, 27 is it? 28? I haven't investigated A* at this stage. I don't think it's the right thing to do. There are people who are getting an average 23 who get a grade A. All I want us to do is to talk to the students who see themselves below 25, 24, 23 and say to them this is do-able. This is is without doubt you know all of these sheets, and I think it is worthwhile sharing these sheets with pupils, all of these sheets have demonstrated that—it's not you as a teacher you know having some gut feeling about a particular student, you know there's some good hard real evidence to support that notion. Our worst case scenario on our performance next year in—er] sorry?*

HC4 *J:] Can I ask a question? (indistinct question about normal distribution)]*

HC5 *C:] I I knew you'd ask that about getting a normal distribution at the end I have done that I I I have and and what (indistinct quick speech) I have shifted that there—quite a normal distribution here and what is interesting is that you're going to actually get quite a good distribution here. Now we know from last year that that distribution has shifted even more from that C middle up through to that B and A*. Now that doesn't show if that's based on you know the worst case scenario this will go down, this will go up and this certainly will continue to shift. (continues) The important thing that I will ask you to do is to share these results with your students. You might need to do it in a sensible sensitive way because for some of them it will be the first time that anybody has said it—now you can't conceal from some students the fact that you are now saying a grade D rather than a grade C—and and you have to do it sensitively and if we don't do it at this stage I think for one thing we're taking this under false pretences and try to do the sort of thing (indistinct) talk with the students talk with the students for whom we are predicting grade D*

(continues with an off record confidential comment comparing with other curriculum areas)

300-363

HC6 *D: Right you know you did a letter to send to parents when pupils are under performing—I did one last year about pupils' attendance if it's noticeable over several lessons over three weeks then]*

HC7 *C:] (both talk simultaneously-indistinct) Could—I mean when we talk about letters home please don't do it alone, come and talk to us about it (indistinct0 er in the communication process there may be occasions when a particular letter may not be appropriate for a particular child. The last item is something which was very much on my mind at the end of last year and if I don't do it now as being an important thought—um it'll escape me (murmur)*

HC8 *B: Can I just say something?*

HC9 *C: Yes*

HC10 *B: I've got Year 11 S2 again for the successive year actually and even though their estimated grades are between E and G—er is there anyone else in a similar position having the same group]*

HC11 *C:] er I haven't*

HC12 *B:] I found it really useful last year]*

HC13 *C:] I haven't got my book with me yes I mean its yes . . . I've got a lot of concerns in year 11 about a lot of students who are playing hell who I'm going to talk to, I'll talk to the Heads of Year and I'm going to start flagging them up because there are problems. What I'll ask from you please is to let me have as soon as possible a short list of please don't make it any more than three names OK four names, I can't do many, of real concerns, concerns that are on overall academic performance. They might be concerns that the person is simply not doing the business not actually going to achieve a great deal.It might be a concern and I think this could be widely the case where you have students stopping other students er if there are any othe rproblems or concerns I don't want to get embroiled in the naughty boy silly girl syndrome er I only do want to attack a dozen cases in Year 12 and Year 10 and I do want to think of strategies for dealing with these first—you may not have them D1 may not have them er D3 certainly has D2 I would imagine—D4—driving it—performing out of their skin*

HC14 *D: What's the deadline for this?*

HC15 *C: if—er er if—now now now we're chasing it if I could do it sooner rather than later, Deirdre. I've left the man aware er let(name of Head of Year) know er is aware er I think he imagines all's quiet on the western front]*

HC16 *J:]How will you tell the students?*

HC17 *C: How will I . . . ?*

HC18 *J: How are you going to introduce this?*

HC19 *C: er I'm not really sure er if you know if er you have any any um any thoughts around this er bring them up, but I don't want to go down the er let's kick them some more route because kicking them hasn't worked I don't really want to go down the route that says well let's stick em on a limb somewhere and exclude them unless we have to but I feel if we don't um make a start on treating this as a big issue the game will get away with us and . . . so the sooner we can identify in real terms er these students we we had er about 30 names did appear at one time er . . . that is a priority—to identify—now we've got some way of doing that certainly did last year in Year 10—I wonder if the list is the same—(1) give me the names of the students who are stopping you doing your job . . . you do your jobs wonderfully well but . . . (unclear) I'm sorry I've taken a lot of time to do that but er it has come out er we'll just be a little bit short on part two three and four er but part two really is er where hopefully if you'd feel able just to tell me er where it's at because I must confess at the moment one of the problems I have is er knowing just where it's ocurring in Year 10, just where it's at. (2) I know there are lots of small classes (4) ooh er I meanwhile er Barbara just talk us through here—some of the things Barbara's started to do she's done (indistinct) to try to get over this massive problem that you're facing*

HC20 *B: (2) Right. er you've caught me on the hop there]*

HC21 *C:] I'm sorry but I'm*

HC22 *B:] Right um what we did really was that we sorted out the scheme of work and divided it into suitable lessons and single lessons and then allocated a particular lesson to a particular person to take responsibility for that person to ensure that they completed it er the set work so we had an actual plan right through the module and so that we'd got the resource material for those lessons. (continues to report on work done with in planning a scheme of work)*

(an aside comment from Eddie)

HC23 *C: Come on we really have got to get our heads round this one because believe you me er I can spot them a mile off I'm sure you can as well and this is going to cause massive problems and it'll go all down the line—it'll cause problems with student behaviour, it'll cause problems in progress, it'll cause problems in student progress, unless you tackle it now and give* it thought and care, we are going to find ourselves er in an impossible situation. Thoughts? Ideas? Come on you're in there, I'm not.

HC24 B: *If anyone wants to have a look at the scheme of work (she explains her suggestions)*

HC25 C: *I er this is really going to make a difference—tackling it*

(discussion of some ideas from Barbara and Deirdre on practical issues of lesson planning and pupil discipline)

HC26 B: *So if anyone wants to look at those they're welcome—if they want to approach it in a different way that's fine but . . .*

HC27 C: *I mean inevitably er er people are going to have different approaches but er keep it systematic er er with good planning I mean it really really is something we must have then then if it doesn't happen . . . it really means you sitting down and (indistinct) the last thing we want is . . . there may be problems with year ten . . . we'll pick them up—you know, we'll pick them up and the last thing we want any of us to do is . . . it's in all our interests . . . my guess is that we've probably already identified the kids who perhaps are in the wrong group. If we have got it wrong we we spent a lot of time . . . it could well be ther are some kids for whatever reason are misplaced. If we can identify them now . . . we can shift them now . . . without any damage to them it's OK er you know we can repair that but if we leave them where they are the chances are the opportunities for change will get less and less and less er and we will find ourselves in a fixed position . . . I'm not inviting wholesale changes—please don't give me a list of ten names*

588

(pause)

HC28 C: *I'm sorry I seem to be dominating all the thoughts but but I think a lot of them are important issues that that . . . er I didn't want to just let this occupy a a short time tonight I am very very truly aware of the the need to spend some quality time particularly with people who've just joined us er on this and er it concerns me I've just looked at . . . for a variety of reasons . . . A level and A level progress is dominating all our time—the problem of course out there is they don't see the broader issue in here—er practical assessment—if it doesn't have attention now we're going to have a problem um the INSET (inservice training day) session is all tied up*

HC29 D: *It's a Whole School activity isn't it?*

HC30 *C: It is. The INSET day for whatever—is again dedicated to A level the the next faculty meeting is is a long time away it's a long long time away*

(murmurings on dates, C talks over this)

HC31 *C: Right. I'll put my cards on the table, I'll be honest with you, if you're asking me what do you suggest what could we do er I'd be delighted if you'd agree to a twilight INSET session it wouldn't need that much time it's not an extra but it's a twilight session now rather than an INSET session that we might be having er sometime after Christmas.*

HC32 *H: I was just going to say that INSET day won't have to come in till March anyway so . . .]*

HC33: *] Yeah it's er the one just before half term is from 8 8.30 till 1 er we have to be careful (laughs) we don't make ourselves (laughs) . . . (talking from others over his words) How do people feel about an extended INSET day?*

HC34 *H: If I have to come in anyway I may as well make it a day.*
643

HC35 *C: So start exercising your minds on . . . . If we could just finish (interrupts Eddie) by my reminding you of . . . I want you to . . . Thanks very much.*

860 (Chris closes the meeting handing out papers)

ANALYSIS

This meeting begins with the usual informal chat as people arrive and settle down around the table. However, Chris signals the beginning of the formal meeting by handing out several sheets of papers to each person as they sit at the table. This not only marks the formal opening but also forecasts a deictic style of meeting.

Chris begins with a fairly long turn introducing the subject of examination results and continues with a demonstration of statistics on the overhead projector. At this stage he holds the floor for about twenty minutes. There are immediately a number of strong declaratives, first person statives such as "I felt", "I gave", "I have to", "I want", "I think", "I'd like to start", which have the effect of asserting status. (HC1) Although he apologises for not giving out the papers before the meeting he then distances himself from that error by using the inclusive first person plural pronoun in saying "that wasn't part of our design, that happened", after which he gives a rationalisation by explaining that he wanted to talk through the contents with them before they spent time on it.

He clearly states his own point of view on the importance of analysing the results by using two intensifiers "I think it really is a very important feature", a strengthener "certainly" and a stressed pronoun "at the top of **my** mind", also backing this up with a reference to a third party who has requested information about estimated grades. He begins the didactic demonstration section of the meeting by using the assertive declarative "I'd like to start by doing just that by examining the process . . . The first set of papers you have . . ." which clearly marks his domination of the process of the meeting and its content. He uses a strongly emotive repetition of the modifier in "wonderful wonderful success" to emphasise his point. When his long turn is interrupted by a relatively quiet and indistinct question from Barbara, he chooses not to ignore it but to pick this up with the terse "yes?" However, he dismisses the query with the personalised "I don't really want to dwell on that" then later more distanced and inclusive third person plural "we don't get any satisfaction going through it again".

Chris then begins to use the overhead projector (OHP) to demonstrate the statistical analysis of the GCSE results, taking again a long turn which amounts to about another fifteen minutes where he holds complete control of the topic apart from one comment from Judith who asks, during one of Chris's pauses "Could I just ask a question?" using the weakener "just" as an apology for her "interruption". Chris answers "By all means" and proceeds to answer the question with factual information. During the long turn the style is a didactic lecturing one using deictics to point out items on the OHP and the sheets in front of the staff. He is explaining figures and expounding on their significance, using informational statives and deictics such as "this column shows", "on this sheet you find", "you'll see from these figures", "one result of this is". The personal pronoun "you" here is not only used as a direct address to the audience but also as a vital part of the authoritative instructional register, firmly establishing the relationship between speaker and listener, that is, one of unequal status, instructor/expert and receiver of information/ instruction.

Chris continues in this register with the following speech events HC2 and 3, during which he passes out a list of students "to show you the process", again demonstrative and instructional, and continuing with the exposition using the OHP. His focus is to identify candidates estimated at a D grade in order to try to improve their result to a C. He again uses strong declaratives such as "I've done it", "I've drawn the line", "I don't think it's the right thing to do", "all I want us to do", which assert his opinion and his authority together. At the same time, he uses some very assertive, if not aggressive, lexis, such as "the students that Deirdre and Judith **drive**", "worst case scenario", "this is without doubt", "good hard real evidence". Again he holds the floor for a long turn, only interrupted once by Judith with the request for permission to speak, "Can I ask a question?" (HC4) and as Chris says "sorry?" at the same time she continues with her question about normal distribution on the graph they are being shown. Chris continues with an explanation of the distribution evident on the graph, and a statement about what he wants the staff to do with the information. The statement is functionally an imperative, "the important thing that I will ask you to do is to share these results with your students", followed by a similar construct in "you might need to do it", "you can't conceal", "you have to do it sensitively", and then finally he uses an actual imperative in "talk with the students for whom we are predicting a grade D".(HC5) After this, he continues with an off-record confidential comment comparing his faculty's practice with the practice of other curriculum areas which could be intended to/have the effect of reinforcing a sense of identity with and belonging to the group (the faculty).

When Deirdre tries to make a comment about the practice of sending out letters to parents of underachievers, Chris talks over her, eventually giving a negative response by indicating that members of staff should not do this without consulting him. He quickly attempts to move on to another topic, but is delayed by Barbara's "can I just say something?" (HC7 & 8) when she attempts to raise a concern about her class and their low achievement, which Chris seems to block although he then goes on to a concern of his about Year 11 pupils in general. The argument is not easy to follow and it is unclear whether he is referring to a widespread problem ("a lot of concerns", "a lot of students") (HC13) or a few cases ("I only do want to attack a dozen cases"), or indeed whether he is referring to achievement ("concerns that are on overall academic performance") or behaviour ("who are playing hell", "students stopping other students") although he says "I don't want to get embroiled in the naughty boy silly girl syndrome". Again this seems to be led by his own action, with many first person singular statives and a request for a list of cases from the staff.

Lexis, again, seems to reflect the assertive if not aggressive jargon associated with business ("flagging them up", "driving it", "performing out of their skin", "chasing it") but there is a sense, because of repetitions and hesitations, that he is almost speaking his thoughts aloud. This continues with the next long turn from Chris (HC19) where he is attempting to reply to Judith's question, "how will you tell the students?" (ie those who are identified as causing problems). He indicates his unease first by repeating her question and then says "I'm not really sure" and throws it over to them by adding "if er you have any any um any thoughts around this er bring them up" and "names of students who are stopping you doing your job". Although he has a long turn he does not in fact address the question asked, but projects the issue on to the staff again in an authoritative distanced register with "you do your jobs wonderfully well but . . ." and "this massive problem that you're facing". He even asks Barbara to report on some work she is undertaking in this area, a request she was not prepared for, although she does fulfil the request. When Eddie makes a lighthearted aside, Chris becomes more direct and assertive in his imperatives, "come on, we really have got to get our heads round this one", using the inclusive first person plural pronoun here, although this changes to the distanced "you" in "unless you tackle it now", and "come on, you're in there, I'm not". His lexical collocations here indicates his assertion, "believe you me er I can spot them a mile off", "massive problems", "it'll go all down the line", "impossible situation". (HC23)

There follows some discussion of ideas from Barbara and Deirdre on practical issues of lesson planning and pupil discipline, and Chris reinforces his previous attempt to involve the staff in finding strategies for dealing with the problem of disaffection among pupils by using intensifiers and repetitions, "it really really is something we must have", "the last thing we want is", "it's in all our interests", "the opportunities for change will get less and less and less." (HC27) But he also places limits on his own involvement by ending with "please don't give me a list of ten names".

After a pause Chris recognises his own position with "I'm sorry I seem to be dominating all the thoughts", (HC28) and then puts forward his idea for a faculty session to work on the problem, "I'll put my cards on the table", "I'll be honest with you", "I'd be delighted if you'd agree to a twilight INSET session",(HC31) again using the first person statives although with a second person conditional addressed to the team. He finally asks the group their opinion directly, "how do people feel about an extended INSET day?" (HC33) and, on receiving positive feedback, he uses the imperative "start exercising your minds on . . ." (HC35)

He ends the meeting with the politeness form, "thanks very much" and hands out some more papers.

Conclusions

Chris uses the strategies of the middle managers in their team meetings at Droverslea such as topic control, use of first person statives, declaratives, and professional jargon. However, the most notable facet of this meeting is the domination of the proceedings by Chris. He takes the most turns and also by far the longest. He holds the floor for the vast majority of the meeting time and even admits his domination himself. It is interesting that on a number of occasions when other colleagues wish to contribute, they ask if they can speak, requesting permission being a clear indication of their recognition of the status distinction between Chris and themselves. This exchange, therefore, does not follow the expected IRF structure, as there is little evidence of response because of the structure which Chris creates in his meeting. This reflects the structure used by Horace and Clive at Droverslea, rather than those of the female managers, but is much more pronounced. He had set the agenda and is the only member of the group to have prior knowledge of it, although he had clearly gone to great lengths to prepare for it with information packs for staff and OHP materials. The register of the meeting is, by and large, didactic, deictic, and reminiscent of a demonstration lecture. This establishes the tone of authority by Chris and reinforces the distinction in status. But this is also reaffirmed in the linguistic strategies he uses.

His speech traits are characterised by the use of active verbs, statives, assertive declaratives and, while he is using the OHP, deictics. There are no examples of supportive responses or of facilitating linguistic features and contributions by others seem on the whole to be dealt with summarily and somewhat dismissively, apart from the two instances where he requests contributions, one from Barbara to report to the meeting without pre-warning, and one from Barbara and Deirdre to elucidate their own ideas on lesson planning and pupil discipline. He elicits cooperation with imperatives, such as "come on, you're in there, I'm not" and only one direct request for the opinions of others, "how do people feel about an extended INSET day?" He on occasion uses politeness forms, "please", albeit with a direct negated imperative, "please don't give me a list of ten names."

His chosen lexis is characterised by assertive business jargon "flagging them up", "driving it", and by emotive modifiers, "wonderfully well", "massive problem", "impossible situation". The tone is of strength yet he seems to be almost thrown by Judith's question about how he intends to tackle a practical situation. Hesitations and repetitions become more apparent and an analysis of the content of some of the speech events indicates ambiguity and lack of a clear focus. This is all the more apparent in contrast to the very confident exposition of the earlier part of the meeting where Chris held the floor for considerable periods of time as he demonstrated and explained the figures he had produced on exam results and estimated grades.

Chris's style reflects a managerial role as leader, figurehead, decision-maker, rather than as facilitator or team-builder. He retains control of the content and process of the meeting through both his planned presentation and his linguistic strategies. The structure of the discourse is characterised by statement, instruction, explanation, rather than by discussion or access; it seems that an open more democratic forum would not be tolerated. Chris himself does not seem to identify with the team, linguistically making a clear distinction between "I think" and "you have to . . ." The strategies used by Chris clearly imply a domination function. There is clear evidence of the masculine frame/schema being brought to this meeting by Chris: dominance, status and task-oriented control of the meeting by the male manager. This, although unlike the overalll picture for Clive and Horace, represents strongly the masculine end of the spectrum of gendered linguistic traits. It was outlined in chapter 5 that the organisational culture of High Ridge differed from the others in the high valuing of its male head of the masculine style of management. This reinforces Chris's gendered language strategies and shows clearly in his more extreme use of the masculine repertoire in this meeting.

High Ridge—Head of Year Eight Pastoral team—Sally

The pastoral team meeting of tutors took place after the end of the school day as it usually did, and consisted of eight members, three women including the Head of Year (Sally) and five men. Peter, Arthur and Neil were all long-standing members of staff at this school, especially Peter, who was a Head of Faculty and had previously been a Head of House under the former system. Arthur was also a current Head of Faculty.

The agenda included arrangements for Activities Week, changes to the personal organisers, attendance, pastoral INSET (inservice training day)day items for agenda, parents' evening and reporting.

TRANSCRIPTION

S—Sally
F—Fiona
B—Barbara
G—Gerald
P—Peter
A—Arthur
N—Neil
E—Eddie

[general informal chat as people arrive and settle down around the table]

HS1 *S: Right—Activities Week. Now by this point, obviously, all kids have signed up for an activity on Tuesday morning. As far as I know there is noone likely with us on the Monday, apart from those people actually absent, and those who have been or are going to be absent I've had letters in for them and you should all be aware of who is . . . going to be away on that Monday. So as far as I know they are all going to be going to Drayton Manor. There are a few who can't afford the full cost . . . and I've talked to them individually and if they come to you and say I'm paying six pounds it's because they're going to pay for their admittance and I'm going to pay for the bus fare—I have actually got some moneys over from last year's Activities Week—we made about forty pounds so I'm prepared to use that to subsidise those kids.*

HS2 *N: That means all staff are going?*

HS3 *S: All staff are going. As I say, there are no Year eight pupils not going as far as I know so all Year eight staff will go.*

N: Free passes?

HS4 *S: Yes, you will all get free passes. We get one free member of staff for every ten children but we can't use those free places for children. So . . . you'll all get your . . . whatever . . .*

HS5 *P: One for every ten?*

HS6 *S: Yes. Yes. So I'm going to ask some of the Year Eleven staff and the office staff if they'd like to come out cos the office staff don't often get chance to get out and socialise with the kids so . . . I think if you remember when we went out to the cinema I asked Pam and Anna if they wanted to come, [murmurs in agreement from F & B] so I may do that again this time cos we've got the places for them—four buses—I've booked them to leave at quarter to eight—er sorry, beg your pardon,quarter to nine but we will be back a little later—we won't be back till about four . . . if that causes anybody any problems?*

HS7 *P: How long does it take to get there, Sally?*

HS8 *S: About—er I think . . . [prompt by someone else] yes, about an hour, an hour twenty minutes.*

HS9 *P: So we're talking about being there about ten o' clock.*

HS10 *S: Well, the gates don't open till ten, so I thought we'd leave about half two—quarter to three time*

HS11 *P: Mmm. So if we actually get two more of the er ladies to come with us we'll have say three members of staff for an hour apiece on-call somewhere]*

HS12 *S:] Yes that's what I intend to do. I intend to have a particular point in the park where there'll always be a member of staff or at least there will be a member of staff there at this time.*

(some discussion about individuals going on the trip)

HS13 *S: So we're all going—I hope that doesn't cause anybody any problems not being back till about four. (someone murmurs "that's fine")The children are aware of that because it was on the letter I sent home. Does anyone have any pupils who haven't yet given back their permission slip?*

HS14 *F: I still don't think I've got one from Sam.*

HS15 *S: She says that she gave you a holiday form and I told her to go and get another one and fill in another one for you. If you've got a problem with her send her to me.*

HS16 *B: If anyone's disgraced themselves—are we going to do what we did last year and say they won't be able to go?*

HS17 *S: I'll take that on merit.*

HS18 *B: Righto.*

HS19 *S: As I say, as far as I know at the moment, there are none not going I mean even the boys that have been a pain and have been on report the great majority of them have tried to do better—I mean, Scott Bown has been great (continues asking individuals about the children in their groups) Now, did Laura give me hers? Because she's one of them that . . .*

(indistinct) (goes through some individual names of pupils) Right Tuesday morning then. The iceskating really took off. . . . I've actually got two coaches going iceskating. There's one coach going bowling. (continues with arrangements and information about numbers, reporting liaison with other Year Heads and suggestions about filling up coaches with pupils from other years.) Generally kids are good when we take them out—we don't have problems with kids messing about when we take them out, do we?

HS20 *P: No*

HS21 *A: No*

HS22 *S: So I said I was quite happy with that. Then there's the local walk. There are about 20 kids who are not going out on Tuesday. I need somebody to—who would be willing to organise to take them on a local walk. (pause)*

HS23 *E: I'll take them if someone could give me a route.*

HS24 *P: I might have something. I might (indistinct)*

HS25 *S: You don't want to go iceskating?*

HS26 *P: (indistinct)*

HS27 *S: OK. Fair enough. (organises who will do what)*

1-140

HS28 *S: So thank you for your help on that. (further comments) Right um regarding money for Activities week, you can send it to me personally whenever you want, but please don't send it to the office—give it to me direct. Jane's eyes lit up when she thought it was raffle money!*

(information on arrangements for the last week.)

HS29 *S: Right, can we move on then? Personal organisers. Now, Arthur very kindly gave me a list of all the pupils in his RG who didn't get or have lost their organiser. We've looked at the organiser and whilst we still think they're a good idea, we've been looking at wanting to make changes to them—principally in the back. I was talking with Patsy and really this termly Record of Achievement I doubt that anyone fills it in—and also the Talking to my Tutor]*

HS30 *N:] I have*

HS31 *P:] I started*

HS32 *S:] so I suggested that perhaps—or rather Patsy and I suggested that perhaps we take those printed sheets out and just put loose plain paper for them to make their own notes on. Now, I know that perhaps you need to look through one (P. talking through S to N & A) Mr Brighthouse!*

HS33 *P: Sorry*

HS34 *S: You need to perhaps look through one but if you have any ideas as to how it could be changed you need to let us know in the next couple of days because obviously we've got to get it done.*

So if you could grab hold of one of your kid's organisers tomorrow, have a quick glance, see if there's any changes you think we could make—I'm not necessarily saying they would be made, but your ideas as you know are always (indisinct)

(discussion on some ideas)

230

HS35 *S: Anyway, attendance and absences. Now, I was very keen on making sure that pupils not signing up for Activities are not ones who were just trying to get two days off—that was why I was making sure I had some communication from home. We talked at the last meeting about a standard letter that could go home if for any reason the pupils weren't bringing in the letters that are needed. Now I wrote this this afternoon and Margaret typed it for me—I hope there are no errors on it . . .*

I'll give you a copy for reference.

280

HS36 *S: I must admit that with all the things we've got to do at the moment that I'm not getting to the registers to check every week.*

308

(P expresses a concern about parents arranging to take holidays in termtime]

HS37 *S:] There's not a lot that we can actually do*

HS38 *S: But I do share your concern, definitely. I think you're right, I think sometimes it's too easy.*

(comment on parental consultation)

HS39 *S: Right, let's just—er—we'll come on to parents' consultations in a moment—Heads of Year pastoral INSET day—now, on the 9th of July the Heads of Year, (Head) and (Deputy Head) actually have an INSET day to look at pastoral issues, possible changes for next year, etc. You'll obviously all stay tutors next year for next year's Year 9. I do believe that Lin Stubbs will take over your RG (to E). (others make comments) So, can I just get back to this INSET day please? Areas are—optional marking of registers system—we may be going over to computerised ones . . . (murmurs from others) effectiveness]*

HS40 *P:] not "optional"—that's the wrong word. Optical?*

HS41 *S: Oh, sorry, beg your pardon. I can't read. Optical.*

HS42 *P: That's computer scanning—it's when]*

HS43 *S:] it's been corrected, hasn't it? Er monitoring the effectiveness of the pastoral system (continues list) and image of pastoral team—and that's not just us—that's you as tutors (continues list). Is there anyone who feels there's something else you'd like me to bring up at that meeting—to discuss—to sort out any areas you're not happy with?*

HS44 *A: Actually I think this is going to upset a lot of people, but there ought to be far more liaison between Heads of Year and Heads of Faculty—there's difficulties—(indistinct) it's not very healthy.*

HS45 *S: I think it was getting better for a while. We were all together for senior management meetings but we've not been together for a long long while, have we? Yeah.*

HS46 *A: These things should be discussed. (mentions a member of SMT who he thinks should be present at the meetings.)*

HS47 *S: Thank you, Arthur.*

HS48 *P: I'd like to question, Sally, the times that we lose assemblies due to other things like exams, which sometimes is unavoidable, but just lately there have been numerous occasions when we've missed an assembly (continues to explain instances)*

HS49 *S: Yes, that's a big problem]*

HS50 *P:] and I think it's about time we did]*

HS51 *S:] I'll admit they're often cancelled far too often by people who're quite capable of doing them*

HS52 *P: (comment on instances) I think far too many of the senior staff back out—they use it as an excuse to back out—excuses for not doing assemblies.*

HS53 *S: I mean, I must admit—was it Wednesday or Tuesday before—I was desperate for an assembly to talk to the kids about Activities Week—just to get them together and talk to them about things like uniform and Activities Week, parents' evening. We just haven't had time—assemblies are just being cancelled—it is a problem—I do share your concern.*
(comments from others)

HS54 *S: Right , let's move on then. Parents' consultations. Obviously, by this point we know who's coming—it's through the computer. (comment on particular pupil) I'm going to go through tonight—if you can just listen for a minute—I'll read the kids' names out and if you know you've had written confirmation one way or t'other then I won't send a letter. (reads list and comments on specific pupils) That's what's going home, anyway. It'll be in the post first thing in the morning. OK?*

181

HS55 *B: You've been busy.*

HS56 *S: I'm a busy woman.*

(comments on reporting)

HS57 *S: I'm going to see Joe, actually, once reports have gone out, I'm going to give him some feedback about the reports because I think some of them—I don't mean the kids' report—I mean what some staff have put in are unreasonable—I mean we talk about consistency and we all say right we'll all write in black and we'll all write on the top of the report and I was amazed to see, you know, to think of the actual members of staff who haven't done that I was appalled! In fact I've even sent some of them back because there's not enough written on them—that they are far too brief—I want more than that.*

HS58 *A: Good. I've seen some like that.*

HS59 *S: Have you?*

HS60 *A: Having said that, most staff are very good.*

HS61 *S: Yes they are, the great majority are.*

(comments from F, A and G on good comments on reports)

HS62 *F: I don't know whether you can bring this up with (Head) but I don't understand why the reports go out after parents evening*

HS63 *S: It has been raised. It has.*

(comments from other staff about this and Sally joins in)

HS64 *S: Anyway, moving on to number 7 on the agenda—does anyone have any other business?*

HS65 *E: Sports Day*

HS66 *S: Oh Sports Day! (comments—gives information) What's Cathy doing? (discussion of arrangements)*

HS67 *S: Anything else? So, Activities Week—keep the money coming in. Any problems just let me know. That's it! Thank you very much. See you tomorrow.*

590

ANALYSIS

This meeeeting also begins with staff having a general informal chat as people arrive and settle down around the table. The atmosphere throughout is one of goodhumoured teamwork and although there is a great deal of aside chatting through the meeting, it is "on task" and commenting on the topics under discussion. It does not become overly intrusive or disruptive, although at one point Sally gives a form of reprimand to Peter (HS32) by saying his name formally *"Mr Brighthouse!"* as he talks across her to Neil and Arthur. The formality of this register suggests that of pupil-teacher rather than colleague to colleague, although it is said in a lighthearted tone and is received good humouredly by Peter who apologises.

Sally opens the meeting with the initiating marker "Right—Activities Week", a reference to the first item on the agenda, speaking in telegraphic style to draw attention to the business in hand. She signals her opening comment with "now by this point . . ." and starts with statives giving information to the team: "kids have signed up . . .", "there is no-one . . ." The first person declaratives (I know, I'm going to, I've actually got, I'm prepared to) are decisive and demonstrate authority and also action and engagement with the day to day tasks, in this case of organising the outings, for example "I've talked to them individually". Her sense of ownership of the organisation is clear in her statement "I'm going to pay for the bus fare", indicating not her own personal funds but her control of the budget. Throughout, Sally displays a concern to show a personal involvement with the pupils and the team affairs, a hands-on manager who pays attention to the practical detail and therefore appears organised, business-like and efficient. She reflects back questions, then expands on them, for example in HS3, when Neil asks, "That means all staff are going?" she responds "All staff are going", rather than simply "yes", then expands "as I say, there are no Year eight pupils not going . . ." These strategies tend to reinforce her decisive and efficient air, by changing affirmatives into declaratives.

A similar effect is shown when Sally uses a full apology phrase "sorry, beg your pardon" (HS6) when there is clearly just a slip of the tongue as she says eight instead of nine. Her pragmatic use of the conditional "if that causes anybody any problems?" (HS6) is also a control strategy implying that she does not expect an affirmative answer, whereas a straightforward interrogative might. Again, the image of efficiency and control is maintained by the use of the pause filler "er" as she buys time to answer a question ("about—er I think") and is, in fact, prompted to the answer by another member of the team, rather than saying "I don't know". This is also seen in her strong declarative response to Peter's working through the logistics of the organisation in HS11 where she gives a positive decisive statement in agreement and even repeats the decisive verb: "Yes, that's what I intend to do. I intend to have . . ." (HS12)

Sally receives supportive responses from her team, minimal responses and murmurs of "that's fine" and there seems to be a well established friendly atmosphere in the working relationship in evidence, certainly on this occasion.

She is quick to recall specific incidents with specific pupils, as in HS15, and details the action she took as well as indicating support for the teacher by the conditional and imperative, "if you've got a problem with her send her to me". She names individual pupils a number of times in HS19, thus indicating her knowledge of them and her personal involvement with their wellfare. When she uses a declarative to indicate her opinion that the pupils are well behaved on visits, she adds a facilitating tag question (do we?) to which other staff respond in agreement, which has the effect of reinforcing her comment.

Again she is decisive in her response to the question about what was to be done about any pupils who misbehaved beforehand, saying "I'll take that on merit" which is accepted by her colleague without questioning her judgement. She organises which staff will be in charge of which event and this again gives the impression of efficiency and organisation.

She uses politeness forms: "so thank you for your help on that" and "please" when giving an imperative, and also softens the imperative by using a lighthearted comment in HS28. She uses the interrogative to function as the imperative as in "can we move on then?" and telegraphic style "personal organisers" to move decisively on in the agenda. In HS29 she uses the inclusive first person plural pronoun: "we've looked at the organiser" and "we still think . . . we've been looking at wanting to make changes to them", which has the effect of providing support for her comments and ideas. Her use of the first person "I doubt" actually then implies third party consent. The ensuing interruptions indicate disagreement but Sally ignores these and continues with "so I suggested" although she immediately self-corrects by adding "or rather Patsy and I suggested that . . ." thus regaining third party consent to the idea and reinforcing its authority.

Sally uses empowerment by requesting input from staff about changes to the personal organisers (if you have any ideas, if you could grab, see if there's any changes you think we could make), using conditionals and modals. She shows support for empowerment by adding "your ideas as you know are always . . ." However, after a brief discussion about some ideas, she marks a desire to move on in the agenda by signalling the next agenda item: "Anyway, attendance and absences," and another decisive marker initiating her own opinion with a first person stative and a strengthening qualifier (very) , "Now, I was very keen on making sure that . . ." She reinforces this with a declarative showing decisive action: "Now I wrote this this afternoon". Her efficiency is again indicated in "Margaret typed it for me—I hope there are no errors on it" suggesting that someone else might have made the errors rather than herself, and "I'll give you a copy for reference."

When a colleague expresses a concern about termtime holidays, Sally first responds negatively (there's not a lot we can do) but then supports his concern and affirms it with the first person stative: "I do share your concern, definitely. I think you're right." (HS38) She then guides the ensuing comments away from this topic with epistemic modality, a modal imperative and a delaying statement: "Right, let's just—er—we'll come on to parents' consultations in a moment" and again with a modal interrogative: "So, can I just get back to this INSET day?"

When she does make an error in reading the word "optical" and Peter points this out, she uses a full politeness form for an apology and a self-depracatory comment: "sorry, beg your pardon. I can't read." (HS41) but she interrupts Peter's attempted explanation of "optical" and continues reading out her list.

Again, she empowers other members of the team by asking if they wish her to bring up any other points at a management meeting. When a team member expresses his concern about the lack of discussion about certain issues, and critisises a member of the SMT by name, Sally at first expresses support then ends his turn with "thank you, Arthur," albeit softening with the politeness term. However, she does affirm Peter's concerns about assemblies with the supportive response "yes, that's a big problem" and reinforces this with the modifier and intensifiers "often, far too often", anecdotal evidence in support, and an intensifying auxiliary "I do share your concern."

When there is some background comment about parental consultations, she regains control of the floor by using the conditional and modal, although she softens the imperative with a hedging weakener: "if you can just listen for a minute." She then asserts control by reading out a list of names and informing the staff of a letter she has written to parents which is going out the next day, which reinforces her efficiency.

She reinforces this by responding to a colleague's comment "you've been busy" with lexical repetiton, "I'm a busy woman."

Towards the end of the meeting, Sally continues her use of first person declaratives as she speaks about the standard of reports written by staff (I'm going to, I think, I was amazed, I was appalled, I've sent) thus showing her opinion, her action and her feelings. She shows authority and decisive action: "I've sent some of them back . . . they are far too brief . . . I want more than that" and she receives support from Arthur: "Good. I've seen some like that." However, when Fiona raises the issue of asking the head about the timing of the reports, Sally uses the distancing passive, "it has been raised."

She ends the meeting with summative comments and reminders of items and then with a polite thanks and an informal friendly greeting, "see you tomorrow."

Conclusions

Sally uses similar strategies to those of all the middle managers at Droverslea regardless of gender: topic control, use of statives, declaratives, professional jargon, as well as softeners and support strategies used by most. However, the most notable feature of this meeting and of Sally's linguistic style is the impression she gives of her efficiency, organisational skills and her business-like approach. The main purpose of the meeting is to provide information, but there is also some discussion of the practical details arising from that information. Like Isabel at Droverslea, Sally is providing a great deal of information to her colleagues and thus uses many statives and declaratives in order to do this. This reinforces her role as a middle manager, one of whose functions is to gain access to information and disseminate it to others. She is also able to explain items further to her colleagues. As with the other managers, she has control of the agenda. She follows a clear IRF discourse structure with participative exchanges balanced throught the meeting.

She asserts her decisions strongly, using first person declaratives to indicate actions and decisions already made : "I'm going to pay", "I have actually got some moneys"(HS1). This reinforces the image of an organised, decisive manager. She shows a high level of control over the progress of the meeting by signalling change of topic, moving the agenda on, and getting the discussion back to the given agenda items: "can we move on then?"(HS28); "can I just get back to this INSET day?"(HS38). She reprimands Peter when he talks across her as she is trying to move the agenda on, but it is done in a light-hearted tone and is accepted by Peter which suggests respect for her authority and a mutually supportive atmosphere. She uses conditionals as imperatives and softened imperatives to assert her control over both the proceedings in the meeting and the daily work of the team, and supportive comments and minimal responses are used both by Sally and towards her by other team members. The issues she deals with are very practical: for example the organisation of the Activities Week and trips out, and she provides information about a host of details which she has anticipated. This appears to be a very "hands-on" manager who controls the day to day business of the tutor team with an eye for detail.

She clearly indicates her personal involvement with individual pupils' concerns, naming them and questioning tutors about particular pupils. This may reflect the demands of her role as pastoral manager but it also seems characteristic of Sally's own personal style. Like Isabel at Droverslea, she reflects a management functioning as organiser, director of tasks within the team, and controller of the processes of those tasks. In terms of Mintzberg's (1973) managerial roles, she fulfils informational roles as disseminator and monitor, interpersonal roles as leader, and decisional roles as resource allocator and negotiator. There is no evidence in this particular meeting of her functioning as spokesperson or intermediary.

Sally's speech strategies reflect all these and there is a good-humoured register in the team. However, unlike Isabel at Droverslea, she does not demonstrate a great concern to achieve consensus by appealing for support and although she accepts comments and allows the floor to others, she does not frequently empower others formally; this happens on one significant occasion where she asks the team to feedback comments to her on the topic of the personal organisers. Nevertheless, like Liz of Droverslea, Sally frequently uses politeness terms, apologies and recognises her error. Her linguistic strategies imply a control function, and although cooperation strategies are also present, her high level of authority, control/monitoring of detailed day to day organisation, and decision-making, could imply a low-level incipient domination function, and there are similarities to Isabel at Droverslea in this respect. However, the feminine frame/schema being brought to the meeting is clear, in Sally's relationship-building, personal involvement, hands-on organisation of the tasks, promotion of cooperation within the team, which is reminiscent of both Iasbel and Liz at Droverslea. Sally does not demonstrate the strong masculine strategies shown by Chris at the same school, but the control strategies she does show and the high business register she uses, indicate that her language use is effected by the organisational culture of the school.

Summary

In this chapter, I have transcribed and analysed the meetings of a male and a female manager of a second school (High Ridge), and have explored the patterns of gender linguistic strategies which have emerged from these. The gender patterns identified in the first school (Droverslea) were confirmed in this second school. However, Chris displayed strategies much nearer to the masculine end of the continuum than any of the other managers, and Sally, although demonstrating many feminine linguistic traits, displayed a strongly driven, business register.

Patterns which I identify in my second set of case studies from the second school (High Ridge) are as follows:

- use by both the male and female managers of topic control, statives and declaratives, use of first person statives, use of professional jargon. However, whereas at Droverslea both men and women used softeners, only the woman used them at High Ridge. Chris used a very high frequency of declaratives and first person statives, and his professional jargon tended to be from a business field rather than specifically education.
- interruptions were handled differently by the male and the female managers.
- in establishing status, the male manager held the floor, used imperatives, and the passive voice, deixis and a didactic register, dismissing empowerment.
- in establishing status, the female manager used empowerment of others, supportive strategies, organisational strategies, business-like register, and the active voice, including anecdotes.
- in handling conflict, the male manager used imperatives, dismissal of questions, distancing strategies.
- in handling conflict, the female manager deflected conflicts, used apology and self-correction.

- in decision-making, the male manager used imperatives and floor dominance.
- in decision-making, the female manager used cooperation and consensus strategies, summarising and inclusive pronouns.

While Sally's linguistic strategies tended to compare closely with those of the female managers at Droverslea, Chris's tended to move much further towards the masculine end of the continuum, with strong features of dominance and little cooperation, support or empowerment of others. The investigation into the organisational culture of High Ridge outlined in chapters 4 and 5, showed that the male headteacher demonstrated a much higher valuing of the masculine style of management than the other three heads. He also clearly used two metaphoric fields during his interview: that of wholeness, associated with ownership and participation, and that of business/industry, associated with a dynamic work ethos. On pages 119-120, I suggested that this could have an effect on the language repertoires used by the managers in this school. The discourse analysis of the interactions of Chris and Sally would suggest that this is confirmed. The effect of the organisational culture has reinforced the masculine repertoire of the male manager, Chris, and influenced the feminine repertoire of Sally. This confirms the idea that male and female managers bring to their team meetings their experience of and pragmatic understanding of a community of practice within middle management, the school and its organisational culture, as well as gender. For different individuals these different but linked communities of practice will assume varying weightings of importance for their own idiolect.

In the case studies in the second school, I have found the patterns of gender differences confirmed. I have also found that the gender similarities follow a similar pattern to those at Droverslea. However, I have found that there are differences between the case studies from different organisational cultures which indicate that other linguistic frames are significant in the choice of language repertoire for middle managers in secondary schools. There needs to be a shift in emphasis in my hypothetical explanation of gender language variation in order to account for the variation found in a different organisational culture.

I begin chapter 8 by analysing the patterns which have emerged and been confirmed in two schools, and continue by testing out these patterns in the final two schools in order to confirm the re-emphasised hypothetical explanation that gender language is one dynamic of variation but that there is also another which is concerned with the frame associated with the specific organisational culture.

CHAPTER EIGHT

SO, WHAT WERE THE PATTERNS FOUND AND HOW CAN WE MOVE FORWARD TO MORE EFFECTIVE MANAGEMENT AND MORE SUCCESSFUL ORGANISATIONS?

Introduction

In the previous two chapters, I have analysed the interactions of middle managers with their teams within the contexts of meetings. I have been looking at the way in which different managers have used language to establish differential status; to deal with critical incidents: the handling of team members in the course of reaching their meeting objectives; the handling of conflicts; and the way that decisions are made within the meetings. The main focus of the research problem was on the identification of any gender differences in the way that language is used for these purposes or any gender similarities which may indicate other linguistic frames or schema, and on whether women's language disadvantaged them in achieving higher managerial positions.

The research questions focused on an investigation of the way that language works in managerial transactions and an analysis of the nature of those linguistic transactions by men and by women. I was investigating whether:

- there were gender differences in the way that language is used by middle managers in communicating to their team members in the specific context of the team meetings, and to analyse the nature of any patterns emerging

- there were gender similarities in linguistic strategies which might indicate other linguistic frames, and to analyse the nature of any patterns emerging
- there were any differences between my case studies of different organisational cultures, which might reflect other linguistic frames
- feminine linguistic strategies play a part in negatively valuing women as managers in secondary schools.

The hypothetical explanation for the existence of gender differences in language and managerial style shown in the literature explored in chapters 1 and 2, is that man and women bring different frame or schema to their interactions with other people (Holmes 1984, Coates 1993, Tannen 1992, 1993, 1994, following frame theory promoted by Minsky 1975, Goffman 1974,1981, Gumperz 1982). I was investigating whether the clear gender differences indicated in the literature were present in my data. These differences can be summarised as follows:

- that women use speech repertoires which suggest support, facilitation, and the empowerment of others, reflecting a feminine profile of co-operation, unity, building relationships and rapport (these corresponded with the feminine cluster of traits identified in the literature on management communication which indicated a supportive, empowering and collaborative style)
- that men use speech repertoires which suggest authority, dominance, and status differentiation, reflecting a masculine profile of competition, striving for status and task achievement (these corresponded with the masculine cluster of traits identified in the literature on management communication which indicated a detached, rational, tough, depersonalised style)

I also aimed to explore another hypothetical explanation for the research problem, which was the idea that there are other strategies employed which raise other issues, for example, the theory that there is an identifiable repertoire associated with the role of the middle manager per se, regardless of gender and that this might also be affected by the particular organisational culture in which it occurred (as in the Community of

Practice theory, Eckert 1990, Eckert and McConnell-Ginet 1992, Holmes and Meyerhoff 1999, Bergvall 1999).

In chapter 6, I showed that patterns were emerging from my data which confirmed those of the literature in terms of the gender differences in managerial linguistic strategies. However, I also found that there were similarities which indicated a "middle manager speak", a choice of language repertoire which reflected a frame or schema identified with middle managers per se and which was common to both men and women in that position. In chapter 7, I provided my analyses of case studies of managers in a different school, with a different organisational culture, whose headteacher had shown, in interview, an incipient valuing of masculine characteristics of management, as outlined in chapter 5. I found that many of the patterns of gender differences and similarities in linguistic strategies were confirmed, but that also there were language features which could be identified with the variation in organisational culture rather than with gender. There needed then to be a shift in emphasis of the hypothetical explanation for the research problem to reinforce the importance of other linguistic frames such as that of the organisational culture of the school. The use of the community of practice as a useful tool for explaining these variations was reiterated in chapter 7.

In this chapter, I explore the comparative patterns emerging from the data from the six case studies from two schools so far. I use a content analysis of agenda items and outline the language function of these. I compare the linguistic strategies used by male and female middle managers which are identified in my data and compare these with the linguistic differences identified in the literature and outlined on page 219. I then test out these patterns in the two remaining schools (Beckfield and Broadmarsh), which were both led by female headteachers.

Table 18: chronology of the analysis process undertaken and described through chapters 6,7 and 8:

Subject, in chronological order of analysis	activity	Patterns confirmed
Clive (Doverslea)	Recorded, transcribed, analysed	Patterns emerging
Liz	As above	Patterns emerging

Horace	As above	"
Isabel	As above	"and hypothesis developing
Chris (High Ridge)	As above, different organisational culture	"
Sally	As above	"re-emphasis in hypothesis
Joe (Beckfield)	Testing key critical areas in different organisational culture, female head	Patterns and hypothesis confirming
Keith	As above	"
Kath & Gladys	Testing key areas	"
Broadmarsh (4)	Testing key areas	Hypothesis confirming

Patterns emerging from agenda items and language function

All meetings were agenda-led; in most cases the agenda was published to team members in advance, apart from Horace and Chris; in all cases the agenda was set by the middle manager. The agenda items and language function of each meeting is shown below.

Table 19: agenda items and language function of each meeting

Name/ manager	Agenda items	Language function
Droverslea Clive (not chairing)	Design of record forms; stock; texts; faculty policy statement; boys' achievement; differentiation strategies (from SMT)	To discuss (issues and practical details)

Liz	Sixth form application process; changes in post-16 structure; pastoral process; diploma of achievement.	To discuss (issues and practical details); to inform A "review & planning meeting"
Horace	Arrangements for Induction days/opening of building; Open Day; tests; NPRA names; Brittany trip cover. (agenda not published in advance; written on Board at start of meeting)	Primary function to inform; secondary function to discuss (practical details apart from challenges))
Isabel (not chairing)	Reports from staff; organisation of field trip; organisation of INSET; Faculty A allowance	Primary—to inform; secondary—to discuss (practical details) To discuss (issues)
High Ridge Chris	Exam results; problem pupils; new syllabus; INSET (No agenda published)	To inform
Sally	Organisation of Activities Week; attendance; INSET; parents' evening; reporting.	To inform; some secondary function to discuss (practical details)

In the main, agenda items were information items, or items requiring discussion of practical details involved in administration/organisation; agenda items for discussion of wider issues of philosophy or principle occurred in only two meetings as a primary function (Clive and Liz) and in part of a third (Isabel) as one agenda item. By the very nature of such meetings, one would expect to see a large proportion of statives and declaratives used to impart information. As all the meetings were agenda-led and that agenda chosen by the middle manager, topic control clearly resides with the manager.

Patterns emerging from research

Reviewing the six meetings from the two different schools I have outlined in the last two chapters, I have found that there is a pattern in the linguistic issues emerging. The following table demonstrates the comparative linguistic tendencies across the managers in both schools.

Table 20: linguistic tendencies by manager and school

Name / manager	Language use (specific)	Linguistic tendencies
Droverslea Clive	Minimal responses; softening commands; empowerment (allowing floor space to others); statives/declaratives; 1st person statives (opinions); professional jargon; supportive interruptions; holding floor; weakeners/qualifiers/hedges; strengtheners/emotives; topic control; argument markers; anecdotes	Many usages imply cooperation, team playing, empowerment of others, yet holding floor, high scoring strengtheners, topic control and argument markers suggest the possibility of incipient domination
Liz	Minimal responses; softeners/facilitative (affective tags); softening commands; politeness forms (apologies); empowerment (allowing floor space to others); statives/declaratives; 1st person statives (opinions); being interrupted with challenges; supportive interruptions; business-like/organisational discourse markers; some strengtheners/emotives; topic control; summations; argument markers; anecdotes	High level facilitating and empowerment of others; challenges marked conflicts within group; conflicts at times dropped unresolved via topic control; high level politeness forms and softeners—avoidance? Status used to defuse/deflect conflict, not resolve it?

Horace	Softening commands; statives/declaratives; being interrupted with challenges; direct imperatives; holding floor; strengtheners/emotives; passive voice; topic control; anecdotes	No supportive minimal responses or facilitative markers (no rapport markers), no empowerment strategies; challenges marked conflict; crisis management (distancing passive voice, imperatives, commanding recorder off) — d o m i n a t i o n but tension from own strategic and operational management internal conflicts?
Name / manager	Language use (specific)	Linguistic tendencies
Isabel	Supportive minimal responses; softeners/ facilitative (affective tags); softening commands; politeness forms; statives/ declaratives; 1st person statives; professional jargon; being interrupted (supportive); supportive interruptions; business-like/organisation markers(high); topic control; summations	Control functions marked: 1st person assertive statives, business-like/ organisational markers high—suggest incipient domination?

High Ridge Chris	Statives/declaratives (high); 1st person statives (high); professional jargon (business); being interrupted (requests for information); direct imperatives; dismissal of questions; holding floor (very high); weakeners/qualifiers/hedges; strengtheners/emotives; passive voice; topic control; use of deictics	High domination markers; deixis marks demonstration mode; didiactic register; rejection of empowerment; dismissal of questions; holding floor highly marked; no supportive or rapport markers.
Sally	Supportive minimal responses; softeners/facilitative (affective tags); softening commands; politeness forms; empowerment (allowing floor space to others); statives/declaratives; 1st person statives; professional jargon; being interrupted for correction; interrupting others back/ accepting correction; high business-like/organisational markers; weakeners/qualifiers/hedges (used as softeners); strengtheners/emotives (used as supportives); topic control; argument markers; anecdotes(high on individual pupils)	Business-like register throughout; provides information; high supportives/ softeners; personalisation (staff and pupils) reinforces common group task; high level control via agenda and informative function.

These linguistic tendencies and strategies can then be analysed in terms of gender similarities and differences as follows:

Patterns of similarity between male and female managers.

Similarities between managers, whether male or female, were as follows:

- Topic control: all the meetings were agenda-led; all managers had set the agenda for the meeting and were the agents in moving from one topic to the next.
- Use of statives/declaratives: many of the agenda items were concerned with the dissemination of information and therefore all the managers studied used statives and declaratives for this purpose. However, one male manager, Chris from High Ridge, used these more frequently than any other manager.
- Use of first person statives: these mark the speaker's personal opinions, and there was found to be little difference between men and women in the frequency of their use, except that again the male manager, Chris at High Ridge, used these more frequently than any other manager.

These strategies reflect the community of practice within the shared pragmatic understandings by middle managers of the nature and methods of conducting team meetings.

The following linguistic devices were found in many of the managers' repertoires, regardless of sex:

- Use of softeners: most of the managers, regardless of sex, with the exception, again, of Chris, used softeners frequently whenever their utterance functioned as an imperative; the most common devices being the use of conditionals, interrogatives and modals.
- Use of professional jargon: the majority of the managers, male and female, used this, although the jargon used by Chris tended to be that of business rather than of teaching.
- Supportive interruptions: there seemed to be no evidence of differences between men and women in the way that supportive interruptions were used
- Being interrupted: most of the managers regardless of sex were interrupted by others during the meeting, but where these

constituted challenges to the manager, they were handled differently by that manager, and this response **did** seem to be gender specific.

Team meetings were regular occurrences at all the schools and therefore a pattern of expectation would have become established amongst the members, about the group's practice, their own individual role and that of the middle manager. It is likely that practices would have become set and mutually understood through a number of influences being brought to bear on the group: the pragmatic understandings of the discourse within the meeting, the shared understandings of the context of the whole school and its practices, and the types and requirements of agenda items, among others.

The first three bullet points indicate a pragmatic understanding of the nature of the meeting, its discourse in terms of topic (content) and language. The next four bullet points reflect the pragmatic understanding by the team members, and especially the agent of the language concerned (the manager in the present study) of the school context and its practices. This embodies the organisational culture of the particular school and also the wider expectations and practices of the field of education and educational management. For example, the use of professional jargon, shared by both sexes, is understood pragmatically by the members of a group whose shared focus is education and whose members will be expected to have an understanding of the semantic field of education. The use of softeners and two-way interruptions, shared by both sexes, are acceptable to the group, even expected, and occurred many times. One explanation for this is that there is a shared understanding that the group comprises a team of colleagues often with other levels of status and responsibility outside this particular community, and that this sense of collegiality militates against linguistic strategies and practices which suggest a hierarchical structure. In most of the meetings there were members who held roles as middle or senior managers in other groups, for example senior managers who also operated as academic faculty members, heads of faculty who also operated as pastoral team members.

A notable example which moved away from the pattern shown at Droverslea, was clearly Chris. He did not use softeners or supportives as the other managers did and his speech features during his transactions with his team showed less co-incidence with the common features used by the other middle managers. His linguistic transactions were marked by high domination features with the rejection of empowerment of team members, considerable holding of the floor to the exclusion of others, a didactic register and demonstration mode. In this way his linguistic strategies as a manager moved distinctly towards the masculine end of the continuum of gendered speech. His language repertoire contained clear examples of the business metaphor used also by the headteacher of his school, High Ridge, during his interview. The female manager from this school, Sally, also used similar business metaphor and a clear business-like register, with high levels of control, although she also used many other features identified with the middle manager style common to both men and women at Droverslea, for example a high level of supportives and softeners. This suggests that the pragmatic understandings of the team members at High Ridge within their team meetings were different in some ways from those at Droverslea. This could be explained in the following way: the community practices at High Ridge have formed within a different organisational culture, one in which the headteacher indicates an incipient valuing of the masculine style of management, shown in his markedly different profile of evaluation from the other heads, as I have discussed in chapter 5. My anticipation following the interview with the head was that this might be reflected in the linguistic strategies chosen by middle managers at High Ridge who aspire to higher management levels, and that those strategies might move closer to the "traditional masculine" end of the continuum (p 120, 132).

The dimension of community of practice of the organisational culture cuts across the dimension of gender here. In other words the repertoires of common practices within that organisational community and of the language which supports them assume a high level of importance along with the repertoires associated with gender. In Chris's case, both the practices of the organisational culture and that of gender reinforce each other, moving his managerial linguistic repertoire closer to the end of the continuum which marks the masculine style. In Sally's case, they do not reinforce each other, since many of her strategies are associated with the feminine style, and she has incorporated both to an extent within her repertoire. In this way, therefore, it is important to look at influences on linguistic repertoire other than that of gender, and it is here that the community of practice provides a useful tool.

Dr Julia Helene Ibbotson PhD, FHEA

Patterns of dissimilarity between male and female managers.

In the three key areas which this research is focusing on (establishing status; critical incidents: handling the team/ dealing with conflict; and decision-making), there were found to be differences between male and female managers, in the following specific areas:

1. **Establishing status:**

    Male managers tended to use the following strategies:

    -   Holding the floor
    -   Using imperatives
    -   Using the passive voice
    -   Retaining tensions

    While female managers tended to:

    -   Use empowerment of others
    -   Use supportive strategies
    -   Use organisational strategies for control (provider of information, controller of topic change, organiser/administrator of topics prior to meeting)
    -   Use business-like register (intonation, moving agenda items on quickly)
    -   Use summarising
    -   Use the active voice

2. **Conflict resolution/ handling conflicts:**

    Male managers tended to:

    -   Use distancing strategies
    -   Use imperatives
    -   Use dismissal mood (terseness)

    While female managers tended to:

- Deflect conflicts
- Use apologies
- Accept correction

3. Decision-making:

Male managers tended to use:

- Imperatives
- Floor-dominance

While female managers tended to use:

- Cooperation strategies
- Consensus strategies
- Summarising
- Inclusive pronouns

These indicate that, although middle managers, regardless of sex, operate the linguistic strategies reflecting the community of practice of the team meeting context, of the given school context and its organisational culture, and of the field of educational management, nevertheless there are gendered differences in the linguistic usage in specific team meeting situations. This is another level of the community of practice: gender and its shared pragmatic understandings, its frame/schema with which each gender approaches the conducting of meetings. It is important, now, to explore the extent to which my data compares with the linguistic strategies identified in the literature as gender-specific.

Dr Julia Helene Ibbotson PhD, FHEA

Comparison, by gender, between linguistic strategies found in my case studies and those suggested by the literature review of previous research.

Table 21: a comparison of the linguistic strategies by gender found in the literature with those found in my case studies.

NB. Those indicated are where usage is assessed as highly marked by a particular male and female manager, not the single use of the feature by any one person.

Functions reflecting gendered frame/ schema (features found in the **literature**)	Gendered linguistic strategies (features found in the **literature**)	Number of **men in my study** using specific feature	Number of **women in my study** using specific feature
Masculine: own status reaffirmed, competition, dominance. Assertiveness, report style	Holding floor	All	0
	Imperatives	2	0
	Passive voice	2	0
	Distancing / depersonalisation	2 2 all	0 0 all
	Dismissals	2 all all	2
	Statives/ declaratives	1	2 all
	Professional lexis		0
	Strengtheners		
	Topic control		
	Negative interruptions/ overlaps		

Feminine: cooperation, consensus, building relationships, rapport, solidarity, support, facilitating others.	Empowerment of others	1	All
	Supportive strategies	1	All
	Organisation/business register	0	All
		0 all	2 all all
	Summations	0	all all all
	Active voice	0	all
	Deflect conflicts	0	2 all all
	Apologies	1	1
	Accept correction	0	2 all
	Minimal responses	2	
	Politeness forms	2	
	Positive interruptions/ overlaps	0	
	Softeners—commands	2	
	Softeners—affective tags	2	
	Epistemic modality—hedges,etc	2	
	Anecdotal evidence		
	Inclusive pronouns		

There is a marked correspondence between the gendered linguistic strategies and functions outlined in the literature review in chapter 2, and the strategies used by men and women managers which were identified in my data. The literature identifies a feminine style of language as using linguistic strategies for support, facilitation, and the empowerment of others, reflecting a feminine profile of co-operation, unity, building relationships and rapport. In my case studies all the female managers used strategies of empowerment, support, deflection of conflict, which help to build solidarity. They all used an organised/business-like register and an active voice, which help to build co-operation in task achievement. They all used apologies, acceptance of correction, politeness forms, softeners (command and affective) and inclusive pronouns, which help to build rapport rather than competitiveness. The only feature which all the men used was the active voice, although two of the three men used a high incidence of the passive voice also.

The literature identifies a masculine style of language as using linguistic strategies for authority, dominance, and status differentiation, reflecting a masculine profile of competition, striving for status and task achievement. In my case studies all the male managers held the floor and used strengtheners, which help to build an image of authority and status differentiation. Two out of the three used imperatives, which have a similar effect. Two out of the three used the passive voice and other strategies which distanced and depersonalised, and dismissals of others, which help to build an image of dominance and status differentiation, none of which were used by the women.

However, there are also areas which overlap between the genders which could only be explained by membership of another linguistic group other than gender. The literature identifies the use of statives and declaratives, topic control and strengtheners as associated with the masculine style. In my case studies I found that all the women also used statives/declaratives and topic control, and two out of the three women used strengtheners, as well as the men. I have already noted in my earlier section on the similarities found between men and women in my data, that these features as well as others found in my case studies marked linguistic strategies used by middle managers in the context of their team meetings.

It is interesting to note that Horace and Chris demonstrate high levels of masculine characteristics in their individual profiles, especially marked by Chris, Liz demonstrates a high level of feminine characteristics, Sally a high level of some feminine characteristics, Isabel and Clive present both masculine and feminine characteristics. These inform the particular manager's ideolect, but that ideolect is also comprised of language repertoires from other linguistic groups.

It is evident that gendered linguistic strategies are important as a differentiator, but also that other language tendencies from other pragmatic groups are also involved in any individual's chosen language repertoire. The idea of the Community of Practice (Eckert 1990, Eckert and McConnell-Ginet 1992,, Bergvall 1999, Holmes and Meyerhoff 1999) is a useful tool for exploring the significance of the similarities and dissimilarities of gendered linguistic practices. If men and women belong to, and reflect in their linguistic usage, different groups, or communities, they also belong, in this present study, to the same group or community, that of the middle manager. Men and women both may reflect, in their choice of linguistic repertoires, their membership of communities within the fields of educational management and of the particular school in which the meetings were taking place. The shared experiences and learning, and hence shared pragmatic understandings, discourse structures and strategies, shape the individual's language repertoire. The individual's idiolect both comprises a profile of different repertoires from different communities, and also may reflect a foregrounding of one of these repertoires during any particular interaction. Thus in Howard's case I argue that in his meeting he foregrounded his gendered linguistic practices, rather than those of the middle manager or of the organisational culture which contextualised the speech event.

Patterns arising in the two schools with female headteachers

I had tested my hypothetical explanation of the research problem in two schools with male headteachers, since this reflects the majority of secondary schools nationally. The patterns of gender similarity/ dissimilarity in the first school, Droverslea, suggested a shift in emphasis from gender differences to gender similarities and a reinforcement of the idea of the community of practice in which gender is seen as only one of a number of interlinking and overlapping linguistic groups. Gender differences were found, but so also were similarities which indicated a community of practice, or communities of practice, comprising the team meeting context, the educational middle management context, and the organisational culture context of the particular school. The question which I then needed to address was whether middle managers in schools with female heads showed similar patterns, in other words whether linguistic strategies used by middle managers in such schools corresponded to those associated with gender and whether there were other linguistic strategies used regardless of gender, or which overlapped the issues of gender, and which therefore indicated other communities of practice arising from other contexts.

I now turn my attention to the two schools led by female headteachers, searching for those **linguistic features** identified in the two schools with male heads in the **key areas outlined**, in order to ascertain whether the same patterns emerged in these different circumstances. I recorded meetings run by two male and two female managers in each school; however, I focused my data search on the key areas only, rather than transcribing large sequences of the meetings. I wanted to pinpoint those features already identified in the previous case studies in order to confirm or question my hypothetical explanation. I have focused my report on my findings on the male managers, since this constitutes the crucial area of possible difference in female-headed schools. I have therefore provided here "dipstick testing" transcriptions and commentaries on the critical sequences in order to test out the patterns already identified. I have then compared these with a review of the female managers' meetings.

Beckfield School

The meetings at this school reflected much the same procedures as the two schools in the main study: they consisted of mainly informative items on a pre-published agenda, with a secondary function of discussion of practical details, the agenda having been set by the manager.

Joe: Head of Science

The science faculty meeting took place after school. The team consisted of four men and four women, and most of the faculty were in posts of responsibility, for example, there were Heads of Year, members of the senior management team (SMT), and a deputy head. The agenda included items on finance, INSET arrangements, KS4 planning, a visit to Jodrell Bank, collection of texts. The language functions identified in the meeting were primarily informative, with a secondary function to discuss practical details. In this, it did not differ from the majority of the meetings already analysed in my previous case studies. In the following extracts of key critical incidents, utterances are designated *J* for Joe, *A, B* or *C* for other department members.

Establishing status

Joe establishes from the start that the meeting is agenda driven, agenda items having been chosen by him.

J: Right, turning to the agenda then. Apologies . . . Minutes of the 9th of the 5th. Any matters arising? There isn't anything I wish to . . . arise. No? . . . (indistinct)

A: Can I just ask about these er irrigating (indistinct)?

J: Well, I'll check that one . . . (indistinct brief discussion, including J's instruction: Keep it locked . . .)

J: I think probably I need to talk to whoever's getting it next year. I'll make sure that's done in time . . .

J: Item 3 dadadada (then indistinct as he dismisses item)

J: Item 4 highlight I've got two things together here er the Walrus revision guides which are meant for Year 10, I hope you've still got a few tucked away somewhere, er I hope you're going to sell them er or get them back to the prep room so we can sell . . . (indistinct) I'm expecting to make a significant profit on that . . . so don't sit on them, please er prep room. Anything else on that one?

J: Right School er advance money has come through. The bid we put in for was 7,890 and er we're actually allocated 7000 which is more than last year um so I don't feel too badly off and er having seen er what they've got in the other faculties I think that's pretty good . . . . It includes a sum of 900 for KS 4 texts so we might be thinking about what we precisely what we want to order there.

Joe establishes immediately that he has control over the proceedings of the meeting by using the agenda items to drive it, and also by demonstrating his authority by stating his view with a first person stative ("There isn't anything I wish to . . .") while inviting the team to comment if they wish by using brief and peremptory interrogatives ("any matters arising?"). When a member of the team raises an issue he responds by taking it on board and reasserting his status again with first person statives ("I'll check . . .", "I need to . . ."). He also reinforces his authority when he glosses over an item and dismisses it, then states his points of information/ instruction on the next agenda item with the declarative ("I've got two things together here"). He uses functional imperatives when he repeats the predicate "I hope" indicating, in fact, a command, but softening it. Again, he uses the imperative, this time a direct imperative, when he says "don't sit on them" but he softens this too with the politeness form, "please". He includes the others when he asks "Anything else on that one?", inviting team members to comment or add. He handles the issue of the budget allocation by stating the information about the amounts and bypassing the shortfall by stating that the amount allocated which was lower than the bid was actually higher than the previous year. He asserts ownership by saying "I don't feel too badly off" and comparing with other faculties to create a sense of group identity, and by using the stative "I think that's pretty good". He also establishes status by announcing a budget for texts and inviting suggestions for spending it by using a modal as a functional imperative ("We might be thinking about . . .")

Critical incidents (handling the team, dealing with conflict)

There are no points of conflict, but points where Joe's handling of the team is apparent. He empowers others by requesting specific reports or items of information from them by name:

J: er Jodrell Bank, Jenny do you want to say anything about it?

He deflects potential conflict or disagreement by continuing the declaratives used to introduce items of information:

J: er we've been talking to or trying to talk to Sheffield University er about a what I call a Maths INSET for us all on pupil learning and the two dates I've got in mind are Thursday the 4ᵗʰ and Thursday the 11ᵗʰ of July. Thursday isn't a very hard day for us so I've tried to fix it for those two, periods two, three and four, but er . . .

C: is that both of those dates?

J: well one or other of those two dates, it's a half day slot, it'd be better before lunch if er . . . I'm negotiating via Rosemary, but er . . . (indistinct)

(other contributions)

C: there is a bit of a problem there, Joe, in terms of cover . . . (explains) . . . so what I'm asking you is . . . (interrupted by another)

J: well the slots I've chosen Thursday 2,3,4 are very very quiet . . . and I was assuming that what money we needed would be taken from INSET budget . . . I'll see what requirements we need for cover. But I was just told in the last meeting that er there would be money available from a TVEI er source for activities designed to raise standards or expectations]

A:] oh well that's perfect

J: I would have thought so

The strong first person declaratives ("I've chosen", "I was assuming that . . .", "I will see", "I was told") are reinforced by the use of strengthening repeated adverbials (intensifiers) ("very, very quiet") which have the effect of asserting his authority to *C* who is raising an objection. He also is able to raise another item of information about possible funding to strengthen his case.

When Joe needs to assert his authority / give orders / ensure that what he wants doing is done, he refers to factual reminders of items on the school schedule, and uses modals and conditionals ("I'd rather", "if you want") as well as strengthening modals which function as imperatives ("I really **must** have"):

J: Just to say two things. Theoretically I should have received your Year 7 and Year 8 reports by now, er quite happy to have them later today or tomorrow (indistinct) time is getting on

C: One or two students are actually absent, (indistinct) what about if I give you half the class that I've done, do you want them with blanks or hold on to the absentees

J: I'd rather have them in as they are and get on with it. I'd rather have the bulk . . . If you want to hang on to the two until Monday . . .

C: alright

*J: (Year 9 and 12 reports) The schedule says that those should reach me by Thursday the 20th which is a week from now. I did mention before I think that I'm intending to be out of school the following Monday to Friday, er so I really **must** have those in by this time next week . . .*

When organising procedures for internal examination marking, he makes clear his requirements by using initially an empowering request for others' preferences ("what do you want to do?"), then a modal and conditional ("I personally would be much happier if . . ."), and finally a functional imperative using a strengthening modal ("I shall want").:

J: Exam marking I wanted to know what you wanted to do about that in terms of marking across the board, in sets (indistinct) or what do you want to do? . . . I personally would be much happier if . . . I shall want raw marks, so don't do anything fancy. Finishing units or attempting to finish units, that's got to be the province of the person in charge of the sets . . . whoever in charge of Year 11 so if that person could find out what

has been accomplished this year and organise . . . (general shaking heads)
You're shaking your heads (laughter)

He asserts his demands further by using a strong declarative ("that's got to be") and then a conditional which functions as an imperative ("if that person").

Decision-making

Joe handles decision-making by involving/empowering others ("are you happy with it?") and by using declaratives which establish prior involvement and agreement regarding the issue ("this is . . . what we agreed . . ."):

J: Um we looked at the design of one of these things last time and er let's . . . this is more or less what we agreed at the KS4 planning meeting um are you happy with it? (pause several seconds)
A: The content bit was a bit small and the cross-curricular links looks a bit big . . .
J: I think it's the length of the word!(laughter)
A: well, there's a big space after curricular,isn't there, don't know how easy it is to move them along a bit
B: is it possible to change it or is it (indistinct)
J: Peter did it and he wasn't very enthusiastic about redoing it (general laughter)
(further discussion about changes)
J: well, I'll see what I can do. I'll take it back and see what I can do about that.

Joe again, later, involves his deputy and a member of the SMT in order to establish a decision:

(deputy presents item on timetabling for sessions to release staff for a parents' function)
J: Just remind us what happens in the er . . . on that day (asks SMT member)
(SMT gives details, followed by general discussion and agreement)

During an item on setting, Joe involves the team by throwing the working decisions over to the team, for presentation of suggestions at a later date:

(setting—discussion. Joe looks at file)
J: Yeah, my calculations suggested that the fast set would be about 26 and then middle 22, bottom 14 . . . (discussion) What Jan is saying I think is that the so-called fast group will have to lose a few people (comments) Well, we've got some work to do on this I think
(further discussion)
J: OK so a fair bit of work to do there in the next few weeks . . . Any other KS4? . . . Item 10. Money.

He uses summation ("what Jan is saying . . . is that . . .") as well as statives ("my calculations suggested that") in order to reinforce the problem and the inclusive first person plural pronoun (we) in order to unite the group in seeking the solution to it. His conclusive ("so a fair bit of work to do there . . .") is followed by the moving-on signal ("any other KS4?") and the actual moving on to item 10.

Keith : Head of Technology

The faculty meeting took place, as usual, after the end of the school day. The team members were composed of three women and five men, one of whom was also a member of the senior management team (SMT). The agenda was published in advance of the meeting and included items such as learning support, Oxford/Cambridge candidates, fabric of the building, faculty representatives, school allowance and directed time. There were reports from three people other than the Head of Department. As in Joe's meeting, the items were informative and the discussions were generally about practical issues. In the following extracts of key critical incidents, utterances are designated *K* for Keith, *A/B or C* for other departmental members.

Establishing status

Keith established the pattern of the meeting by introducing the minutes of the last meeting and continuing with the first main agenda item.

K: Right you've all got copies of the minutes and agenda. (pause) Are those a true record of what took place? OK right item 2 then . . . Learning Support. This information came to me in the last few days and I've put the information in with the agenda, OK, so if you can all look at that . . . It's to inform staff that from next September they've he's going to monitor the statemented students. This is the proposed system . . . . subject staff will be asked to fill these sheets in . . . . We're asked to look at this and to make suggestions as to (indistinct)

(discussion)

Like Joe, Keith establishes his control over the proceedings immediately. He uses quite a formal register ("are those a true record"," this information came to me in the last few days") which helps to create a feeling of authority. He uses declaratives ("I've put the information . . .", "it's to inform staff", "this is the proposed system") and introduces the discussion of the document by using the inclusive pronoun and the passive ("we're asked to . . ."), which empowers the team members to give their responses.

He uses empowerment frequently, for example by requesting others to speak to or introduce agenda items:

K: Now, Ida you want to speak to this item,4
A: Yes now this won't take long . . . (gives information about arrangements)

He uses supportive responses to their contributions:
(following colleagues' reports on various meetings, ICT, raising achievement etc, each holding the floor for several minutes)

K: Yes, it will need looking at again

and empowering questions:

K: Where will the funding come from?

Half way through the meeting Kevin leaves the room to see to a student and leaves the second in the department to continue with items 7,8,and 9 on the agenda, returning in time for the last item. He re-asserts his status by introducing the agenda item and with an initiation signal ("right."). He concludes the meeting business with an assertive declarative ("that's it"):

K: Right, directed time . . . (discussion) . . . OK, right, fine. (item of AOB), right, that's it.

Critical incidents and decision-making

As with Joe, Keith receives no direct points of conflict to deal with, but where a colleague expresses dissatisfaction with the design, purpose and administration of some forms to fill in, he handles this by showing support for her argument, even by continuing it, and then hands the floor to a colleague whom he asks to speak to the item with further information:

(Item 2 Learning support forms for staff to fill in)
A: I would suggest or it's just a point that would occur to me that if this was officially given to me by Cynthia or Dave you know I know it will take their time and I know how busy they are but if you just have a blanket pile of these in the faculty. . . . if he'd just come to me personally and just done something simple like put the name in, the form, the subject and then just said you'll know about this youngster , you know what his problems are . . . you know I would feel it you know I'd be more inclined . . .
K: because if it is statemented kids then they could actually do a proforma with the name, form, already there and possibly things the staff ought to be aware of to be on the form already . . . there are generalisms which er er comments that could just make us . . . put the signals out to us
A: like organisation, comprehension . . .
B: yeah, yeah key words that would make life easier for us cause then we could actually target that
K: OK yeah (asks colleague to speak to the item)
(further discussion along these lines)
C: problem is . . . this is the first time I've seen these and I'm still wondering where they might be generated from . . . . (continues)
(long pause while colleague minutes the item, K helps her)
K: right . . . Right then, next one, Oxbridge candidates.

Keith therefore handles critical incidents and decision-making by empowering others to "take charge" of (take responsibility for) the proceedings, without conceding his own status. This may be either the whole group in discussion or one colleague presenting an item. The sequence above where a colleague is unhappy with the actions of other staff outside the team, is reminiscent of the sequence shown in Horace's meeting (Droverslea) where he is seemingly caught in a tension between strategic and operational policy-makers, finds himself making critical comments about named members of the SMT and handles the crisis by removing the tape recording. Keith, however, seems not to feel personally threatened by the comments of his colleague and is able to agree with her without compromising his status, and withdraws by handing the floor to another. He therefore deflects the conflict, in a way similar to that of the female managers in the other two schools.

Conclusions

Both the men used empowerment; Joe (head of Science) asked directly for opinions of other members, either as a general request or as individuals by name ("Just remind us what happens . . ."; are you happy with it?") He used modals and conditionals as imperatives, although he also used strengtheners, strong stressing intonation and modal auxiliaries for emphasis when his utterances were effectively functioning as imperatives: "I really **must** have those in by . . ."; "I **shall** want . . ."; "If that person can find out . . ."; "We **did** say . . ." He tended to use frequent strong first person declaratives and summations: "I've chosen . . ."; "I was assuming that . . ."; "my calculations suggest that . . ."; "I think what . . . is saying is that . . ." These techniques are reminiscent of Clive's at Droverslea and suggest the appearance of cooperation and consensus while covering an incipient domination function.

The other male manager, Keith (head of Technology) used the empowerment of others by asking members to speak to three agenda items, one giving a full report and holding the floor for several minutes. His responses to others were supportive and empowering: "Yes, it will need looking at again; where will the funding come from?" The floor was shared between the members with reports and discussion of items.

Both these male managers used linguistic strategies nearer to the feminine end of the continuum. In establishing status, they used empowerment of others and organisational strategies for control, rather than the masculine strategies of holding the floor, using imperatives and the passive voice. Few areas of conflict arose in either case study, but both men deflected potential conflicts rather than confronting them, in a similar way to the women in the previous case studies. They used functional imperatives but not the distancing strategies or dismissal found in two of the three other case studies involving male managers. However, on the other hand, they did not use the apologies and acceptance of correction used by all the female managers. In decision-making, they tended to use the co-operation and consensus strategies found in the female managers' language repertoires, both using empowerment of others, although Joe's use of strengtheners and strong first person declaratives reflected a masculine style.

The gendered differences in linguistic repertoires, as far as the men were concerned, were not as marked in the two case studies in the school with the female head as they were in the two schools with male headteachers. Both the male managers here demonstrated some important characteristics more associated with the feminine style of managerial language, such as the empowerment of others, consensus strategies and conflict deflection. They used politeness forms, softeners for commands, and the inclusive pronoun, but they also used strategies associated with the masculine style such as strengtheners, and did not use strategies characteristic of the women managers in the other two schools, such as apology and acceptance of correction. Language associated with the gender similarities in the previous case studies and that associated with the context of the middle manager's team meetings, such as the use of topic control and of statives/declaratives, were seen here.

This suggests that there were linguistic practices other than those of gendered practices coming into play here and supports the idea of different communities of practice, for example that of the school's organisational culture, overlapping and interlinking within managers' interactions with their team.

In checking my findings with the data from the female managers' meetings at Beckfield, I found that both the women, Kath and Gladys, used organisational strategies to assert status, empowerment of others and supportive responses. Kath was the head of Modern Languages and her team meeting consisted of five members, four of whom were women.

In establishing status, Kath used topic control; she introduced items from the agenda which she had produced beforehand. She also used statives: "The last faculty meeting we had, we outlined special needs policy"; "I've had one or two letters back from parents"; "I want to . . ."; "The Head called me in and asked me . . . I said yes . . .". She used questions and softeners as functional imperatives: "could you perhaps do . . . ?"; "I think it would be helpful if you", rather than direct imperatives. She used supportive minimal responses and the inclusive pronoun "we/us" on a number of occasions, which helped to create a feeling of unity in the team: "let's . . . anyway, let's . . ."; "we've got to". Kath used empowerment frequently throughout the meeting, often in the form of monitoring, using questions to check agreement: "is that OK?" ; "how do you feel about that?"

There were no points of conflict to deal with, but in *decision-making*, Kath used empowerment: "tell me exactly what I've got to ask"; "what do you think?" and self-effacements: "well, beggars can't be choosers"; "I don't know, that's what we've got to choose from". She used softened imperatives through statives and conditionals: "I'd like to get it sorted"; "I wondered if we could"; "we need to make sure that whoever has it can keep it clean"; "so if anybody could spare a bit of time that weekend . . ."

Gladys was a head of year and her team meeting consisted of nine members of both sexes. In establishing status, she also used topic control by introducing the agenda items and by reading through the minutes of the last meeting and talking through matters arising, providing team members with information. She used statives and first person declaratives frequently: "I think . . ."; "I felt . . ."; "I don't mind if . . ."; "I will let you have"; "it's because the pupils have . . . increasingly year ten have . . ."; "what I'm proposing for them to do is"; "I gave them the first task today"; "I did talk to several colleagues to say what do you think"; "the option choice I have taken further, I wrote to . . ." She also used the inclusive pronoun: "we could get them to . . ."; "we can"; "we need", and positive modals like "it could be trailblazing" which helped to create unity and team effort. She used empowerment by inviting another member of staff to report on a topic and by asking for responses: "what has feedback been like?" Gladys also used functional imperatives rather than direct imperatives, using statives: "it means keeping a check on . . ."; "we need to keep a careful check on . . ."; "I think this needs reinforcing." She frequently used supportives, such as minimal responses and "yes, yes"; "yes, it can be as lighthearted as you want to make it."

Again, there were no points of conflict during this meeting, but *in decision-making* Gladys, like Kath, used empowerment: "do you think it sounds a reasonable idea to . . . ?" and functional imperatives, softening with statives and the inclusive pronoun: "the only thing we've got to be really firm about is . . ."; "we need to be really firm in making sure that . . ."; "I think we've got to be very firm about that"; "perhaps that's something we need to look at."

Both women in this school used linguistic strategies nearer to the feminine end of the continuum, including the self-effacements, apologies and acceptance of correction used by all the women in the previous case studies, but not found in the language strategies used by the men in this school. Both used hedges and weakeners such as "really", "you know", "sort of", "perhaps." Both used topic control by means of setting and driving the agenda items and both used the statives/declaratives and softeners which characterised the language of middle managers' interactions in their team meetings found in the previous case studies regardless of gender. Again, as in the previous schools studied, both men and women used the following linguistic strategies: topic control, statives/declaratives, first person statives, softeners functioning as imperatives, professional jargon, and supportive interruptions.

Both the male and the female managers established status by using organisational strategies, being the information provider, using supportive strategies of various types, and most obviously by using empowerment of others, both by using others to report on agenda items and by directly asking others to contribute or provide their opinions on a particular issue. These are associated with the feminine style. There were no occurrences of holding the floor for any length of time by the manager, no direct imperatives, nor use of the passive voice, which are associated with the masculine style.

There were no discernible conflicts during the meetings and no identifiable tensions arising between the team members and the middle managers.

In making decisions there appeared to be no discernible difference between the genders here, both tending to fit the feminine functional tendencies of cooperation and consensus, using summation and inclusive pronouns in the process.

However, the women used more specific "feminine" linguistic traits such as hedges, weakeners, softeners, while the men used more specific "masculine" linguistic traits such as strong declaratives, strengtheners, and stressed intonation.

In conclusion, the common features for both sexes found in the previous schools were also present at Beckfield, but the gender differences identified at Droverslea and High Ridge were not found in this school, and indeed, managers of both sexes used linguistic strategies mainly focused on cooperation and consensus, in other words feminine strategies. The gendered community of practice has been submerged into the school / organisational culture group; the latter has become of greater importance than gender in the choice of linguistic field. I then wished to see whether these patterns were confirmed in the other school with a female head.

Broadmarsh School

The organisational culture of this school, headed by a very "hands-on" female headteacher who encouraged the use of experiential learning for both pupils and staff, promoted an in-service training (INSET) approach to team meetings. This meant that two of the meetings researched included a short business meeting for the whole team for a few minutes at the start, then moving on to small group/paired working parties on a set topic of development. A third meeting comprised a group discussion based on items from a questionnaire produced by the senior management team and which involved sharing teaching practices, similar to an INSET session. The fourth meeting consisted of a team of only four who worked together on administrative and standardisation matters. The nature of the meetings was therefore very different from those in the other three schools and this inevitably had an implication for comparison.

Patrick was the head of English with a team of seven members of both sexes. The only agenda item in this meeting was the discussion of a questionnaire document produced by the senior management team (SMT) concerning the sharing of good practice in classroom matters, such as behavioural issues in lessons, the delivery of the merit rewards/ sanctions policy, the use of resources. *In establishing status*, Patrick used topic control as he introduced the items in the questionnaire. The topics had not been chosen by him, as they were imposed from the SMT. He delegated a team member to write the minutes which formed the report of the team discussion to be fed back to the SMT. He then read through each given question and the members of the team discussed their practical strategies used in the classroom, in response to each issue. He used statives frequently: "I'll just read this to you straight, that's the best thing, I think"; "I've asked Paul to"; "now, I think that's a fair thing to say"; "I think we can say"; "I think that." He did not hold the floor for any longer than the other team members, and used empowerment in encouraging the members to discuss and to state their opinions and strategies, without interruption. He frequently used supportives and politeness forms: "thank you for your input"; "thank you very much."

There were no conflicts, although during the discussion members at times disagreed with each other. At one point, Patrick disagreed with a member of the team who made a comment about her handling of the threat of sanctions. However, he responded with a supportive followed by a disjunct: "yes, but that's distinct from receiving bad behaviour from pupils and . . . what you're talking about is . . ." When the colleague further explained her point of view, Patrick responded with a disclaimer and supportive: "right, no, no, what I meant was, exactly what you say . . .", "I just think there are some pupils who . . ." On a hypothetical point on the questionnaire, he used a stative, which was received by positive colleague support: "I'm not happy about that. I think it causes terrible resentment." Throughout the meeting Patrick frequently responded to others' contributions with supportives: "yes", "sure", "absolutely", "I share your concern", "mmm", with many positive minimal responses.

In decision-making, Patrick tended to use summative statements: "so you tend to . . . ?"; "right, so you think . . ." where he summarised his colleague's ideas. He used first person statives, as did his colleagues during the discussion: "The one I try is."; "In my own case I . . ."; "I always"; "have to say that I don't do that"; "I tend to . . ."; "I plough all my efforts into . . ."; "my feeling is that"; "I think it's just a question of reminding ourselves at meetings . . ." He used empowerment in the form of questions: "does anyone ever.?"; "how does the team feel about.?"; "yes, but how, how?" He used a final summative, using the inclusive pronoun as a softened imperative: "OK, so we'll have a big splash on year ten."

Ivan was the head of Humanities and his meeting consisted of nine members of both sexes. His meeting consisted of a short business agenda for the whole team together and then the "main agenda" as he called it, which involved discussions in pairs on different items in the development plan. These arose from the whole school development plan originated by the SMT and concerned prioritising targets for the department and discussing ideas on how to achieve them. Each pair reported back at the end of the session. Therefore, as with Patrick's meeting, the discussion base was rooted in empowerment.

In establishing status, Ivan used topic control as he introduced items on the business agenda at the start of the meeting. He read through the minutes of the last meeting which frequently included: "Ivan suggested that . . ." and used statives to inform the members of the team about the action which he had taken. He also used statives and agreement monitoring: "we agreed at our last meeting that we'd concentrate on development planning"; "what I'd like to do is . . ."; "OK?"; "would you agree?" He used statives frequently: "I'll see to that"; "I've had"; "I've said I'd like." He used softened imperatives: "but they must go in the book, please, otherwise I won't know about it"; "I'd like you to . . ." He then gave the team instructions for the paired working groups by using statives and softened imperatives: "I'll tell you what I want to do, me included"; "there's already been some team input"; "I'll give some little pieces of paper"; "I'd like you to put on the card"; "for you to write down". He used conditionals as softened imperatives and monitored agreement: "so if we looked at . . ."; "I'd like you to . . . or don't you want to do that?"

Again, there were no points of conflict in this meeting. *In decision-making*, Ivan used statives, softened imperatives, modals and frequently the inclusive pronoun: "OK I'll note that"; "so we'll wait to hear"; "when I get back I'll be asking you what groups you'd like to teach next year"; "I suggest that"; "so I think that could be a good idea for the school." He clearly used empowerment throughout this meeting through its structure. The team members decided through majority vote the priorities for pair work. The individual pairs chose the topic they wanted to discuss. The pairs were empowered in their groups to offer their own opinions and were invited to report back to the meeting at the end.

Both the men, Patrick and Ivan, used empowerment. Patrick functioned first of all as the information provider, then using another member of the team to write the minutes as a report, he asked for discussion of an SMT document. He used co-operation and consensus seeking strategies in his meeting, and he demonstrated a high level of rapport strategies. Ivan also functioned as an information provider, then moved his team on to paired work on targets followed by a plenary for feedback reports. He also used co-operation and consensus seeking strategies.

Cheryl was the head of upper school pastoral team and her meeting consisted of sixteen members of both sexes and included three heads of faculties, middle managers in their own right. As with Ivan, Cheryl used a short time at the beginning of the meeting for the business agenda and then moved the team on to small group discussions of different topics. During this period for most of the time she was dealing with administrative tasks such as photocopying, although she also moved around the groups as they were working. The small group work arose from items on the business agenda, the issues arising from "bronze awards" and records of achievement.

In establishing status, Cheryl used topic control as she introduced items on the business agenda which she had produced beforehand: "you will have noticed that on the agenda"; "Sharon has asked if she can have ten minutes to report . . ." She read through the minutes of the last meeting herself and commented on action taken. She used supportiveness features and politeness forms: "thanks for that"; "you've provided a stable structure for careers support." She frequently used functional imperatives rather than direct imperatives, through softeners, inclusive pronouns and conditionals: "it will mean that . . ."; "we're going to try to target"; "if you know that . . . you could try to . . ."; "there are one or two things we need to think about"; "; "if you've got someone who . . . you could also indicate"; "what I'd like you to do . . ." She used statives: "The other issue is . . ."; "when I first came we had"; "it was quite useful"; "I'd like"; "we're going to try to give year ten tutors."

There were no conflicts. In decision-making, Cheryl used empowerment in frequently asking for opinions, at times also using self-effacements: "what I'm not clear about in my own mind . . . is whether to . . . don't know what you feel about that but I'd like to hear"; "so shall I titivate that one up and then get it to you all to try . . ." She used statives and also monitoring for agreement: "what I'd like year ten tutors to do is . . . OK?"; "what'd like you to do over the next few weeks is . . . OK?"; "what I propose is . . . OK?"; "can I suggest that?" She used summarising strategies to then move on to decisions: "so can I suggest, then, that.?"; "I think as long as you year ten tutors are happy that . . . then I think I could . . ." and empowerment: "I'm quite interested . . . for the year ten tutors to give this some time . . . could come up with some useful strategies for this . . ."

Clearly empowerment was an important strategy as the structure of the meeting was based on the subsequent small group work which took up the rest of the meeting.

Gertie was the head of the Learning Support team and her meeting consisted of four women. The agenda was focused on administrative matters and standardisation of practices, and consisted for the most part of a discussion amongst all four and sharing of practice. In establishing status, Gertie used topic control as she read out the minutes of the last meeting and talked through matters arising from them and action she had taken. She therefore functioned as information provider. She used frequent declaratives: "I will mention it and see what she says"; "I've had a sheet from Linda about capitation"; "I've got some that . . ." She used statives and conditionals to soften imperatives: "you'll need to make sure that . . ."; "letters have gone out, so you'll have to let them know . . ."; "if you've got your IEPs, then can I put them in for photocopying?" She used self-effacements: "I don't understand it"; "I'll have to go and check." She also, like the other managers at this school, frequently used the strategy of empowerment: "any other things on that?"; "so you and I will share"; "suggestions on that for next meeting please."

There were, again no points of conflict in this meeting. In decision-making, Gertie used softened imperatives rather than direct imperatives: "we need to be thinking about what we want to order . . ."; "so if you can be thinking"; "if you can come up with some ideas"; "the other thing I wanted to do was to . . . could you take your folders and sort them out?"; "so if we can think about that"; "so I think we could quite easily manage those." Throughout the meeting, Gertie frequently used the inclusive pronoun we/us, conditionals and modals. She also clearly used empowerment in the discussion during the meeting, not only by sharing the floor, but also by directly asking the others' their opinions: "do you reckon we could?"; "I wondered if we could do a brainstorm, what do you think, Jan?"; "what do we think about picking up all the stage ones up to and including year nine?"

Both the female middle managers, Cheryl and Gertie, used organisational strategies and a business-like register for the control function. They were in control of the agenda and of topic change, and had organised administration prior to the meetings. They functioned first of all in the meeting as information provider, holding the floor. However, Cheryl then moved her team on to working in small groups for the rest of the meeting thus empowering the participants. Gertie kept her small group together, but used empowerment by including all her team in a brainstorming session to discuss the issues already produced for the meeting. Both women used self-effacing strategies which were not identified in the linguistic usage of the men.

Again, as in the previous schools studied, both male and female managers used the following linguistic strategies:

- topic control,
- statives/declaratives
- first person statives
- softeners functioning as imperatives
- professional jargon
- supportive interruptions and other supportive techniques.

Both the male and the female managers established status by:

- using organisational strategies
- being the information provider
- using supportive strategies of various types
- and most obviously by using empowerment of others, both by using others to report on agenda items, by using group discussion and by using working groups and feedback.

There were no occurrences of holding the floor for any length of time by the manager, no direct imperatives, nor use of the passive voice.

There were no discernible conflicts during the meetings and no identifiable tensions arising between the team members and the middle managers.

Decision-making across all meetings was achieved through empowerment through meeting content (brainstorming, small group work, discussion groups) and therefore appeared to be arrived at through the consensus of the members, although how far the nature of the materials prepared ahead of the meeting influenced these decisions was difficult to assess.

In conclusion, the common features found in the previous schools were also present at Broadmarsh, but the gender differences identified elsewhere were not found in this school, and indeed, managers of both genders used linguistic strategies mainly falling into the feminine tendencies group, focused on cooperation/consensus outcomes. Again, as with Broadmarsh, the gendered community of practice has become subsumed under the greater importance of the school community of practice.

However, the type of meeting where small groups split off from the main group to work together on an aspect of the agenda task, is more representative of INSET sessions than the usual team meetings researched in all the other schools. Moreover, the teams also held other INSET sessions using a similar pattern at other times on the calendar. This appeared to be unusual generally in comparison with other schools, but typical of this particular school, and reflected the headteacher's stated aims and vision. In many ways, the "collegiality" observed at Broadmarsh could be said to be "contrived", after Hargreaves' definition (1998), reflecting a situation in which a simulation of collegiality is contrived through "compulsory cooperation" required of teachers and management teams, driven by the headteacher and operated through working parties structured by given whole school plans in order to implement a non-negotiable agenda. The operational management of such contrived collegiality as observed at Broadmarsh appears to advantage feminine styles of management and linguistic strategies, with its focus on cooperation and consensus.

Conclusions

The significant finding at this stage of the research is that within the two schools headed by female headteachers middle managers tended to manifest linguistic strategies and traits in their meetings generally associated with females and that these schools demonstrated among male managers a greater focus on co-operation, consensus, unity and rapport-based discourse than the males in the schools with male headteachers. Just as, at High Ridge, Chris (strongly) and Sally (in some respects) demonstrated a move towards masculine strategies, which reflected the valuing of masculine styles by the headteacher of their school, so also the middle managers of both sexes at Broadmarsh and Beckfield moved towards the feminine end of the linguistic continuum.

Although clearly all managers have their own idiolect which is reflected in the commentaries on the linguistic use identified in each meeting, and each individual's style is composed of devices from a number of different linguistic groups, they also belong to a social/professional/occupational group from which a sociolect arises, informed and shaped by the shared experiences, pragmatics and shared discourse structures/strategies. The framework of the Community of Practice, outlined in chapter two, is useful here, the community being defined by the membership of the group and by those practices in which the membership engages as a joint enterprise, and in which gender is one of a number of diversities which impinge upon the group (Eckert 1990, Eckert and McConnell-Ginet 1992, Bergvall 1999, Holmes and Meyerhoff 1999). The speech community of the model essentially arises from a shared enterprise and involves a shared repertoire of joint resources for negotiating meaning, which could be seen in my fieldwork as specialist terminology, linguistic routines, shared discourse which reflects a common perspective on the part of the world in which the meetings engage. These pragmatic understandings between the members of the group give rise to those linguistic features which are shared by both genders and can be regarded as anticipated/expected middle manager-speak within the contexts of this type of team meeting, such as the use of first person statives, the use of softeners where there is a functional imperative, the use of professional jargon.

An outline of the way in which the community of practice model works in my research is as follows:

- The community of practice in my research comprises both (a) the team meeting context which I am directly analysing, and (b) the wider school context in which the meeting takes place, reflecting the particular organisational culture of the school in question, and by extension, (c) the influence of the field of educational management. Each of (b) and (c) influences (a), but each of the three "levels" are also separate communities. In other words, the team meetings are communities of practice separate yet closely linked to (and interdependent on) the other communities.

- Issues of status are present both for the community and for the individuals involved ("core" and "peripheral" members of the Community of Practice model). The "core members" could be seen as the middle managers and the "peripheral members" the members of the team, within the context of (a), the pastoral or academic team meetings. However, core members of (a) could be peripheral members of (b) and vice versa. In other words there may be members of the senior management team in any faculty team, although the middle manager is not a member of the SMT. Expectations, and equally diversity, of language repertoires indicating issues of status within the context of (a), the team meetings, are therefore influenced by idiolect, sociolect, gender and the membership of a number of other communities of practice.

- Issues of a middle manager's status are shown in the key areas of my research: establishing status, critical incidents—handling the team interactions, handling conflicts, reaching decisions.

- Issues of similarities and differences in the way in which male and female middle managers use the speech repertoires at their disposal in order to handle the key sequences of their meetings can be seen as issues of diversity within a continuum of "gendered practices" and which are also influenced by other shared practices both within and without the meetings.

- In some cases, for example in the two schools led by female headteachers in my case studies, the gendered community of practice, as far as the male managers were concerned, had become subsumed under the greater influence of the school (organisational culture) community of practice. This was particularly observed in the contrived collegiality of Broadmarsh, where the organisational culture was marked by working party/INSET style team meetings required by the headteacher to implement school policy. This effect was also discussed in regard to the linguistic repertoire chosen by Chris at High Ridge.

However, it is clear from my case studies that there was a difference in the range of linguistic strategies accessible to men and women. The male middle managers had at their disposal a range of strategies from the feminine end of the continuum, and were able to apply these where the situation required them, as, to an extent at Droverslea, and clearly at Broadmarsh and Beckfield. On the other hand, the female middle managers demonstrated few masculine strategies, apart from the use of statives, topic control, and to an extent strengtheners and professional lexis, all of which were associated with the contextual language of middle managers' meetings. None of the women used holding the floor, imperatives, dismissals or distancing and depersonalising strategies associated with the masculine style.

Whatever the organisational culture and whatever the gender of the headteacher, there was still an imbalance between men and women in the management structure of all four schools and this was outlined clearly in chapter 4. Therefore, the common use of feminine linguistic strategies across both genders at the two schools with female heads did not imply that women gained greater access to higher managerial positions than men in these schools. Men were still able to gain more faculty management positions and more senior management positions. It is possible to conclude that a factor in the valuing of men above women in management posts could be that of the greater flexibility of linguistic range which men demonstrate, or the greater access men might have to the diversities of communities of practice.

Summary

In this chapter, I have explored the patterns emerging from my data and argued that there were gender differences (gendered practices) in linguistic usage in the meetings analysed in my case studies. These are especially evident in usage reflecting the masculine/feminine frame/schema outlined in the literature review: the masculine approach being status and task-oriented, competitive, dominance driven, while the feminine approach is led by a desire for team-building, consensus and cooperation. However, I also argue that there are other influences on language choices in any given repertoire: for example, that of the community of practice of the school itself, its organisational culture, and of the field of educational management.

In conclusion, I support my argument, exemplified in the case studies, that there are differences in the way that male and female middle managers use linguistic strategies in managerial interactions with their teams these differences arise from the different frames/schema they bring to the situation; these frames can be identified as gendered communities of practice in which shared experiences and pragmatic understandings of gender shape discourse gender variation in linguistic usage is part of a continuum of both sexes' gendered linguistic practices there is an identifiable middle management frame which is common to both genders gendered linguistic practices may be subsumed under other linguistic practices, for example that of the field of educational management or of the particular school itself and its organisational culture the feminine style of management was valued in theory by both male and female headteachers, although in practice there was a significant under-representation of women at middle and senior management levels in all the four schools in this study academic (faculty) team leadership positions were more available to women in the schools headed by women than in those headed by men the feminine linguistic repertoire may mismatch the management style incipiently valued by male headteachers who form the majority of assessors for promotion to senior levels of management. I also raise the question of whether headteachers of both sexes value the greater linguistic range that men show, being able to adapt to both masculine and feminine styles where appropriate to the organisational culture.

CHAPTER 9

THE WAY FORWARD

On a linguistic level, my research has implications for the progress of gender linguistic research. Much of the research in this field over the last couple of decades has concentrated on the nature of gender differences. In investigating gendered language within real managerial/leadership interactions in team meetings I have looked at the nature of the linguistic strategies used by male and female middle managers/leaders and the way that language works in a specific managerial context. I have seen that in my case studies there were linguistic strategies used, which overlapped those of gender. Although I have found gender differences in strategies used and explained these by reference to frame and schema theory, indicating that men and women bring to their interactions frames reflecting their previous, socially constructed gender experiences, I have also found that there are other frames brought to the situation. Linguistic strategies in common between male and female managers corresponded with the requirements of the team meeting management itself and indicated a commonality of prior experience and practice between both sexes.

I have found that the models of the community of practice, outlined by Eckert and McConnell-Ginet (1992) and further developed by Bergvall 1999 and Holmes and Meyerhoff 1999, a useful tool for explaining these dimensions. This approach moves on from both the deficiency/dominance and the difference models of gender linguistic variation to a model of diversity which challenges assumptions of polarised gender differences. It interprets evidence of similarity and dissimilarity in gender repertoires as issues of diversity within a continuum of gendered practices. These practices are established by membership of a group and they are informed and shaped by shared experiences, shared pragmatics and are reflected in shared discourse strategies. Gender is then seen as one of a number of diversities which influence language variation. In my case studies, other diversities can be seen as the practices of middle management, and of the organisational culture of the particular school.

On a practical level, my case studies have shown that a balance of management and communication style is required in schools. It is my belief, as I have shown from the literature, that this applies also to other institutions and businesses. Whatever the access to management posts may be for women in reality, the feminine style of management and language is **overtly** valued by headteachers in schools. What may be **covertly** valued, however, is access to masculine communication strategies which men are more able to achieve than women. Thus, women may often not be regarded as "talking the walk".

But what indeed is "talking the walk"? If it is about assertiveness, aggression, dominance, do we need this climate at this time? Talking the walk could just as easily be about a manager or leader determined to create a cohesive (not divided) team, one which has an ethos of working collaboratively (not in a negative and competitive way). Talking the walk could just as easily be about encouragement and support of each individual so that each one plays a significant part, and so that there are more junior colleagues coming up behind.

We have seen that such teams are successful, and that they are more than holding their own in these new darker days of recession. In the persistent climate of change in education, industry and in the current global economic recession, it is important to maintain a balanced management team and to value the feminine communication and management style in the practice of promotion for women within schools and other businesses. It is logical that an overt valuing of the feminine style most associated with the female sex should result in greater promotional opportunities for women.

There are, of course, many other factors involved in the under-representation of women in educational management, and Davidson and Cooper (1992) discussed some these in regard to the "glass ceiling" effect. Use of language and the way this reflects management style is only one such factor. However, my case studies indicated that men were assuming more feminine styles of language and management in secondary schools, and therefore I argue that a movement towards feminine strategies **should** imply an opening up of the field to potential women managers and leaders. Whether it is in practice is another question. But this is what we should be advocating now.

Because gaining more women leaders will lead to greater success in difficult times, whether this is within the business or the educational field. Underlying the issue of increasing women's access to management and leadership posts in schools, is the issue of whether this would improve schools' effectiveness. OFSTED guidelines in "Framework for the Inspection of Schools" (1993) and in "Improving Schools" (1994) state that two of the conditions for schools' improved effectiveness are strong leadership and a valuing of open and consultative management. Harrison (in Bell and Harrison 1995) discusses the idea that an effective school needs team management, more open lines of management and active consultative management. These approaches are appropriate to the feminine style of management and communication; as my case studies showed, feminine strategies are concerned with team-building, co-operation and empowerment.

One implication of my study is that those who make the appointments to middle and senior educational management, that is, mainly heads and governors, should be aware that the skills and characteristics which they overtly value, do, in fact, correspond closely to those at the feminine end of the continuum. It is not a question of positive discrimination, which the male headteachers of Droverslea and High Ridge rejected, but of being aware of the implications of those skills which are currently valued in middle managers. We need to make a more critical examination of gender assumptions than we have done hitherto. We need to take another look at the models which are currently being used in recruitment decisions. So CEOs and senior leaders in business and the professions need to think more about sex—or at least the gender characteristics which will benefit their management teams, and finally the effectiveness and success of their institution.

A second implication is that of professional development of staff. Evetts (1994) showed that even women who had achieved headship of a school were aware of the personal struggle it had been to reach that level. Her respondents in her study of career histories made it clear that the women concerned perceived the criteria for management promotion up the career ladder as being geared to the masculine style. Whether there are elements of this or not, it is important that women are made aware of the skills and characteristics which are valued by headteachers in assessing qualities for management. Both Davidson and Cooper (1992) and Evetts (1994) discussed the undermining effect on women's self-image and self-value of the perception that management norms are male-orientated.

If staff development focused on the feminine strategies which heads claim to value in their management teams, then surely women would feel more self-confident about applying for such positions. My case studies showed that heads claimed that women did not apply for management posts when they became available. In order to recruit more female managers, therefore, there needs to be a more intensive drive to demonstrate to women that the feminine style of collaboration, team-building and relationship-focus **is** appropriate to educational management, and, I would argue, to leadership in other fields of business, even more so in times of global recession, and that women should be more confident of offering themselves for promotion.

It is not a question of training courses for "women into management" of which many have been available in the past, since the highlighting of Davidson and Cooper's "glass ceiling" in the early 1990s. These have tended to focus on assertiveness training for women and in consequence to reinforce gender stereotypes of management and leadership. These training courses clearly say "women are not assertive enough"; they are deficient in their professional practice. In other words they have reflected the old saying "why can't a woman be more like a man?"

Most of all, I believe that it is, as my work has shown, a question of diversity which needs to be understood not only by the assessors but also by the potential candidates. Professional development needs to focus, not on simply trying to persuade women that they should apply for management positions, nor on trying to change women's managerial, leadership or communicative style, but on convincing them that feminine styles of management, leadership and communication **are** valued, and, if anything, on supporting them to develop feminine strategies further. There is surely an argument that men need to be trained to communicate with their teams in a more feminine way, focusing on team-building and collaboration, valuing the ideas and contributions of others.

It is, however, a question of understanding the different approaches to communication which people bring to their communicative engagements, along with their different "frames". Not only do women need to learn more about the effectiveness of some masculine communicative strategies, but also men need to learn about the effectiveness of feminine strategies, and both need to learn how these can operate successfully together. Only then can we develop effective team working, management and leadership strategies, and institutions fit for purpose in the second decade of the twenty first century and beyond.

Women can be empowered to "talk the walk" that is needed for success, but on their own terms, not to emulate the way that men communicate. And institutions can position themselves for the post-recession era, as long as CEOs (or headteachers in the case of schools) think more strategically about the positives which women bring to the workplace.

Most women cannot always directly influence senior management and CEOs' views of female applicants for leadership posts, because they may well not be included in the senior team or the interviewing panel, or else they find themselves, even in 2012, marginalised within it. But what we women can do for ourselves is be confident that research shows that women in leadership and management are a force to be reckoned with, that teams with female leaders are successful and effective. So, my advice as a result of my study is:

To the women seeking promotion and standing in their institutions,

- do what you are good at
- do not let anyone persuade you that you need to adapt your style to a more masculine one—or to be more like anyone else! Be yourself.
- focus on building relationships within your team; a happy sharing team is a productive one
- encourage and support others, show CEOs and senior leadership that you are happy to share your skills for the greater good of the company or institution
- ensure that you talk about what you are doing for company/ institutional growth and development
- do not be afraid to be the "wife" or "mother" figure—the nurturing one who ensures that the team's tasks run smoothly and that the outcome is successful. These should not be derogatory terms.
- learn to delegate; you are not the only one who can do the task well; trust in your colleagues
- mentoryour colleagues and then let them fly. It may feel like you are at times creator of your own demise if those colleagues rise higher than you. But believe that your work is for the larger

team/ the company/ the greater good—and that you WILL be recognised for it.

- remember that at the end of the day colleagues, senior leaders and company directors remember positively those who they enjoy working with, not those they have to fight with.
- be confident of your leadership and use language which reflects this. Talk about what you have done (use the "I" word more); talk about what the team has done together , or needs to do ("we need to . . .", "it would be really good if we . . . .", "let's build on our success last month . . ."); be specific about what you want and when ("can I have those reports by Friday?")
- remember that women are some of the most successful managers and leaders: look at Anna Wintour (British: publishing), Laura Ashley (British: business), Nicola Horlicks (British: finance), Hilary Clinton(American: politics), Angela Merkel (German: politics), Gina Rinehart (Australian: mining industry), Amanda Staveley (British: finance broker), Karren Brady (British: business/ football management), Susan Greenfield (British: academic) . . . . and the list goes on . . . .

Let me know if this book resonates with your experience, of your difficulties and of your successes at
juliaibbotson@btinternet.com
www.juliaibbotson.com

REFERENCES AND FURTHER READING

Abbott, P. & Wallace, C. (1997) *An Introduction to Sociology: feminist perspectives* (London: Routledge)

Adair, J. (1988) *Effective Leadership* (Reading: Pan)

Adler, N. and Izraeli,D. (1988) *Women in Management Worldwide* (New York: Sharpe)

Adler, S., Laney, J., Packer, M. (1993) *Managing Women: Feminism and Power in Educational Management* (Bucks: Open Univ. Press)

Andrew, C., Coderre, C., & Denis, A. (1990) Stop or Go : Reflections of women managers on factors influencing their career development, IN *Journal of Business Ethics* pp361-7

Antal, A. and Krebsbach-Gnath, C. (1993) Women in Management in Germany:East, West and Reunited IN *International Studies of Management and Organisation* Vol 23 No 2 pp 29-69

Balderson, S. and Broderick, A. J. (1996) Behaviour in teams: exploring occupational and gender differences IN *Journal of Managerial Psychology* Vol 11 no 5 pp33-42

Ball, S. J. (1987) *The Micro-politics of the School* (London: Routledge)

Barthes, R. (1990) from Alexander, J.C. & Seidman,S. (1990) *Culture and Society: contemporary debates* (Cambridge: Cambridge University Press)

Bell, J. & Harrison, B. T. (1996) (ed) *Vision and Values in Managing Education* (London: Fulton)

Benfari, R. (1991)*Understanding Your Management Style* (New York: Lexington Press)

Berman, J. (1982) *The managerial behaviour of female high school principals: implications for training* Paper—American Educational Research Association (March) NewYork

Bergvall, V. L. (1999) Towards a comprehensive theory of language and gender, IN *Language and Society* Vol 28 pt 2 pp273-293

Blase, J. & Anderson, G. (1995) *The Micropolitics of Educational Leadership: from control to empowerment* (London: Cassell)

Bloor, M. (1978) On the analysis of observational data: a discussion of the worth and uses of inductive techniques and respondent validation IN *Sociology* Vol 12 pt 3 pp545-552

Bottery, M. (1994) *Lessons for Schools? A comparison of business and educational management* (London: Cassell)

Bouchard Ryan, E., & Giles, H.(1982) (ed) *Attitudes towards Language Variation* (London: Edward Arnold)

Brenner, O., Tomkiewicz, J. and Schein, V. (1989) The relationship between sex role stereotypes and requisite management characteristics IN *Academy of Management Journal* Vol32 pp662-669

Bryman, A. (1995) *Quantity and Quality in Social Research* (London: Routledge)

Cameron, D. (ed) (1990) *The Feminist Critique of Language: a reader* (London: Routledge)

Cameron, D. (1992) *Feminism and Linguistic Theory* (London: Macmillan)

Cameron, D. (1997) Theoretical Debates in Feminist Linguistics: questions of sex and gender IN Wodak, R.(1997) (ed) *Gender and Discourse* (London: Sage)

Cantor, D. and Bernay, T. (1992) *Women in Power: the secrets of leadership* (Boston: Houghton Mifflin Co)

Chomsky, N. (1965) *Aspects of the Theory of Syntax* (Cambridge Mass: MIT Press)

Clampitt, P. (1991) *Communicating for Managerial Effetciveness* (USA: Sage)

Clarke, L. and Teddlie, C. B. (1987) Gender-related Communication Barriers of Managers: acomparative study of men and women IN *The Delta Pi Epsilon Journal* Vol29 no 115-26

Coates, J. & Cameron, D. (1989) (ed) *Women in their Speech Communities* (London: Longman)

Coates, J. (1993) *Women, Men and Language* (London: Longman)

Coates, J. (ed) (1998) *Language and Gender : a reader* (London: Longman)

Coe, T. (1992) *The Key to the Men's Club: opening the doors to women in management* [British Institute of Management Report] (London: BIM)

Cockcroft, S. (1999) *Investigating Talk* (London: Hodder and Stoughton)

Cohen, L. & Manion, L. (2007) *Research Methods in Education* (London: Routledge)

Cooper, G. & Lewis, S. (1995) Working together: men and women in organisations IN *Leadership and Organisation Development* Vol 16 pt 5 pp29-31

Coulthard, M. & Montgomery, M. (1981) (ed) *Studies in Discourse Analysis* (London: Routledge & Kegan Paul)

Coulthard, M. (1992) *Advances in Spoken Discourse Analysis* (London: Routledge)

Coulthard, M. and Brazil, D. (1992) Exchange Structure IN Coulthard, M. *Advances in Spoken Discourse Analysis* (Milton Keynes: OUP)

Creemers, B. P. M. (1994) *The Effective Classroom* (London: Cassell)

Darking, L. (1991) The Equalisers IN *TES* May 3

Davidson, M. & Cooper, C. (1992) *Shattering the Glass Ceiling: the Woman Manager* (London: Paul Chapman)

Davidson, M. & Ferrario, M. (1992) A comparative study of gender and management style IN *Management Development Review* Vol 5 pt 1 pp13-17

Davidson, M. & Cooper, C. (1993) *European Women in Business and Management* (London: Paul Chapman)

Davidson, M. & Burke,R. (ed) (1994) *Women in Management : current research issues* (London: Paul Chapman)

DfEE (1992 and 1997) *Statistics of Education: Teachers, England and Wales*

DfES (2001) *Statistics of Education: Teachers in England* (including teachers' pay for England and Wales)

Eckert, P. (1990) The Whole Woman: sex and gender differences in variation IN *Language and Change* 1 pp245-267

Eckert, P. and McConnell-Ginet, S. (1992) Think practically and look locally: language and gender as community—based practice IN *Annual Review of Anthropology* 21 pp461-490

Ely, M. et al (1991) *Doing Qualitative Research: circles within circles* (London: Falmer)

Evetts, J. (1994) *Becoming a Secondary Headteacher* (London: Cassell)

Fagenson, E. (ed) (1993) *Women in Management : trends, issues and challenges in managerial diversity* (Ca. USA: Sage)

Fairclough, N. (1989) *Language and Power* (Harlow: Longman)

Fasold, R. (1990) *Sociolinguistics of Language* (Oxford: Blackwell)

Fauth, G. C. (1984) Women in Educational Administration: a research profile IN *Educational Forum* 49 (1) pp65-79

Ferrario, M. (1991) Sex differences in leadership style : myth or reality? IN *Women in Management Review* Vol 6 pt 3 pp16-21

Figueroa, P.M.E.(1981) *Writing Research Reports* (University of Nottingham School of Education)

Firth, J. R. (1964) On Sociological Linguistics IN Hymes, Dell (1964) (ed) *Language in Culture and Society* (New York: Harper Row)

Foucault, M. (1970) *The Order of Things* (London: Routledge)

Foucault, M. (1979) Sexual discourse and power from Foucault, M (1979) *The History of Sexuality* Vol 1 An Introduction (London: Penguin)

Fowler, R., Hodge, B., Kress, G. & Trew, T. (1979) *Language and Control* (London: Routledge)

Gale, A. and Cartwright, S. (1995) Women in Project Management: entry into a male domain? a discussion on gender and organisational culture IN *Leadership and Organisational Culture* Vol 16 no 2 pp3-8

Gayle, B. and Preiss, R. (1991) *Gender and the use of Conflict Styles* (presented at the 14th annual Communicating Language and Gender Conference) (Milwaukee, Wisconsin, USA)

Giddens, A. (1989) *Sociology* (Oxford: Blackwell)

Glaser, B. G. & Strauss, A. L. (1967) *The Discovery of Grounded Theory* (Chicago: Aldine)

Goffman, E. (1974) *Frame Analysis* (New York: Harper Row)

Goffman, E. (1981) *Forms of Talk* (Oxford: Blackwell)

Graddol, D. & Swann, J. (1992) *Gender Voices* (Oxford: Blackwell)

Gray, H. L. (1989) ch.4 Gender considerations in school management: masculine and feminine leadership styles IN *Human Resource Management in Education* Richards & Morgan (ed) (Milton Keynes: OUP)

Gross, N. and Trask, A. E. (1964) *Men and women as elementary school principals* (Final Report No2) (Cambridge MA, Harvard University Graduate School of Education)

Gross, N. and Trask, A. E. (1976) *The sex factor and the management of schools* (New York: John Wiley)

Gumperz, J. J. (1982) *Discourse Strategies* (Cambridge: CUP)

Habermas, J. (1987) *The Theory of Communicative Action* (London: Polity Press)

Hall, V. (1996)_*Dancing on the Ceiling: a study of women managers in education* (London: Chapman)

Hall, V. (1997) Dusting off the Phoenix IN *Educational Management and Administration* Vol 25 pt 3 pp309-324

Halliday, M. A. K. (1978) *Language as Social Semiotic* (Kent: Edward Arnold)

Hammersley, M. (1992) Some reflections on ethnography and validity IN *Qualitative Studies in Education* Viii pp195-203

Hammersley, M. (1992) *What's Wrong with Ethnography?* (London: Routledge)

Hargreaves, A. (1998) *Changing Teachers, Changing Times* (London: Cassell)

Harris, A. (1994) Breaking the Glass Ceiling for Senior Executives IN *HR Focus* March 94

Hearn, J. et al (ed) (1989) *The Sexuality of Organisation* (London: Sage)

Hite, L. M. & McDonald, K. S. (1995) Gender issues in management development: implications and research agenda IN *Journal of Management Development* Vol 14 pt 4 pp5-15

Holmes, J. (1984) Hedging your bets and sitting on the fence: some evidence for hedges as support structures IN *Te Reo* 27 pp47-62

Holmes, J. (1997) *Sociolinguistics* (Harlow: Longman)

Holmes, J. & Meyerhoff, M. (1999) The Community of Practice: theories and methodologies IN *Language and Society* Vol 28 pp173-183

Hymes, D. (1964) (ed) *Language in Culture and Society* (New York: Harper Row)

Hymes, D. (1968) The ethnography of speaking IN Fishman, J (ed) *Readings in the Sociology of Language* pp99-138 (The Hague: Mouton)

Hymes, D. (1972) On Communicative Competence IN Pride, J. B. & Holmes, J. (ed) *Sociolinguistics* (Harmondsworth: Penguin)

Hymes, D. (1974) *Foundations in Sociolinguistics: an ethnographic approach* (London: Tavistock)

Kmetz, J. and Willower, D. (1982) Elementary School Principals' Work Behaviour IN *Educational Administration Quarterly* 18 (4) pp62-78

Kanter, R. (1977) *Men and Women of the Corporation* (New York: Basic Books)

Labov, W. (1971) Variation in Language IN Reed, CE (ed) *The Learning of Language* (New York: National Council of Teachers of English)

Labov, W. (1972) *Sociolinguistic Patterns* (Philadelphia, USA: Univ. of Philadelphia Press)

Lakoff, R. (1975) *Language and Women's Place* (New York: Harper Row)

Lave, J. and Wenger, E. (1991) *Situated Learning: legitimate peripheral anticipation_*(Cambridge: CUP)

Lawton, D. (1992) *Education and Politics in the 1990s—conflict or consensus?* (London: Falmer)

Loden, M. (1985) *Feminine Leadership* (New York: Times Books)

Loden, M. (1987) Recognising Women's Potential: no longer business as usual IN *Management Review* (USA) Vol 76 no 12 pp44-46 Dec 1987

Lindesmith, A. R. (1968) *Addiction and Opiates* (Chicago: Aldine)

Marshall, J. (1995) Gender and Management: a critical review of research IN *British Journal of Management_*Vol 6 Special Issue pp53-62

Martin, N. J. and Willower, D. J. (1981) The managerial behaviour of high school principals IN *Educational Administration Quarterly* 17 (1) pp69-90

Maurer, T. J. and Taylor, M. A. (1994) Is sex by itself enough? An exploration of gender bias issues in performance appraisal IN *Organisational Behaviour and Decision Processes* Vol 60 no 2 pp231-251

Mills, A. J. (1988) Organisation, Gender and Culture IN *Organisational Studies* IX 3 pp351-369

Minsky, M. (1975) A Framework for Representing Knowledge IN Winston, P. (ed)(1975) *The Psychology of Computer Vision* (New York: McGraw-Hill)

Mintzberg, H. (1980) *The Nature of Managerial Work* (New York: Harper Row)

Morrison, A., White, R., and Van Velsor, E. (1987) *Breaking the Glass Ceiling* (Reading Ma: Addison-Wesley)

Mortimore, P. & J. (ed) (1991) *The Secondary Head: roles, responsibilities and reflections* (London: Paul Chapman)

Murphy, J. (1993) *Restructuring Schools* (London: Cassell)

National College for Leadership of Schools and Children's Services (2009) (NCLSCS)

NEDO (1990) *Women Managers: the untapped resource* (London: Kogan Page)

O'Barr, W. & Atkins, B. (1980) Women's language or "powerless language"? IN McConnell-Ginet et al (ed) *Women and Language in Literature and Society* pp93-110 (New York: Praeger)

Office for Standards in Education (1993) *Framework for the Inspection of Schools* (London: HMSO)

Office for Standards in Education (1994) *Improving Schools* (London: HMSO)

O'Grady, W., Dobrovolsky, M., Katamba, F. (1997) (ed) *Contemporary Linguistics* (Harlow: Longman)

O'Sullivan, F., Jones, K. & Reid, K. (1990) *Staff Development in Secondary Schools* (Kent: Hodder & Stoughton)

Ozga, J. (1988) *Schoolwork—Approaches to the Labour Process of Teaching* (Milton Keynes: OUP)

Ozga, J.(1993) (ed) *Women in Educational Management* (Milton Keynes: OUP)

Parry, J. (1969) *The Psychology of Human Communication* (London: Univ of London Press)

Pemberton, C. (1992) From stew to salad: men and women managers as contributors to organisational diversity IN *Industrial and Commercial Training* Vol 24 no4 pp12-15

Pitner, N.J. (1981) Hormones and Harems: are the activities of superintending different for a woman? IN Schmuck, Charters & Carlson (ed) *Educational Policy and Management* (New York: Academic Press)

Powell, G. N. (1990) One more time: do female and male managers differ? IN *Academy of Management Executive* Vol 4 no3 pp58-75

Powney, J. et al (2003) *Teachers' Careers: the impact of age, disability, ethnicity, gender and sexual orientation* (Research Report 488, DfES, University of Glasgow)

Prichard, C. and Deem, R. (1999) Wo-manageing Further Education: gender and the construction of the manager in the corporate colleges of England IN *Gender and Education* Vol 11 no 3 pp323-342

Pride, J. B. & Holmes, J. (ed) (1972) *Sociolinguistics: selected readings* (Harmondsworth: Penguin)

Raconteur Media (2010) *Women Mean Business* (published in The Times, Nov 30 2010) containing articles by Maitland, A. *Addressing the global gender gap*; Khalilizadeh, A. *Leading from the front*; Whittle, S. *He said, she said*. Also available online at www.raconteurmedia.co.uk

Robinson, W. S. (1951) The logical structure of analytic induction IN *American Sociological Review* Vol 16 pp 812-818

Rosener, J. (1990) Ways women Lead IN *Harvard Business Review* Nov/ Dec 1990 pp119-125

Ruderman, M. N., Ohlott, P. and Kram, K. (1995) Promotion decisions as a diversity practice IN *Journal of Management Development* Vol14 no 2 pp6-23

Saville-Troike, M. (1982) *The Ethnography of Communication* (Oxford: Blackwell)

Scheerens, J. (1992) *Effective Schooling: research, theory and practice* (London: Cassell)

Schick Case, S. (1988) Cultural differences, not deficiencies: an analysis of managerial women's language IN Rose, S. & Larwood, L. (ed) *Women's Careers: Pathways and Pitfalls* (New York: Praeger)

Schratz, M. (ed) *Qualitative Voices in Educational Research* (London: Falmer)

Shakeshaft, C. (1989) *Women in Educational Administration* (USA: Sage)

Sinclair, A. (1993) Approaches to Organisational Culture and Ethics IN *Journal of Business Ethics* Vol 12 no 1 pp63-73

Sinclair, J. and Coulthard, M. (1975) *Towards an Analysis of Discourse: the English used by teachers and pupils* (Oxford: OUP)

Sinclair, J. and Coulthard, M. (1992) Towards an Analysis of Discourse IN Coulthard, M. (1992) (ed)_Advances in Spoken Discourse Analysis* (London: Routledge)

Silverman, D. (1993) *Interpreting Qualitative Data : methods for analysing talk, text and interaction* (London: Sage)

Someck, B. (1995) The contribution of Action Research to development in social endeavours: a position paper on Action Research methodology IN *British Educational Research Journal* Vol 21 no 3

Spender, D. (1990) *Man-made Language* (London: Routledge)

Statham, A. (1987) The gender model revisited: differences in the management styles of men and women IN *Sex Roles* Vol 16 no 7/8

Stevenson, R. (1993)*Language, Thought and Representation* (Chichester: Wiley)

Stokoe, E. (1997) An evaluation of two studies of gender and language in educational contexts: some problems in analysis IN *Gender and Education* Vol 9 no 2 pp 233-244

Strachan, J. (1993) Including the Personal and the Professional: researching women in educational leadership IN *Gender and Education* Vol 5 no 1 1993 pp71-80

Strachan, J. (1999) Feminist Educational Leadership: locating the concepts in practice IN *Gender and Education* Vol11 no3 pp 309-322

Strauss, A. & Corbin, J. (1990) *Basics of Qualitative Research : grounded theory procedures and techniques* (Ca., USA: Sage)

Strauss, A. (1993) *Qualitative Analysis for Social Scientists* (Cambridge: CUP)

Stubbs, M. (1983) *Discourse Analysis: the sociological analysis of natural language* (Oxford: Blackwell)

Sydie, R. (1987) *Natural Women, Cultured Men* (Milton Keynes: OUPress)

Tannen, D. (1992) *You Just Don't Understand: women and men in conversation* (London: Virago)

Tannen, D. (1993)(ed) *Gender and Conversational Interaction* (New York: OUP)

Tannen, D. (1994) *Gender and Discourse* (New York: OUP)

Tannen, D. (1994) *Talking from 9 to 5 : how women's and men's conversational styles affect who gets heard, who gets credit, and what gets done at work* (New York: Morrow)

Taylor, S. & Bogdan, R.(1984) *Introduction to Qualitative Research Methods* (USA: John Wiley)

Tong, R. (1989) *Feminist Thought* (London: Unwin Hyman)

Treicher, P. and Kramarae, C. (1983) Women's Talk in the Ivory Tower IN *Communication Quarterly* Vol 31 no 2 pp118-132

Troman, G. (1996) No Entry Signs: educational change and some problems encountered in negotiating entry to educational settings IN *British Educational Research Journal* Vol 22 no1

Trudgill, P. (1972) Sex, covert prestige and linguistic change in the urban British English of Norwich IN *Language and Society* Vol 1 p179-95

Trudgill, P. (1974) *Sociolinguistics* (Harmondsworth: Penguin)

Trudgill, P. (1978)*Sociolinguistic Patterns in British English* (London: Edward Arnold)

Van Maanen, J. (ed) (1995) *Representation in Ethnography* (Ca., USA: Sage)

Vygotsky, L. S. (1962)*Thought and Language* (Mass, USA: M I T Press) (written in 1934, English translation 1962)

Vygotsky, L. S. (1978) *Mind in Society* (London & Mass: Harvard University Press)

Walford, G. (ed) (1991)*Doing Educational Research* (London: Routledge)

Wardhaugh, R. (1993) *Investigating Language: central problems in linguistics* (Oxford: Blackwell)

Wenger, E. (1998) *Communities of Practice* (Cambridge: CUP)

Wilkins, B. and Andersen, P. (1991) Gender Differences and Similarities in Management Communication IN *Management Communication Journal* Vol 5 no 1 pp 6-35

Wodak, R. (1997) Some important issues in the research of gender and discourse IN Wodak, R. (ed)_*Gender and Discourse* (London: Sage)

Wolcott, H. (1995) Making a study "more ethnographic" IN Van Maanen, J. (ed) (1995) *Representation in Ethnography* (Ca., USA: Sage)

Woods, P. (1986) *Inside Schools: ethnography in educational research* (London: Routledge)

Yin, R. K. (1989) *Case Study Research: design and methods* (USA: Sage)

Youngman, M.B. et al (1979) *Essential Empirical Concepts* (University of Nottingham School of Education)

Zimmerman, D. & West, C.(1975) Sex roles, interruptions and silences in conversation IN Thorne, B. & Henley, N. (ed)_*Language and Sex Differences and Dominance* (Mass, USA: Newbury House) pp105-129